COMIC TALES
OF THE
MIDDLE AGES

Recent Titles in
Contributions to the Study of World Literature

COMIC TALES
OF THE
MIDDLE AGES

AN ANTHOLOGY AND COMMENTARY

MARC WOLTERBEEK

Contributions to the Study of World Literature,
Number 39

Greenwood Press
New York • Westport, Connecticut • London

Copyright Acknowledgments

The author and publisher gratefully wish to acknowledge permission to reprint "'Unibos': The Earliest Full-length Fabliau (Text and Translation)," edited and translated by Marc Wolterbeek. Originally published in *Comitatus* 16 (1985).

Every reasonable effort has been made to trace the owners of copyright materials in this book, but in some instances this has proven impossible. The publisher will be glad to receive information leading to more complete acknowledgments in subsequent printings of the book and in the meantime extends its apologies for any omissions.

Library of Congress Cataloging-in-Publication Data

Wolterbeek, Marc.
    Comic tales of the Middle Ages : an anthology and commentary / Marc Wolterbeek.
      p. cm. — (Contributions to the study of world literature, ISSN 0738-9345 ; no. 39)
    Includes bibliographical references (p.) and index.
    ISBN 0-313-27737-0 (alk. paper)
    1. Latin poetry, Medieval and modern—Translations into English.
2. Latin poetry, Medieval and modern—History and criticism.
3. Tales, Medieval—Translations into English. 4. English poetry—Translations from Latin. 5. Tales, Medieval—History and criticism. 6. Latin poetry, Medieval and modern. 7. Comic, The, in literature. 8. Tales, Medieval. 9. Literary form. I. Title.
II. Series.
PA8164.W6   1991
871'.09003—dc20   90-47533

British Library Cataloguing in Publication Data is available.

Copyright © 1991 by Marc Wolterbeek

Library of Congress Catalog Card Number: 90-47533
ISBN: 0-313-27737-0
ISSN: 0738-9345

First published in 1991

Greenwood Press, 88 Post Road West, Westport, CT 06881
An imprint of Greenwood Publishing Group, Inc.

Printed in the United States of America

The paper used in this book complies with the Permanent Paper Standard issued by the National Information Standards Organization (Z39.48-1984).

10 9 8 7 6 5 4 3 2 1

Uxori meae

Contents

viii   Contents

Preface

I have always been intrigued with origins, particularly with the rebirth of "modern" culture during the late Middle Ages. The years preceding the Twelfth Century Renaissance have held a strong fascination for me, as fundamental cultural changes and new literary trends effected the great transition from the Dark Ages to the High Middle Ages.

Thanks to the pioneering efforts of early scholars, many works of literature that once lay buried in little known manuscripts are now published, albeit disparately in minor journals. Thus I have been able to conduct much of my preliminary research in this country and only during the later stages of my work did I need to visit various libraries and sites in Europe.

In my study of tenth- and eleventh-century literature, I discovered that one area of literary activity has been largely ignored by American, British, and French critics, and even German critics who were aware of this activity still had a limited view. I experienced much excitement as I came across impressive comic narratives that had been neglected by scholars who deal with medieval comedy: *Unibos*, a full-length fabliau in Latin, composed over a hundred years before the first French fabliaux; Radulfus Tortarius' ribald tale about Sincopus, who castrates himself in order to join a religious order; Warnerius of Rouen's wild "Satire against Moriuht," depicting a wandering Irish scholar who is raped by Danish pirates and repeatedly sold into slavery before belching forth verses at the Norman court.

My "discovery" of these and other seminal works in the history of medieval comic literature led to this volume, in which I edit and translate early comic tales accessible to only a few scholars until now. One of these stories, Warnerius' "Satire against Moriuht," has not even been critically edited, while most of the *nugae*—Egbert's and Hildebert's epigrams, Fulcoius' and Radulfus' epistles—as well as Warnerius' and Peter's satires, have never been translated. The longer texts are edited and translated in the appendix of this book; shorter works are edited and translated in my extended commentary.

I would like to thank three individuals who have been most helpful to me in my efforts to translate the Latin. Professor Edward Steidle of Stanford University helped me turn *Unibos* into idiomatic English; Professor Phillip Damon of the University of California, Berkeley, and Professor Robert Smutny of the University of the Pacific both spent long hours with me pouring over crabbed corrupt Latin as we attempted to understand writers who composed their works nearly a thousand years ago.

I am also grateful to the librarians of the Bibliothèque Royale of Brussels, the Bibliothèque Nationale of Paris, the Bibliothèque Municipale of Beauvais, the Biblioteca Apostolica Vaticana, the British Library, Cambridge University Library, Trinity College Library, and the Bodleian Library.

Introduction

From late Antiquity to the High Middle Ages, a period of over five hundred years, both comic drama and comic narrative declined in the West. With the closing of the Roman theaters in the fifth and sixth centuries, only private productions of classical comedies were possible, while mimes and other public performers continued to enact lower forms of drama that were not worthy of print. Comic narrative waned even earlier, for after the masterful works of Petronius and Apuleius, sustained comic narration is virtually nonexistent before its re-emergence in the tenth and eleventh centuries. During these transitional centuries between the Carolingian and Twelfth Century Renaissances, three genres maintaining significant structures mark a new beginning, as they anticipate in form and theme the comic literature of the High Middle Ages. The *ridicula*, "funny stories" recounted in rhythmic verse, are essentially primitive fabliaux having close ties with live performance; the *nugae*, "trifles" of scholarly Latin poets writing in metrical verse, reveal a classicizing tendency similar to that of the late twelfth-century *comediae elegiacae*. The *satyrae* rarely achieve narrative structure, but the few narrative satires that are extant offer penetrating insights into contemporary life. Although these poems have definite generic ties with late comic literature, what is striking is how the writers' sense of humor differs from that of later storytellers. These poems, then, are important not only to the literary historian interested in the origins of medieval comic genres, but also to the humanist fascinated with man's sense of humor and his attitude about the value of literature at the dawn of the High Middle Ages.[1]

Throughout Antiquity and the early Middle Ages, writers use the term *ridiculum* to mean "a laughing matter," "a jest," or "a joke," in a non-generic sense. For Cicero, as for Quintillian, "the word *ridiculum* is the most general in meaning, and consequently the most colorless of all terms" (Grant 101). However, in the tenth and early eleventh centuries, three poems, all belonging to the famous *florilegium* known as the Cambridge Songs, use the term generically to identify themselves:[2]

Advertite
omnes populi,
ridiculum
et audite, quomodo
Suevum mulier
et ipse illam
defraudaret.
(Pay attention, everybody, and listen to a funny story about how a wife cheated a Swabian and he cheated her.)

In gestis patrum veterum   quoddam legi ridiculum,
exemplo tamen habile,   quod vobis dico rithmice.
(In the tales of our forefathers I read a funny story, yet useful as a moral tale, which I recount to you rhythmically.)

Quibus ludus est animo   et iocularis cantio,
hoc advertant ridiculum;   est verum, non ficticium.
(Those who would like to hear a jest and a funny song should listen to this *ridiculum*—it's true, not fiction.)

These poems present tales of human deceit and presumption, and they employ one of two formal structures, sequence or rhythmic hymn.

Such content and form link them closely with four other poems in the same manuscript.[3] One of these tales, *De Lantfrido et Cobbone*, has sequence form in the Cambridge collection and hymn form in a Parisian manuscript. The latter version claims "oral stories" ("fabule") as its source:[4]

Quodam tempore fuerunt   duo viri nobiles,
sicut fabule testantur   et scurrarum complices. . .
(Once upon a time there were two noblemen whom popular stories, told by minstrels, have made famous. . .)

The *Modus Florum*, a sequence in the Cambridge manuscript, belongs to a subgenre, for it labels itself a *mendosa cantilena* ("lying song"):[5]

Mendosam quam cantilenam ago,
puerilis commendatam dabo,
quo modulos per mendaces risum
auditoribus ingentem ferant.
(I compose a "lying song," which I recommend for little boys [to sing]. Through lying little measures they will bear great laughter to listeners.)

All of these poems are brief comic narratives consisting of one or two episodes. Five of the seven have prologues that identify the sources and genre of the poems.

Another eleventh-century poem that may be labeled a *ridiculum* is the lengthy *Unibos*, which, like the shorter stories of the Cambridge manuscript, uses the Christian hymn structure to depict human deceit and presumption. Like *De Lantfrido et Cobbone, Unibos* is a "fabule," and its prologue claims actual performance as a source:[6]

1. Rebus conspectis seculi   non satiantur oculi,
   Aures sunt in hominibus   amicae novitatibus.
2. Ad mensam magni principis   est rumor Uniusbovis;
   Praesentatur ut fabula   per verba iocularia.
3. Fiunt cibis convivia   sed verbis exercitia.
   In personarum drammate   uno cantemus de bove!
4. Natis natus ridiculis   est rusticus de rusticis;
   Natura fecit hominem   sed fortuna mirabilem.

(Men's eyes are never filled enough by the remarkable sights of this world. Their ears are ever eager to hear new tales.

As a play with witty words, the story of Unibos is presented at the table of a great prince.

There are guests at the feast, a bandying of words. Accompanied by performing actors, let us sing of Unibos!

Son of ridiculous sons, he is a peasant from peasants. Nature made the man, but fortune produced wonders.)

Unibos has five episodes and is nothing less than a full-length fabliau of the eleventh century. Surprisingly, this poem has been completely ignored by British and American critics.

Only German scholars, most recently Jürgen Beyer and Joachim Suchomski, seem to have any appreciative knowledge of *Unibos*. Beyer places the *ridicula* in the broad German category of *Schwank*, which "designates any genre of coarse (for example, obscene) content . . . [and] refers to a definite historical genre (for example, the fabliau) that primarily treats coarse material" ("Morality" 15, note 2). Beyer makes the Ciceronian distinction between *ridiculum dictum* and *ridiculum factum*, theorizing that the genre emerges as the *Schulschwänke* of Theodulf of Orléans (circa 760-821), which are little more than riddles or jokes (*Schwank* 68-72). Once of source of comedy moves from human speech to human action, the *ridiculum dictum* becomes a *ridiculum factum*, a single episode whose economy of expression increases comic effect. According to Beyer, the latter type of *ridiculum* defines the extant specimens of the tenth and eleventh centuries, including *Unibos*. Beyer claims that in all there are under twenty *Schulschwänke*, and he includes in that number five of the Cambridge Songs. He also considers a passage of the twelfth-century *Alda*, an elegiac "comedy," as a *ridiculum factum*, and he classifies several of Petrus Alfonsi's *exempla* as *Schwänke*.

The broad connotations of the German term *Schwank* lead Beyer to place several different genres into a single category, and his thesis, although it is often illuminating, is undermined by a failure to acknowledge generic distinctions. Selecting a group of poems composed over a five-hundred-year period, Beyer places *ridicula, exempla, comediae elegiacae*, and fabliaux into a single category. Further, he overlooks a number of comic *exempla*, epigrams, and epistles of the eleventh century, such as those written by Egbert of Liège, Hildebert of Lavardin, and Fulcoius of Beauvais. Finally, Beyer's use of a Ciceronian dichotomy has questionable validity, since for Cicero himself *ridiculum* is "the most colorless of all terms."

Joachim Suchomski, in *"Delectatio" und "Utilitas": Ein Beitrag zum Verständnis mittelalterliche komischer Literatur*, takes a purely literary approach to a large number of comic narratives, including several of the Cambridge Songs and *Unibos*, and he contends that many of these stories are not comic at all, but instead they are ethical tales ending with "moralistiche *utilitas* zu suchen."[7] Suchomski believes that despite the testimony of three prologues and the authority of Ernst Curtius (433-35), *ridiculum* is not a generic term, for the poets themselves use the term indiscriminantly.[8] While Suchomski's thesis raises an important concern facing these early storywriters—that is, their conflict between comic impulse and moral intent—his position that these stories are not comic is untenable, and his argument that the *ridiculum* is a non-generic term is weak.

Peter Dronke's brief article, "The Rise of the Medieval Fabliau: Latin and Vernacular Evidence," classifies seven of the Cambridge Songs as *ridicula* and analyzes two of them closely, yet like other British and American critics, he fails to mention *Unibos*. Dronke uses the term *fabliau* to describe the *ridicula* as well as the comic narratives of William IX, Duke of Aquitaine, and in *Poetic Individuality in the Middle Ages,* he labels the episode concerning *rufus* in the *Ruodlieb* as a "fabliau." Dronke's term, like Beyer's, is valid as a descriptive, generalizing label for these poems, and like Beyer, Dronke jumps, with a momentary pause around the year 1100, from the early eleventh-century *ridicula* to the late twelfth-century *comediae elegiacae*. By seeking similarities rather than differences, both critics use broad terms that do not distinguish specific genres.

Further, the theses of Beyer, Suchomski, and Dronke are not comprehensive: if they had been aware of a single poem, the eighth epistle of Fulcoius of Beauvais, their conclusions would have no doubt been greatly altered, for this epistle is a late eleventh-century rendition of the snowchild story, a tale taking form as the *Modus Liebinc* in the Cambridge Songs, which these critics emphasize heavily because it also exists as an elegiac "comedy," school exercise, and Old French fabliau.[9] Since Fulcoius writes at the end of the eleventh century, after the compilation of the Cambridge Songs and before the careers of William IX and Petrus Alfonsi, he could provide an important link in the history of late medieval comic literature. If this poem were known to the critics, they may have been led to investigate the comic tradition among the so-called learned Latin poets writing primarily in France during the latter half of the century.[10] But just as *Unibos* has been much neglected by modern scholarship, the trifles of poets like Fulcoius have also been largely ignored.

Both the content and form of the eight extant *ridicula* distinguish these poems from related genres, notably fables and fabliaux.   All three genres characteristically possess frames, prologues and epilogues enclosing the narrative, but the fables' heavy moralizing tempers humorous potential, while the *ridicula* and fabliaux often end with amoral statements that do not undermine the humor of the narrative. The obvious difference between fables and *ridicula* is length: in the fables, narrative is reduced to minimal proportions and details are lacking; in the *ridicula*, as in the fabliaux, extended length permits fuller presentation of conflict, character, and theme.

Not only do the *ridicula* and fabliaux generally supersede the fables in narrative development, but characters and themes are also qualitatively different. Talking animals never appear in the *ridicula*, and animals that do appear are not overtly personified. In fact, allegory is never explicit in the *ridicula*, whereas in the fables and beast-epics, perhaps because animals are personified, allegory is obvious, Finally, whereas fables avoid erotic subject matter, the *ridicula* often treat erotic themes, though they avoid the indecency of the fabliaux.   Both *ridicula* and fabliaux reveal dependency and advancement upon the age-old fables.

The outstanding characteristic of the *ridiculum* is its formal structure, which at times achieves excellence. Of the three poems using the sequence form, one of them, the *Modus Liebinc*, has been described as "so crystal clear and beautifully sounding that it must have been created by a master who was at least as expert in the arts of singing and harp-playing as in that of elegant diction" (Meyer quoted in Dronke, "Rise of the Fabliau" 179). Sequences, as is well known, originally consist of words set to melodies as purely mnemonic devices for improvisation during church services, and the alternating strophes, with exact syllabic correspondences, are sung by semichoruses.[11] Once a certain melody is established, it is given a title and can be used for sacred or profane subject matter; in other words, the melody is a skeleton to which a poet adds a lyric or narrative.   Peter Dronke has demonstrated that sacred sequences do not necessarily antedate profane ones, for "the melodies of a fair number of ninth and tenth century sacred sequences have secular, not sacred, titles" ("Beginnings of the Sequence" 57). The *ridicula* in sequence form, therefore, are not simple parodies of sacred sequences.   But were these profane sequences actually performed—that is, sung, like the religious sequences during church services? The question is complicated by the fact that medieval drama was in its infancy at the time these sequences were popular. Associated with the trope, another improvisation in the church services, early drama involved impersonization, whereas the sequences, according to authorities like Karl Young, were sung without pantomime, although they belong to the same milieu as early medieval drama.[12]

The formal structures of the rhythmic *ridicula* are keys to understanding the history of the genre, for several Carolingian rhythms also use the Christian hymn strophe to recount comic subject matter.[13] The *Cena Cypriani*, for example, uses the same fifteen-syllable rhythmic lines as the French version of *De Lantfrido et Cobbone*. Another Carolingian rhythm, which describes a tippling monk from Angers, "has no fellow until the time of the Cambridge Songs. It stands, therefore, as a lonely landmark, suggesting . . . the same Teutonic humour which gave birth to several of the songs in that collection" (Raby, *SLP* 1:218). But the earlier rhythms, though generically akin to the *ridicula*, differ in a most fundamental way: they have thin plots or no plots at all. The Christian hymn strophe, because of its simplicity, its prosaic nature, permits the composer to concentrate more on matter than on form, much like the Old French octosyllabic couplet of the twelfth and thirteenth centuries.[14]

The prologues of the *ridicula*, in addition to labeling themselves generically, provide remarkable comments about the origins and nature of poetic composition. Only one of these poems claims a written source: the *Vitae patrum*, or, as the poet puts it, "in gestis patrum veterum."[15] Other Cambridge Songs suggest oral origins as well as oral performance of the songs themselves. The *Modus Florum*, the "lying song," commends itself to singing by boys ("puerilis commendatam dabo"), and it is possible that this sequence is intended for the "Boy Bishop" during the "Feasts of Innocents or Boys" as described by E. K. Chambers.[16] The prologue of the Parisian version of *De Lantfrido et Cobbone* calls the poem a "useless song" ("ociosa cancio") that is nonetheless performed by "scholars playing" ("scolastici ludentes," perhaps referring to clerics playing instruments or merely having a good time); further, the origins of this tale are "popular stories" ("fabule") and "minstrels" ("scurrarum complices," literally "the allies of jesters," synonymous, according to Gaston Paris ["Lantfrid" 287], to *jongleurs*). The most impressive statement about origins and performance occurs at the beginning of *Unibos*, where the poet asserts that "tidings" ("rumor") of Unibos are presented as a "fabula" at the "table of a great prince"; he then exhorts his audience, "accompanied by a performance of actors" ("in personarum drammate"), to sing of Unibos. Numerous allusions to banquets and marketplaces as the locales of theatrical performances by *mimi*, *scurrae*, and *histriones* attest that the prologue of *Unibos* is not pure fiction, and curiously enough, much of the action in the poem occurs at markets and public squares.[17]

Two poets living when songs like those in the Cambridge manuscript were popular—during the late tenth and early eleventh centuries—illustrate the nature of public performances where stories like the *ridicula* were presented. Froumond of Tegernsee (born c. 960), who writes obscure comic poems in metrical verse, imagines himself a *ridiculus* or jester entertaining the boys:

Si facerem mihi pendentes per cingula caudas
  Gesticulans manibus, lubrice stans pedibus,
Si lupus aut ursus, vel vellem fingere vulpem,
  Si larvas facerem furciferis manibus,
Dulcifer aut fabulas nossem componere, menda,
  Orpheus ut cantans Euridicen revocat,
Si canerem multos dulci modulamine leudos
  Undique currentes cum trepidis pedibus,
Gauderet, mihi qui propior visurus adesset,
  Ridiculus cunctos concuteret pueros.
Fistula si dulcis mihi trivisset mea labra,
  Risibus et ludis oscula conciperem.
Veridicax minor est vobis quam ligula mendax,
  Diligitis iocos en mage quam metricos.
(If I made tails dangling on my belt,
Pantomiming with my hands, quick on my feet,
If I [pretended to be] a wolf or a bear or wanted to impersonate a fox,
If I made a mask with sleight of hand,
If I knew how to compose sweet stories or lying songs,
Like Orpheus, singing, calling back Euridice,
If I sang many songs to sweet melodies,
Moving everywhere with anxious feet,
Anyone present to look at me closely would rejoice,
And laughter would shake all the boys.
If the sweet pipe touched my lips,
I would receive kisses with laughter and play.
A truthful tongue means less to you than a lying one,
And you love playful poems, as it were, more than metrical verse.)
(81-82; poem 32, lines 33-46)

Froumond pleads with his students to make metrical songs instead: "Come, friends, let us vie in metrical song" ("Eia, confratres, certemus carmine metri," line 63).

Another poet, the satirist Sextus Amarcius, writing in the mid-eleventh century, also gives a lengthy description of a performing artist displaying his talent. Most important, in this description Sextus alludes to three of the songs located in the Cambridge manuscript, one of which is the story of the snowchild.[18] He first attacks mimes who steal from their aristocratic listeners:

Quid loquar astantes ficta ditescere laude
Mimos? hi dominis astu per verba iocosa
Plurima surripiunt etiam scalpente datore
Sinciput; exhausto decrescit copia cornu.

(What should I say about these mimes hanging about and becoming rich
on feigned praise?
In their cleverness, with playful words,
They steal much from the lords, even the ham from the titillated giver;
Plenty diminishes when the horn is emptied.) (15; book 1, lines 403-6)

Still criticizing the *mimus*, Sextus gives an inventory of the performer's themes:

Ille fides aptans crebro diapente canoras,
Straverit ut grandem pastoris funda Goliath,
Ut simili argutus uxorem Suevulus arte
Luserit, utque sagax nudaverat octo tenores
Cantus Pytagoras et quam mera vox Philomele
Perstrepit.
(He frequently adjusts his melodious flute up a fifth
So that the sling of the shepherd may fling down great Goliath,
So that the cunning Swabian may deceive his wife with a like fraud,
So keen Pythagoras may disclose the eight tones of song
And the nightingale may burst forth with such a clear voice.) (17; book
1, lines 438-43)

It is possible that Sextus Amarcius had the Cambridge manuscript before him
when he composed this passage, though Beyer's suggestion that Sextus himself
may have been the compiler of the manuscript seems unlikely, since the satirist
is so critical of mimes (*Schwank* 67, n. 12). His allusion to the snowchild story,
in which "the cunning Swabian" outtricks his unfaithful wife "with a like fraud,"
is strong evidence that this story belonged to the public performer's repertoire.
Not coincidentally, mimes appear within the *Modus Liebinc*, where they
contribute to the decadence of the wife:

Nec interim
domi vacat coniux;
mimi aderant,
iuvenes secuntur,
quos et inmemor
viri exulis
excepit gaudens
atque nocte proxima
pregnans filium
iniustum fudit
iusto die.
(Meanwhile, his wife is not idle at home; mimes attend her, and
forgetful of her wandering husband, she joyously receives youths who

follow [them]. On the following night she conceives a son, and she
bears the illegitimate one on the appointed day.)

Sextus' mimes, who deftly play one tune after other for their listeners, have
entered the fiction of the sequence and are self-mockingly ridiculed by the poet.

Several other medieval texts make allusions to actual performances, and a
few pre-eleventh-century works, like the *ridicula*, claim oral presentation. The
prologue of the ninth-century *Cena Cypriani*, for instance, is "un prezioso
documento di rappresentazione scenica medievale," and the metrical dialogue
Terentius et Delusor is "un vero e proprio mimo rappresentato, forse nella
scuola, su una vera scena, e non un'esercitazione puramente letteraria."[19] This
fragmentary drama is an argument between the aged Latin playwright, who
composes old stories ("fabules, dico, vetus veteres"), and a young poet claiming
superior artistic skills. When the angered Terence threatens to attack the young
man, the latter says in an aside, "How well this old man plays the fool for me!"
("Quam bene ridiculum mihi personat iste veternus!") Critics date this play
anywhere from the seventh to tenth centuries; it is rare evidence of a comic
dramatic tradition very early in the Middle Ages.

Evidence from allusions and from statements within the *ridicula* themselves
make it clear that these works were intimately linked to live performances, that
they even may have been performed themselves in their current state. *Terentius
et Delusor*, being pure dialogue, is a drama in the modern sense; performances
by mimes, on the other hand, required jesters ("scurrae") who pantomimed while
minstrels or *jongleurs* ("scurrarum complices") recited the story. Hence the
presence of narration instead of speech in a poem does not rule out possible
performance. Froumond's testimony, contrasting his own metrical compositions
with the "playful" productions of mimes, suggests that rhythmic hymns achieved
live performance; Sextus' criticism of mimes reveals that stories extant in
sequence form, such as the *Modus Liebinc*, were also performed, though perhaps
in another form.[20] Later evidence that mimes performed the *ridicula* is found in
Walter Map's *De nugis curialium*: describing Clodoanus as a well-lettered man,
Walter explains that he is degenerated by becoming a mime, so that he devoted
himself completely to rhythms and jests ("degeneravit in mimum, ut totus in
rithmis et ridiculis ocupetur," 189). Although Walter's use of the term
ridiculum is probably non-generic, this twelfth-century writer nonetheless
associated mimes with rhythmic poetry. Both sequence and rhythm originate
within the church, but they apparently become the property of mimes at a very
early date.

Strictly speaking, the *nugae* are school exercises specifically designed to
improve a beginning writer's skill in composition. Their emphasis is therefore
upon verbal and rhetorical skills, and the exercises of the eleventh century hardly
differ from those written throughout the Middle Ages. An example of such a
poem, *Nugae poeticae*, placed erroneously among the works of Marbod of

Rennes ("Carmina" column 1685), illustrates the mundane nature of such compositions:

> Altus mons, firmus pons, libera frons, vitreus fons,
> Arbor nux, sacra crux, leo trux, bona lux, vigilans dux,
> Candida nix, nigra pix, homo frix, aqua Styx, volucris strix,
> Fertile rus, corruptio pus, et amica luto sus,
> Longum crus, curvat grus, rodit mus, redolet thus.
> Est mordax dens, estque memor mens, est patriae gens,
> Urbis plebs, virtus spes, omnia res, graditur pes.
> Cogit vis, turbat lis, in tribus aequivocat glis.
> Ditat dos, vernat flos, stillat ros, acuit cos.
> Uxor fratris glos, mugit bos, cuncta trahit mos.
> Dat sors, aufert mors, resonat vox, furta tegit nox.
> Jus carnis, vis rectoris, id est jus juris utrumque.
> (High mountain, stable bridge, free garland, clear fountain,
> Nut tree, holy cross, wild lion, good light, watchful leader,
> White snow, black pitch, Phrixean man, water Styx, screech-owl bird,
> Fertile field, corrupting pus, swine friend to mud,
> Long leg, crane bends, mouse gnaws, incense smells.
> The tooth is biting, the mind remembers, the race of the home,
> The populace of the city, strength hope, everything a thing, the foot steps.
> Force compels, strife disturbs, the dormouse is called the same thing among the masses.
> The gift enriches, a flower blooms, a rose drops, a flintstone sharpens.
> A wife is sister-in-law of a brother, the ox bellows, custom endures everything.
> Fate decrees, death carries away, the voice resounds, night conceals thefts.
> The law of the flesh, the power of the rule, this is the law and both are of the law.)

The poem utterly sacrifices meaning to rhetorical play: words and ideas remain obscure, and transitions are lacking.[21] This production is a rather typical exercise indulged in by nearly every important writer of the eleventh century.[22]

But the term *nugae* has a broader meaning than merely a rhetorical exercise, and this meaning is apparent in three important retractions by eleventh-century writers. Guibert of Nogent's retraction of his youthful verses (64) sheds light upon their contents: as a youth, he says, he learned worldly letters ("saeculares litterulas") and put aside the "universal seriousness of religious literature for this ridiculous vanity" ("ita ut universa divinae paginae seria pro tam ridicula vanitate seponerem"), which consisted of Ovid's poetry, Virgil's *Eclogues*, and "amatory charms" ("lepores amatorios"). Moreover, Guibert did not at all abstain from the "bafoonery of writers of trifles" ("et scriptorem nugantium nequaquam scurrilitatibus temperabam"). Though Guibert's profane works are not extant, his retraction reveals their nature: they included classical imitations, amatory epistles, and the writing of trifles.

Although Marbod of Rennes does not use the word *nugae* in his retraction, he spent his youth composing verses much like Guibert's. Marbod opposes "sweetsounding tunes, harmonious words" ("dulcisonos numeros, concinnaque verba") to "seria," yet his retraction is apologetic in tone, for "it was fitting that youth sing playful songs" ("juvenem cantare jocosa decebat," "Carmina" col. 1693-94). Until Walther Bulst's publication of Marbod's love poetry, it was believed that many of his youthful productions were lost.[23] The eleven poems published by Bulst include several amatory letters exchanged with women, a satire against a prelate, and what Dronke considers "a lady's lament in a tragic romance" (*Medieval Latin* 214). Baudry of Bourgueil, Marbod's friend, would consider such productions *nugae*, for he too writes a multitude of friendship poems to women and, more than any other eleventh-century poet, he uses the term *nugae* and its cognates to describe his poetry, a *genus jocundius* ("playful genre," 123; poem 147, line 43). For Marbod and Baudry the *carmen iocosus* consists, above all, of love letters, though mildly humorous narratives do appear in both poets' works.

Fulcoius of Beauvais, in an epistle considering various poetic genres, says a *carmen* has a "playful subject" ("res est iocunda," 253; poem 17, line 29), and in his retraction to his *Uter*, consisting of letters, epitaphs, and *nugae*, he explains why he wrote it:

> Non ut stent feci sed utrum quid scribere possem.
> Nullus opus primum pictorque faberque reservat.
> Fac, precor, ut pereat prior experientia.
> (I made them not so they would remain, but to be able to write in each [genre].
> No painter or craftsman keeps his first work.
> Let this first experiment, I beg of you, perish.) (267; poem 26, lines 5-7)

The epitaphs and the *nugae* of the *Uter* have, unfortunately, been lost—if they were ever written—but the metrical letters remain, though Fulcoius also committed them to Vulcan along with the rest of the *Uter*.[24] Among these letters, as has been mentioned, is the story of the snowchild, which Fulcoius, acknowledging popular origins, calls a *frivola* (229; poem 8, line 60). Several other of Fulcoius' epistles are tales of deceit and seduction; these works, like the *nugae*, are part of his *prior experientia*. Such poems may be described as *epistolae nugatoriae*; more simply, we may call them *nugae*.

The term *nugae* may be used loosely to categorize a number of comic narrative poems composed during the late tenth, eleventh, and early twelfth centuries. These *exempla*, epigrams, epistles, and exercises are quite different from the trifles of earlier centuries, for even in the late tenth century poets demonstrate a renewed interest in comic narrative, whereas before this time comic narratives are scarce during the Middle Ages. Most important, however, is a profound change in stylistic clarity occurring in the course of the eleventh century. By the end of the century a flowering of poetry and classicism that is the forerunner of the Twelfth Century Renaissance results from the pioneering educational efforts of such schoolmen as Gerbert of Aurillac and Fulbert of Chartres during the early eleventh century. This change is immediately apparent when comparing such writers as Froumond of Tegernsee and Egbert of Liège, who write in the late tenth and early eleventh centuries, with poets like Hildebert of Lavardin, Fulcoius of Beauvais, and Radulfus Tortarius, writing at the end of the eleventh and beginning of the twelfth centuries. The earlier poets flaunt their learning with obscure rhetoric and strange vocabulary, and the result is esoteric, precious, and often incomprehensible. Later eleventh-century poets, on the other hand, write with clarity and fluidity, no doubt a result of better training in the masters. True, they still indulge in obscure exercises such as the *Nugae poeticae*, but they also compose epigrams, epistles, and other extended comic narratives that, though they are the prurient excursions of otherwise orthodox churchmen, reveal a concern for excellence of style.

Though the eleventh-century *nugae* have a unique history and a very peculiar humor, they are nonetheless linked generically to school exercises written before and after this century. The brief narratives of Theodulf of Orléans are not *ridicula*, as Beyer contends, but rhetorical trifles, like Theodulf's non-narrative *De bilingue*.[25] The *nugae* also have direct links with the twelfth-century elegiac "comedies," which, according to Tony Hunt, "represent *oeuvres de transition* between the *imitatio auctorum*, or school exercise, and the courtly narrative presented to a patron" (155). These lengthy poems are the sort of productions an aging prelate would retract, and the retractions of later medieval writers are indeed quite like those of the eleventh century.[26] The *nugae* of the eleventh century, then, have an easily identifiable generic context, yet they reveal a change in consciousness about literary stylistics as well as about the nature and validity of comic literature.

The rebirth of venality satire during the eleventh century has often drawn the attention of literary historians. This century "produced Europe's first pamphlet war of propaganda, the 'libelli de lite' of the Investiture Contest. The Contest developed in clergy and laity alike a consciousness of the evils of simony so strong that the corrupting power of money was reborn as a theme of satire and flourished for the rest of the Middle Ages" (Yunck 47). With few exceptions, this satire is non-narrative in nature.[27] An examination of early comic narrative would not be complete, however, without consideration of two satirical narratives falling outside the realm of venality satire: the first, written by Warnerius of Rouen ("Satire" 193-210) in the early eleventh century, is an attack upon a wandering scholar who is twice sold into slavery; the second, composed by Peter the Painter (*Carmina* 121-27; poem 16) at the end of the century, criticizes an adulterous woman who meets her lover while her husband believes she is praying for him at church. These poems, unlike venality satires, do not attack greed, but lechery, and their humor is sardonic and obscene, approaching the frontiers of tragedy; moreover, neither possesses high artistic expression or form, though their creators are familiar with classical and patristic satire. In addition to having a historical interest, these poems are unique literary productions and are therefore difficult to compare to other comic narratives of the time. Warnerius' attack is something like a *comedia*, something like a fabliau, but his sense of humor is most unusual, and Moriuht, the *scholasticus*, is drawn vividly, apparently from real life. Peter's *De matronis*, laden with the platitudes of the contemporary misogynistic tradition, introduces the intriguing notion of *falsa religio* ("false religiosity"), yet the cuckold's worship of his unfaithful wife is quite different from the troubadours' quasi-feudal, quasi-religious adoration of their ladies. Both works, then, are original satires, and their ribald comedy ranges from the ludicrous to the obscene.

With the exception of the short *ridicula*, modern scholarship has imperfectly understood the comic tradition immediately antedating the *comediae elegiacae* and the fabliaux, for the comic *nugae* of scholarly Latin poets have largely escaped the notice of the major critics of medieval comedy, and the important *Unibos*, a complex Latin fabliau of the eleventh century, has claimed the attention of only a few scholars. Obviously a thorough evaluation of this early tradition is necessary for a competent understanding of the late medieval comic tradition.

Probably the most striking characteristics of this early literary production are the foreignness of its childlike humor and the primitive nature of its comedy, containing the formal elements of comic structure and characterization, but lacking broad unifications and quick inversions.[28] Indeed, the comic structure and comic characterization of these early stories enable us to identify them as comedies, for we often fail to recognize their distant humor. Sometimes even the basic storyline is difficult to decipher, and earlier or later analogues, when they exist, are necessary tools to understand otherwise incomprehensible narratives. The *ridicula*, the more "popular" genre, are generally easy to understand, though their humor is not always easy to appreciate. Stylistically the *ridicula* and the Old French fabliaux are close, and certain generic links suggest that the later vernacular tales are the offspring of the earlier, clumsier Latin stories. But the fabliaux, especially in their humor, offer striking evidence of a change in mentality during the transition from Latin to vernacular modes of expression.

The generic relation of the *nugae* with earlier trifles and with the later *comediae elegiacae* is more obvious.[29] Both *nugae* and *comediae*, for instance, employ the rhetorical processes of amplification and abbreviation when handling a given theme, and both genres share certain topoi demonstrating their affinity. The *comediae*, however, maintain more complex narrative structures, and they are a more homogenous genre than the *nugae*. Generic similarities, therefore, reveal the evolution of medieval comic genres, yet evolution itself, involving change, is the key to perceiving the birth of modern humor.

NOTES

1. It is important to distinguish comedy and humor from the outset. Comedy is a manner of presenting situations and people, and it tends to be objective and universal. Humor, on the other hand, is revealed in subject matter and implies the author's involvement in his work; it is subjective and varies from time to time, place to place, person to person.

2. Karl Strecker's edition, *Die Cambridger Lieder*, still remains the best. See poems 14.1a; 35.1; and 42.1.

3. *Cambridger Lieder*, poems 6, 15, 20, 24.

4. *Cambridger Lieder*, poem 6; Strecker edits the Parisian version on pp. 18-20.

5. *Cambridger Lieder*, poem 15. The title *Modus Florum* means "the melody of Florus," probably an unknown composer who created the musical structure of this poem. Similarly, the *Modus Liebinc* is "the melody of Liebinc," perhaps an unidentified poet. Schupp (30) considers the possibility that this Liebinc is identical to a historical Liuppo or Liupo.

6. Langosch, ed., *Waltharius* 252-305; and "'Unibos'" 49-75.

7. Suchomski fails to see humor in the *Modus Liebinc* ("In über der Hälfte des Gedichts fehlt jeder komische Zug," 102), and he perceives heavy moralizing in other *ridicula*, including *Unibos* (103-10).

8. See Suchomski 106: "Dass *ridiculum* jedoch keinerlei formale Vorstellungen implizieren kann, zeigt der Dichter des Mönch Johannes, indem er seine Quelle—also die Prosanekdote—als *ridiculum* bezeichnet."

9. Fulcoius of Beauvais, "one of the most distinguished literary figures of the eleventh century" (191), is not even mentioned in Raby's *History of Secular Latin Poetry in the Middle Ages*. For the elegiac comedy *De mercatore* and the school exercises about the snowchild, see Cohen, *La comédie latine* 2:260-78. Text and translation of *De l'enfant qui fu remis au soleil* may be found in Harrison 381-89. Texts and translations of the *Modus Liebinc* and Fulcoius' *Epistola VIII* are located at the back of this book, pp. 136-39 and 176-81.

10. Among the theorists of comic narrative, only Suchomski mentions the scholarly Latin poet Marbod (69-70). He fails to consider, however, learned poets who compose true narratives: Egbert of Liège, Hildebert of Lavardin, Fulcoius of Beauvais, Radulfus Tortarius, and Petrus Pictor, among others. More recent scholars of the Old French fabliaux (Muscatine, *The Old French*

Fabliaux; Bloch, *The Scandal of the Fabliaux*) also neglect to mention the comic narratives of these early learned Latin poets.

11. See Young 1:183.

12. The sequences, or proses, are actually forms of tropes. But Young (1:188 f.) considers tropes "in the more restricted sense"—those linked with the rise of liturgical drama.

13. The rhythms employ three types of Christian hymn form: Ambrosian rhymed couplets in iambic dimeter (*Sacerdos et Lupus, De Iohanne abbate, Unibos*); rhythmic adonic tercets consisting of dactyls and spondees or trochees (*Alfrad, Heriger*); and rhymed tercets with fifteen-syllable lines (*De Lantfrido et Cobbone*, Parisian Version). Strecker gives copious notes about metrics in his edition.

14. The Ambrosian rhymed couplet, with each verse containing eight syllables, is nearly identical to the Old French verse form. See Nykrog 248 and Schenck 16.

15. *Cambridger Lieder*, poem 42. Strecker prints the text from the *Vitae patrum* on p. 100.

16. *Mediaeval Stage* 1:368-69: "This term [Feast of Boys] must have been familiar by the end of the eleventh-century for it lends a point of sarcasm to the protest made by Yves, bishop of Chartres, in a letter to Pope Urban II against the disgraceful nomination by Philip I of France of a wanton lad to be bishop of Orléans in 1099:

eligimus puerum, puerorum festa colentes,

non nostrum morem, sed regis iussa sequentes."

17. See Ogilvy 603-19. Allusions to markets and public squares occur in the following strophes of *Unibos*: 12-13, 30, 57, 197-98.

18. Sextus 17. The songs referred to are poems 10, 12, and 14 of Strecker's edition.

19. Franceschini 300-301. The text of *Terentius et Delusor* is printed by Winterfeld in Hrotsvitha, *Hrotsvithae Opera* xx-xxiii. See Chambers 2:326-28.

20. Hence the two versions of *De Lantfrido et Cobbone*, a sequence in the Cambridge manuscript and a hymn in the Parisian manuscript, may attest to differing modes of performance. Sequences, of course, occur within liturgical dramas.

21. Several phrases of this poem remain enigmatic. "Libera frons," for instance, may mean "free garland" or "unrestrained brow," and the idea that "the dormouse bears the same name among the masses" may refer to the fact that this creature was a delicacy among the Romans and therefore eaten by the upper classes.

22. Other similar exercises were written by Hildebert (*De oppositis*, "Carmina" col. 1446) and Fulcoius (*Mellifluae Meldi*, "Epistolae" 196-97).

23. "Liebesbriefgedichte Marbods," in *Liber Floridus* 287-301. Raby (*SLP* 1:333) notes the "pieces of questionable character" in Migne (171: col. 1717 f.),

and Suchomski (66 f.) considers one of these poems (IV. *Satyra in amatorem puelli sub assumpta persona*) a *nugae*.

24. Colker (*Fulcoius* 196-97) prints a poem that "may have belonged to the *nugae*." The piece is a "metrical letter on the food products of Meaux and Beauvais," and like the *Nugae poeticae*, it is highly obscure.

25. *MGH, Poetae Latini aevi Carolini* 1:552. Theodulf uses the term *nugax*, "trifling."

26. See Raby (*SLP* 2:109 and 323) for the retractions of Giraldus Cambrensis and Peter of Blois. Pope Pius II (Aeneas Silvius Piccolomini) composed one of the first Renaissance comedies in Latin (the fifteenth-century *Chrysis*) and later retracted it along with other trifles of his youth. See Aeneas Silvius Piccolomini, *Chrysis* 5-6. Also see Suchomski 71.

27. Only the *Tractatus Garsiae*, among the venality satires, achieves true narration—or, more exactly, dramatic structure. See "Tractatus Garsiae," *MGH, Libelli de lite imperatorum et pontificum* 2:425-35; Yunck 70-78.

28. Unification is a technical method of the joke described by Freud: it involves "the eliciting of a more intimate connection between the elements of [a] statement than one would have had a right to expect from their nature" (39). Inversion is a technique of comedy described by Bergson: "if you reverse the situation and invert the roles, you obtain a comic scene" (121).

29. Many writers of the *nugae*—Hildebert, Radulfus, Petrus Pictor—lived in the early twelfth century, when the first *comediae elegiacae* (*Ovidius puellarum* and *Pamphilus*) were being written. Dronke's dating of the earliest *comedia* ("A Note on *Pamphilus*" 230) is unconventional: "A tentative approximate chronology might be: *Ovidius puellarum*, c. 1080; *Pamphilus*, c. 1100; *Facetus*, c. 1130-40." Hunt (129-31) and Beyer (*Schwank* 158) place *Pamphilus* in the late twelfth century, but this work is mentioned in a mid-twelfth-century *accessus*, indicating that it was already known in the first half of the twelfth century.

Chapter 1

Ridicula: Funny Stories
in Rhythmic Verse

"Sic fraus fraudem vicerat"—"Thus fraud had conquered fraud"—concludes the *Modus Liebinc*, and this "moral" of the poem characterizes the nature of the comedy found in all of the *ridicula*. They all depict deception, and usually the deceiver is unmasked at a climactic scene of recognition, yet often the characters' roles are inverted—that is, the deceiver is himself deceived—and hence there is a doubling of lies, of fictions. Somebody is always caught in his own trap, whether that trap is a lie or a presumption, and the result is one character who evokes admiration through his cunning and another who provokes laughter through his stupidity. All of them reveal a fascination with man's ability to lie, to pervert language, and most often they celebrate *ars*, craftiness. Hence the world of the *ridicula* mocks credulity while it emphasizes materialism. The "moral" of the *Modus Liebinc* extends beyond the confines of the simple funny story: it is a commentary on the nature and limits of fiction itself.

The formal structures and characterization of the *ridicula* enable us to identify them as comic stories, and this is important, for often the humor escapes the modern reader. The pervasive theme of fraud conquering fraud leads to what Henri Bergson calls inversion, obtaining a comic scene by making the situation turn upon itself and by reversing the characters' roles (121). In two of the *ridicula*, the *Modus Liebinc* and *Sacerdos et Lupus*, inversion is explicit. In the first, the adulterous wife tells her husband that she has conceived her illegitimate son by eating snow; years later, the husband sells the boy and tells his wife that her son melted in the torrid heat. In *Sacerdos at Lupus*, the priest is literally caught in his own trap: he finds himself at the bottom of a pit that he built to capture the wolf. The "moral" of this poem is a concrete version of the *Modus Liebinc*'s: the wolf uses the priest, "by whose cunning he was captured, as a ladder" ("et cuius arte captus est, illo pro scala usus est").

In several of the *ridicula*, inversion is implicit in the reversal of the recognition scene. In the *Modus Florum*, the king is *not* supposed to call the

Swabian a liar, and by doing so, he is outtricked by the Swabian. The Swabian's trick consists of calling the king his servant, of reversing their roles. In the story of little John, the cellmate pretends not to recognize the protagonist and mocks John's earlier vows, and thus John's roles, as ascetic and cellmate, have been reversed, or inverted. The unmasking of the lying *propheta* by Heriger is a recognition of the liar, and like the *Modus Florum*, this poem is a sort of lying contest, but in this case the liar is supposed to be called a liar. The very act of recognition or exposure entails a reversal of situation or character, and this reversal, whether explicit or implicit, is a form of inversion.

While we today may have difficulty appreciating the childlike humor of these narratives, the writers themselves were at times uncomfortable with their own audacity, for they no doubt perceived these funny stories as racy affairs—hence their need for "morals" terminating the narratives, framing the useless tales in the manner of the fable writers. Yet the "moral" endings of the *ridicula* are curiously amoral, and one gets the impression that these writers often identify their own activities with those of their protagonists. Five of the eight *ridicula* praise or ridicule liars, and the emphasis on lying within the fictions implicates the poets, the makers of fictions, and the listeners or readers, who must accept or reject these fictions as true.[1] The prologue of *Sacerdos et Lupus* indicates that the composer's consciousness about fiction is not simple:

> Quibus ludus est animo   et iocularis cantio,
> hoc advertant ridiculum;   est verum, non ficticium.
> (Those who would like to hear a jest and a funny song should listen to
> this *ridiculum*—it's true, not fiction.)

While the authenticating aside "est verum, non ficticium" may mean little more than the modern comedian's claim that he saw something "on the way to the club," it is nevertheless possible that such an introduction to a poem celebrating *ars*, man's *ingenium*, tests the listener's credulity and allies the poet with the protagonist, a creator himself.[2] Like the lying Swabian of the *Modus Florum*, the poet himself is a liar, a composer of *mendosa cantilena*.

The *ridiculum* with the simplest narrative structure, the *Modus Florum*, is little more than a suitor's contest familiar to the world of folklore, while the elegant physical structure of this sequence is in sharp contrast to this mundane subject matter. The formal structure is corrupt yet impressive: the first strophe, or prologue, corresponds in syllabification to the last, and the interior strophes, 2a, 2b, 3a, 3b, likewise correspond to each other, as the singing by semichoruses is duplicated.

The narrative structure does not exactly correspond to this strophic arrangement, though it too possesses a frame. The four-line prologue identifies the genre, and the last two lines of the poem offer a "moral":

4. Sic rege deluso Suevus falsa
   gener regius est arte factus.
(Thus when the king was tricked, the Swabian became a royal son-in-
law because of his deceptive cunning.)

The first two alternating strophes, 2a, and 2b, are a straightforward exposition
setting the terms of the lying contest; the rest of the poem consists almost
entirely of the Swabian's lie, and thus the story is largely a dramatic speech.

The Swabian, having heard of the king's offer, begins a mundane account of
his hunting expedition, and he thereby leads his listener into accepting the
veracity of his tale:

3a. "Raptis armis ego
    dum venatum solus irem,
    lepusculus inter feras
    telo tactus occumbebat.
    Mox effusis intestinis
    caput avulsum cum cute cedo."
("When I was hunting alone, with my weapons in hand, I struck down
a young hare, along with other wild animals, with my spear. After its
intestines poured forth, I cut off its head, tore it away with the skin.")

Having captured the king's attention, the Swabian introduces the miraculous and
builds suspense by mentioning a charter:

3b. "Cumque cesum manu
    levaretur caput,
    lesa aure effunduntur
    mellis modii centeni,
    sotiaque auris tacta
    totidem pisarum fudit.
    Quibus intra pellem strictis,
    lepus ipse dum secatur,
    crepidine summa caude
    kartam regiam latentem cepi . . ."
("When I raised the cut-off head with my hand, a hundred measures of
honey poured from the wounded ear and just as many peas poured out
of the fellow ear. When these were stripped and the hare was cut up,
within its skin, at the very base of the tail, I found a royal
charter . . .")

The Swabian has managed to make his lie believable and to arouse the king's
interest. He also piques the listener's interest by mentioning the contents of the

charter not in this antistrophe, sung by semichorus, but in the following strophe, sung by full chorus:

> "Que servum te firmat esse meum."
> "Mentitur," clamat rex, "karta et tu!"
> (". . . which proclaims that you are my servant!" "Liars," exclaims the king, "both the charter and you!")

In order to trick the king, the Swabian insults him. Since the king is *not* supposed to call the Swabian a liar, the "recognition," by which the king acknowledges the suitor's real status, is ironic, for the king should have avoided it.

Again the formal elements of comedy assure us that somebody at some time thought this story was amusing. Indeed, this simple story is remarkably similar to the joke about Serenissimus recounted by Freud (68-69):

> Serenissimus was making a tour through his provinces and noticed a man in the crowd who bore a striking resemblance to his own exalted person. He beckoned to him and asked: "Was your mother at one time in the service of the palace?"—"No, your Highness," was the reply, "but my father was."

Structurally, of course, this story is quite different: its comic effect derives from "ready repartee" rather than verbal entrapment. But Freud's comments about this joke shed some light on the story of the lying Swabian: "a joke shows the way in which the insult may be safely avenged—by making use of the technical method of unification in order to take up the allusion and turn it back against the aggressor . . . The question asked by the aggressor had itself the character of a joke with the technique of allusion" (104). In both Freud's joke and in the Swabian's trick we find the aspect of unification, "the eliciting of a more intimate connection between the elements of [a] statement than one would have had a right to expect from their nature" (Freud 39).

The emphasis on speech in the *Modus Florum* almost makes it what Beyer calls a *ridiculum dictum* (*Schwank* 68-72), yet the comedy lies both in the speech and in the involuntary reaction of the king. The admirable Swabian is responsible for building suspense to a climax, but the reversal is the source of laughter. Just as the man in the crowd reverses the situation by suggesting that Serenissimus is the bastard, the Swabian in the *ridiculum* reverses his relation with the king by calling him his servant. Both stories contain an implicit inversion, and they both reveal safe ways of attacking a socially superior person: by making a joke or lie. In a different context the lying Swabian would be punished, perhaps executed, for calling the king his servant, but since the king himself has condoned the lying contest, the Swabian may say anything and remain safe. The liar's cleverness lies in his recognition of this fact: by saying his worst, he adroitly leads the king outside the realm of play into the "real" world.

So in *Modus Florum*, a socially inferior character who has acute mental faculties is admirable and a socially superior character who, one may assume, is usually clever at recognizing jokes is reduced to a mentally inferior status and thus becomes a laughingstock. Freud explains how stupid characters provoke laughter and clever ones admiration (195-96):

> . . . a person appears comic to us if, in comparison with ourselves, he makes too great an expenditure of his bodily functions and too little on the mental ones; and it cannot be denied that in both of these cases our laughter expresses a pleasurable sense of the superiority which we feel in relation to him. If the relation in the two cases is reversed—if the other person's physical expenditure is found to be less than ours or his mental expenditure greater—then we no longer laugh, we are filled with astonishment and admiration.

Freud's comments apply universally to comic characters, and in the *ridicula*, the quality of cleverness cuts through all classes—the admirable figure may be a bishop or a peasant—while stupidity may also be found anywhere: among town leaders or a rustic priest. The characters of the *ridicula*, consisting of deceivers and the deceived, alternately reveal the themes of *ars* or cunning on the one hand and stupidity or physicality on the other. Thus the simple comedy of the *ridicula* may lack pointedness, but it nonetheless possesses universal characteristics.

The *Modus Liebinc* is one of the great poems circulated during the tenth and eleventh centuries, and it is the only one of the three sequences that is technically perfect in form. This poem presents a doubling of the situation found in the *Modus Florum*: it contains two speeches that are lies and thus creates a clear case of inversion, as the poem's "moral" emphasizes. Again low content contrasts with high form, as a simple, cruel story is cast in a highly ornate structure. The mockery of a quaint superstition and the husband's cruel vengeance hardly amuse a twentieth-century audience, yet this subject matter continued to delight audiences throughout the Middle Ages and well into the Renaissance, demonstrating how different today's humor is from that of the past.

Unlike the *Modus Florum*, whose first and last strophes, corresponding with each other syllabically, establish a strong formal frame, the *Modus Liebinc* consists of five pairs of strophes terminated with a single strophe. The first two strophes correspond structurally, but not thematically:

1a. Advertite,
    omnes populi,
    ridiculum

1b. Constantie
    civis Suevulus
    trans equora

et audite, quomodo   gazam portans navibus
Suevum mulier   domi coniugem
et ipse illam   lascivam nimis
defraudaret.   relinquebat.

(1a. Pay attention, everybody, and listen to a funny story about how
a wife cheated a Swabian and he cheated her.

1b. A little Swabian, a citizen of Constance, carrying his goods in
ships across the sea, left his wanton wife at home.)

The first strophe (1a) is simply a prologue, and as Dronke reveals, the call to
attention ("Advertite,/omnes populi") parodies familiar Biblical passages
("Medieval Fabliau" 280):

> The Latin singer summons his audience *as if* he were a fairground
> performer clamoring for their attention. And yet the words he chooses
> also have more solemn parallels and connotations: "Audite et populi
> attendite—Laudate eum, omnes populi." I think the poet meant these
> connotations, and meant the contrast, the leap from "Advertite, omnes
> populi" to "ridiculum." For a moment he leaves the audience in
> suspense whether his persona will be that of a sacred singer or comic
> entertainer, but swiftly he reveals that the solemn overtones were
> intended parodistically.

The opening is identical with an apparently lost sequence by Heribert, Bishop of
Eichstatt (1021-42), and scholars have suggested that *Modus Liebinc* is a parody
of Heribert's religious sequence or that Heribert himself, perhaps, composed the
Modus Liebinc.[3] Neither of these assumptions seems likely, however, since the
Modus Liebinc was probably popular in the tenth century, long before Heribert's
bishopric; further, the early existence of secular titles for religious sequences, as
has been noted, is strong testimony that the *ridicula* are not simple parodies of
religious models. The presence of religious parody, as we shall see, is difficult
to establish in this *ridiculum* as well as in others.

The second strophe (1b) begins the narration and introduces a thematic
parallelism that is maintained throughout the poem: "rich merchant on the seas
. . . wanton wife alone at home." The next pair of strophes depict "the uproar
of the ocean and the uproar at home" (Dronke, "Medieval Fabliau" 280):

2a.	Vix remige	2b.	Nec iterim
	triste secat mare		domi vacat coniux;
	ecce subito		mimi aderant,
	orta tempestate		iuvenes secuntur,
	furit pelagus,		quos et inmemor
	certant flumina,		viri exulis
	tolluntur fluctus,		excepit gaudens

post multaque exulem   atque nocte proxima
vagum littore   pregnans filium
longinquo nothus   iniustum fudit
exponebat.   iusto die.

(2a.   Scarcely did he cleave the harsh sea with his oars than lo!
suddenly, a tempest arises, the deep rages, the winds contend, and the
waves are borne up. After much turmoil the north wind lands the
wandering exile on a far-off shore.

2b. Meanwhile, his wife is not idle at home; mimes attend her, and
forgetful of her wandering husband, she joyously receives youths who
follow [them]. On the following night she conceives a son, and she
bears the illegitimate child on the appointed day.)

Dronke points out the "sardonic touches" of this description in "a narrative
detail—'meanwhile the wife is not idle at home'—in the wordplay (*filium iniustum
fudit iusto die*) and in the performer's self-mocking allusion to *mimi*, as ushering
in and typifying the wife's attempt at wicked *dolce vita*. Here as at the opening,
the poet—who may also have been the first performer—ironically half-accepts the
mime-player's role, even while pretending to accept the conventional hostile
view of it" ("Medieval Fabliau" 280-81).

The poet's narrative and dramatic skills are further demonstrated in the
following pair of strophes (3a, 3b) describing the husband's arrival and the
wife's lie. "As the husband returns," says Dronke, "there is a sinister suspense
about his behaviour—first kisses (even though he at once sees the little boy),
then the seemingly neutral question, at last bursting into a murderous threat"
("Medieval Fabliau" 281). The wife's lie, like the Swabian's, draws upon
folklore motifs, but unlike the Swabian's, her fiction is impromptu and poorly
executed.[4] Also, the Swabian in the *Modus Liebinc* is far craftier than the
tricked king of the *Modus Florum*: he remains silent. In other words, there is
recognition, but hidden recognition.

In the Cambridge manuscript a lyrical strophe intrudes into the sequence at
this point, and because it fits into the poem neither thematically nor structurally,
it is never edited as part of the poem.[5]

Nam languens amore tuo
consurrexi diluculo
perrexique pedes nuda
per nives et frigora
atque maria rimabar mesta,
si forte ventivola
vela cernerem
aut frontem navis conspicerem.

(Languishing for love of you, I arose at dawn and made my way bare-
footed across snows and cold, and I searched the desolate seas to see

if I could find sails flying in the wind or catch sight of the prow of a ship.)

Unlike the rest of the *Modus Liebinc*, this stanza contains rhyme, and it does not have a corresponding antistrophe with equal syllabification. In the sequence, the wife has just explained that she ate snow "in the Alps" (3b); in this passage, a woman is apparently near a seashore, perhaps climbing a snow-covered mountain overlooking a large body of water such as Lake Constance.

Dronke imagines that "in the German musical manuscript from which the English collection copied its words these lines may well have been written in the margin because they could be sung to the same tune as this pair of stanzas in the sequence, or perhaps because they had themselves provided the tune" (*Medieval Latin* 276). The English copyist may have mistakenly thought the lines should be inserted: "here too a woman is speaking, and the occurrence of 'nives' here as in the sequence may have given the impression of continuity." But Dronke adds that "it is less easy to be sure that the lines themselves are not fragmentary. Are they perhaps out of a lyrical narrative? Could she who is speaking be Alcyone waiting for Ceyz, or Phyllis for Demophoon—or for that matter Yseult watching for Tristan? Or is it a complete song, a Latin *winileod*?" Dronke concludes that the song draws "inspiration from a living tradition of 'cantigas de amigo,'" and he compares the intrusive passage to the "cantigas marineras," a sub-genre (*Medieval Latin* 277).

Only Dronke raises this possibility. Other scholars agree that the strophe is spurious, but they do not speculate about its presence in the Cambridge manuscript.[6] Karl Strecker points out that the additional strophe in the *Modus Liebinc* does not occur in the Wolfenbüttel manuscript, which also contains the poem, and he concludes that neither of these manuscripts is a copy of the other; instead speculates Strecker, an "Ursequenzensammlung" accounts for both the Cambridge and Wolfenbüttel collections (*Cambridger Lieder* xiii).

Neither Dronke, Strecker, nor any other scholar mentions an eleventh-century rendition of this story by Fulcoius of Beauvais. This later version is important when assessing the status of the strophe beginning "Nam languens," for in Fulcoius' story the wife claims to have eaten snow on a seashore, not in the Alps. When the husband returns home after his long voyage, Fulcoius' wife says:

"Coniugis oblitum dum quero nocte maritum,
Dum iuvat insanos amplexus reddere, vanos
Quaerere concubitus, vehemens hoc visito litus,
Quem sic arderem tanquam te, sponse, viderem.
Te non audivi, mea vota videre nequivi.
Cum magis exarsi, nivis hoc in gutture sparsi.
Pro te consumpsi, vice seminis ignea sumpsi."

("When I was seeking my husband, forgetful of his wife, at night, at the time when it is most pleasing to exchange heated embraces, to seek fruitless coition, I was burning with passion and I visited this shore; I was burning for you as if I saw you, my husband. I did not hear you, nor could I see my prayers. When my passion blazed even more, I sprinkled snow in my throat. I took it in place of you; burning, I took it in lieu of your semen.") (228; epistle 8, lines 25-30)

Although the speaker in "Nam languens" gazes at the sea in the morning ("diluculo") while Fulcoius' Ida visits the shore at night, in other respects the unusual locale is similar, as both women walk through snow in order to scan a large body of water.

Fulcoius provides evidence that "Nam languens" may be thematically related to the *Modus Liebinc*. If this is so, an early scribe may have placed the thematic variation in a manuscript margin and a later copyist perhaps mistakenly thought that this alternate version belonged to the sequence. Certainly "Nam languens" does not belong to the sequence *Modus Liebinc*, as both its rhyme and meter reveal. But from Fulcoius we discover that these lines, rather than being a lyrical narrative about a romantic heroine or a complete Latin *wineleod*, perhaps offer a glimpse of an alternate version composed sometime between the creation of the *Modus Liebinc* and Fulcoius' eighth epistle.

The following two strophes in the manuscript (4a, 4b) are "laconic, showing the merchant's cunning and his greed without comment, as he takes the boy with him and sells him as a slave" (Dronke, "Medieval Fabliau" 282). Then occurs the husband's fiction, based on that of the wife, who must remain silent though she knows her husband is lying:

5a.	Ingressusque domum	5b.	Tempestate orta
	ad uxorem ait:		nos ventosus furor
	"Consulare, coniux,		in vadosas sirtes
	consolare, cara:		nimis fessos egit,
	natum tuum perdidi,		et nos omnes graviter
	quem non ipsa tu		torret sol, at il-
	me magis quidem		le nivis natus
	dilexisti.		liquescebat."

(5a. After entering his house, he says to his wife: "Console yourself, my wife. Console yourself, my dear. I have lost your son, whom not even you loved more than I.

5b.   "A storm arose and a raving wind drove us, exhausted, into sandbanks full of shoals, where the sun burned all of us fiercely, melting him who was born of the snow.")

This fictional voyage echoes the flux of the real voyage undertaken years earlier: the "tempestate orta" and the "ventosus furor" are direct verbal echoes of strophe

2a. Further, this speech, with its delaying tactics ("Consolare, coniux/consolare, cara"), its hesitation to reveal the "truth," parodies the wife's previous hesitancy ("Mi . . . /mi coniux") as "she thinks of a lie wherever she can." And again there is hidden recognition. The husband's story at first contains nothing preposterous: the stormy voyage he says he undertook is realistic, for after all, it closely resembles the "real" voyage described by the poet. The transition to the miraculous is smooth and inevitable: the son melted in the heat. This method of drawing the listener in by beginning with the believable and ending with the miraculous is the liar's best ploy. The verbal echoes and strophic parallelism create aesthetic excellence and contribute to comic effect, as repetition is one of the bases of comedy.[7]

The final strophe of the *Modus Liebinc*, which Dronke believes provides "symmetry with the opening, framing the black comedy in a statement of mathematical detachment" ("Medieval Fabliau" 282), has been called superfluous by German scholars:[8]

> 6. Sic perfidam
>   Suevus coniugem
>   deluserat;
>   sic fraus fraudem vicerat:
>   nam quem genuit
>   nix, recte hunc sol
>   liquefecit.

(Thus the Swabian deceived his unfaithful wife. Thus fraud had conquered fraud. And him whom snow engendered, rightly the sun melted.)

This tendency to sum up or "moralize" at the end of a story is characteristic of the *ridicula*, as it is of the fabliaux. Beyer sees such "pseudomoral justifications of the negative Schwank" as formal, structural aspects of the genre that reflect the rise of the fabliaux from fables. "The concept 'morality through the negative in man,'" says Beyer, "could not be replaced with the formulation 'comedy through the negative in man' before the second half of the twelfth century" ("Morality" 31).

> Obviously because of the mighty influence of the medieval church, the comic intention . . . was at first not strong enough to compensate for the vulgar elements. At least four hundred years elapsed before the comic *fabulae otiosae*—due to the literary acceptance of the fabliaux towards the end of the twelfth century—overcame the odium of sinfulness which had caused them to be confined in the ecclesiastical penitentials since the eighth century. ("Morality" 22)

Beyer's theory may explain the rarity of secular comic narratives before the twelfth century, yet in the *ridicula*, comedy, not morality, seems to be the final aim. Also, the *Modus Liebinc*, far from being confined to a penitential, is located in a *florilegium*, a collection of classical and medieval works that perhaps served as a primer or textbook (Cambridge MS. Gg. 5.35), and it is also wedged into a blank space of an Italian manuscript holding Persius' *Satires* (Vat. Palatinus 1710).[9] What is more surprising about the *Modus Liebinc* is the amoral "moral": "Thus fraud had conquered fraud." The poet sees the husband's victory over his wife as acceptable behavior: perpetrators of fraud should be vanquished by their own methods. This is hardly a Christian or even a practical moral like those of the fables.

But the creator of the *Modus Liebinc*, though he may not be a Christian moralizer, refrains from overt parody of religious ideas or institutions. The husband's parody of the wife's speech within the fiction, like the poet's parody of Biblical language in the prologue, is a sure indication that this composer is capable of linguistic mockery, yet he fails to exploit the potential parallel of the miraculous conception through eating snow and the Immaculate Conception.[10] In this respect the *ridicula* differ from the Old French fabliaux, in which parody of religion is sometimes obvious.[11] In the *ridicula*, religious parody remains latent, unexploited.

Whereas writers of a later age may discern the parodic potential of the folktale, in the *ridicula*, the source of humor is not religious or literary parody, but mockery of human actions, intentions, and beliefs. Such mockery is carefully framed by sententious "morals" whose usefulness is already undermined by their essential amorality. The black humor of *Modus Liebinc* and its realistic mockery of superstition continued to fascinate storytellers throughout the Middle Ages and Renaissance, but its subject matter fails to amuse a modern audience, repulsed by the husband's cruel vengeance upon his wife, unimpressed by the mockery of a quaint but dead superstition.[12] Yet, this *ridiculum*'s technical excellence and vivid detail make it the best rendition of a story with multiple variants, and the poet, "undoubtedly a master of form who understood well the Latin sequence of his time," proves himself a master at blending high style with low matter.[13]

The only *ridiculum* existing both as a sequence and as a rhythm is *De Lantfrido et Cobbone*, and a comparison of its two forms, though both are fragmentary, provides insight into the difference between the two dominant structures of the *ridicula*. In addition to existing as a sequence in the Cambridge manuscript, this story is extant in a tenth- or eleventh-century French manuscript (B.N. lat. 242), and its rhythmic, fifteen-syllable lines are the same used in the ninth-century *Cena Cypriani*.[14] Though both texts are very corrupt—the French rhythmic version, for instance, contains several lacunae, and at one point in the manuscript (strophe 12), an earlier section intrudes into the narrative—the essential story is easily understood.

Nowhere is the stylistic difference between sequence and rhythm sharper than in the prologues of the two versions. The Cambridge Song's extended prologue (1a, 1b, 2a, 2b) poeticizes a passage from Isadore's *Etymologia*, and it reveals a peculiar eleventh-century tendency to flaunt a technical knowledge about music.[15] This precious prologue, distinguishing three form of music, *rhythmica*, *organica*, and *harmonica*, no doubt impressed the medieval listener. The prosaic prologue of the Parisian version, in contrast, is apologetic in tone, and the poet makes his didactic intentions clear:

1. Cum insignium virorum   gesta dictis fulgeant,
   dulcibus ecce iam decet   ut modolis clareant,
   quatinus illorum facta   fidem nobis augeant.
2. Sepe namque, que videtur ociosa cancio,
   pura nobis imputatur   fidei devocio,
   ceu scolastici ludentes   canimus in timpano.

(1. Since the deeds of distinguished men glitter in words, it is fitting, here and now, that they resound in sweet melodies because their actions increase our faith.

2. For often, we finally judge what seems a useless song as the holy zeal of our faith when we scholars, playing, sing it to a timbrel's beat.)

The difference in style is immediately discernible: the sequence, commencing with a three-stanza sentence, is dense with nouns, and it displays a considerable technical knowledge both of music and of composition; the rhythm, in contrast, with each stanza containing a single sentence, has a much more colloquial language, and its consistent rhyme and rhythm constitute a much simpler form.

This difference is also obvious in the narrative exposition: the rhythm reveals popular, oral sources of the story, and its fairytalelike beginning ("Quodam tempore") marks a less elevated artistic form. The sequence mentions no such oral origins; rather, Biblical allusions underscore the literary formality of this composition.[16]   The sequence's verbal play on the two friends' equality introduces a theme popular throughout the later Middle Ages.[17]

3. Quamvis amicitiarum
   genera plura legantur,
   non sunt adeo preclara
   ut istorum sodalium,
   qui communes extiterunt
   in tantum, ut neuter horum
   suapte quid possideret
   [nec] gazarum nec servorum
   nec alicuius suppellectilis;
   alter horum quicquid vellet,
   ab altero ratum foret;

more ambo coequales,
in nullo umquam dissides,
quasi duo unus essent,
in omnibus similes.

(Although one may read about many kinds of friendship, there never
has been a more remarkable one than that of these two companions,
who experience so much together that neither of them possessed
anything of his own, neither riches nor servants nor household goods
of any kind; if one of them should desire anything, it would be guessed
at by the other; in this way they were both equal, in nothing ever
separate, as if two were one, in all things alike.)

This absolute equality, as well as the exceptional ability of the duo to read each
other's minds, is contradicted by the narrative that follows, for Lantfrid is not
only unable to read his friend's mind, but he also proves utterly inferior in
mental capacity.

Like the *Modus Florum* and the *Modus Liebinc*, lies are at the center of *De
Lantfrido at Cobbone*, where they are tests to prove Lantfrid's friendship.
Cobbo's stated motivations for his feigned need to return to his homeland differ
slightly in the two versions: his brothers and relatives need him in the
Cambridge Song (st. 4); his servants and neighbors create troubles in the Parisian
rhythm (st. 5-6). In the rhythm a lacuna occurs after Cobbo informs Lantfrid
about his departure, for in the following strophe (st. 7), Cobbo is again "first"
to speak, and his offer of wealth induces Lantfrid to make his own offer:

7.   Primus Cobbo ad Lantfridum   dixit inter epulas:
     "Multas valde tesaurorum   posui divicias,
     quas tibi fieri volo: mihi dono capias."
8.   Lantfridus ei respondit: "Meum est hoc facere.
     Tu trans mare me venisti   visitando querere;
     ego tibi multa bona   debeo [rependere]."

(7. Then Cobbo said to Lantfrid when they were at table: "I have put
aside a great deal of my wealth, I want it to become yours: take what
I give you."
8. Lantfrid replies: "It is *my* duty to do this. You have crossed the sea
to live with me; I ought to repay you for the many favors I have
received from you.")

Whereas in the rhythmic version Lantfrid offers to give his wealth to the parting
Cobbo, in the sequence he offers to become an exile for his friend, and by this
act he will repay his friend for his love (st. 5). Cobbo's request for his friend's
wife lacks a solid causal relationship with Lantfrid's speech in the sequence (st.
6), and the wife does not emerge as a character; the setting changes often, and

the yielding of the wife lacks realism.   In the rhythm, on the other hand,
Lantfrid's offer of money leads Cobbo to request the fair Segesvita:

> 9.   "Dic mihi, quomodo tu vis   fieri placabilis?"
>   ....
>   "Uxor ad amandum tua   mihi est amabilis."
> 10. Cuius uxor Segesvita   fulgebat in talamis,
>   splendor solis utque lune   rutilat in radiis,
>   ac pre cunctis speciosa   videbatur feminis.
> 11. Cobbo tantum perscrutare   volens amicitiam
>   ....
>
> (9. "Tell me, how would you most like to be pleased?" . . . "You
> would behave like a true friend if you gave me your wife to enjoy."
> 10. Lantfrid's wife, Segesvita, glittered in her room. The brilliance
> of sun and moon reddens in her rays, and she seemed more splendid
> than all other women.
> 11. Cobbo, wanting to test Lantfrid's friendship . . .)

After a spurious strophe (st. 12), the poet describes, in straightforward fashion,
Lantfrid's gift (st. 13).   Despite its fragmentary state, the rhythm has
chronological and causal order surpassing that of the sequence. Furthermore,
Lantfrid does not seem quite so stupid: in the rhythm he is "paying close
attention to his friend's faithfulness" (st. 13), but in the sequence, "without
hesitation Lantfrid gave his hand/to the other's hand cheerfully" (st. 6). The
rhythm, though inferior in technical form, possesses greater realism in
chronology, causality, and characterization.

   In the final scenes of the story, the sequence, which is far more developed
than the truncated rhythm, offers a superior rendition. In the Cambridge Song,
Lantfrid, whose fidelity is pressed to the limit, uses three forms of music—string,
voice, and percussion—as he urges his friend to keep faith (st. 7); Lantfrid states
that Cobbo's seduction of his wife is shameful, a disgrace committed by one
brother upon another. This detail is missing in the rhythm, in which Lantfrid
simply repeats, "Cobbo, fidem teneas!" (st. 14). Also, in the sequence, Cobbo's
revelation of his intentions has the ring of a moral: "Iam non est, quod
experiatur ultra" (st. 8); in the rhythm, the "moral" purpose has already been
stated within the story by the poet (strophe 11: "Cobbo tantum perscrutare volens
amicitiam"). The extremely brief conclusion of the rhythm is apparently altered
more than the rest of the poem, and the result is that the end of the sequence is
"plus détaillé et plus pittoresque" (Paris, "Lantfrid" 183).

   The formal structures of the poems illustrate some key differences between
sequences and rhythms.   In general the sequences tend to disregard the
relationship of formal structure and narrative structure, particularly in the case
of dialogue, which in all three sequences can begin almost anywhere in a strophe
and often spills over into a following strophe, perhaps for suspenseful effect. In

the rhythmic hymns, on the other hand, with their short strophes of two or three lines, quite often the structural units follow the narrative development faithfully: whenever a character begins a speech, typically a new strophe occurs. In the sequences, strophic parallelism leads to verbal echoes and thematic mockery, as demonstrated in the *Modus Liebinc*. But in the case of *De Lantfrido et Cobbone*, the rhythm, except for the end, is more detailed and generally clearer than the sequence, and it contains a greater concern for realism. However, it is an oversimplification to conclude that the sequences have an overwhelming concern for form, whereas the rhythms value content over structure. The hymns too reveal awareness of poetic structure, and in some of the rhythmic *ridicula* this structure effectively complements the comic tale.

Such correlation adds to the aesthetic excellence of *Heriger*, in which deflation of august figures and clever repartee between speakers contribute to effective comedy. The lying *propheta* or boaster[18] claims to have visited heaven, a paradise where divine figures are reduced to human proportions. Bishop Heriger, revealing humor with his ironic quips, is a superior character arousing admiration; the false *propheta*, making errors in his account of an alimentary heaven and finally admitting he stole from Christ's table, is an inferior character provoking laughter. The process by which Heriger catches the *propheta* in his own lie contains a move from dissimulation to revelation, from bewilderment to illumination, and thus exemplifies the universal tendency of comic inversion, by which the trickster is outtricked.[19] The structure of the poem, consisting of statement and reply, leads to a final recognition of the liar's true nature.

Heriger, one of the two *ridicula* lacking a prologue, is thematically close to the *Modus Florum*, for the *propheta*, who claims to have seen hell "girded by an extremely thick forest" ("accinctum densis undique silvis"), lies like the tricky Swabian. As bishop, Heriger must patiently listen to this report and determine its authenticity, yet he is capable of joking even at the beginning of the presentation:

> 3. Heriger illi   ridens respondit:
>   "Meum subulcum   illuc ad pastum
>   nolo cum macris   mittere porcis."
> (Laughing, Heriger replied to him. "I'd better not send my swineherd
> there to feed his lean swine.")

The "selva oscura" which has epic dimensions in Dante's *Inferno* is here rejected as a possible feeding ground for pigs, and Heriger generates comedy by reducing what is frightening and mysterious to mundane size. The unexpectedness of such a reply reveals Heriger's skepticism regarding the *propheta*'s voyage at the outset, though the boaster himself is unaware of the irony. He too is responsible for reduction of the supernatural: he saw Christ "joyful, sitting and eating" ("Christumque vidi/letum sedentem et comedentem"):

5. "Iohannes baptista   erat pincerna
   atque preclari   pocula vini
   porrexit cunctis   vocatis sanctis."
("John the Baptist was the cupbearer and offered cups of excellent wine
to all the saints who were summoned together.")

Christ becomes a mere human with physical needs, and John the Baptist has
more in common with Ganymede than a Christian saint. Heriger is again ready
with a witty, ironic repartee:

6. Heriger ait: "Prudenter egit
   Christus, Iohannem   ponens pincernam,
   quoniam vinum   non bibit umquam"
(Heriger replied.   "Christ behaved wisely by making John the
cupbearer, since the Baptist never drinks wine.")

Heriger's reply reveals sound memory of the Bible and also foreshadows the
boaster's theft of liver from the heavenly banquet.[20] The suggestion, however,
that John the Baptist could possibly drink wine at the expense of others is doubly
preposterous, for John does not drink to begin with, and furthermore, he is a
saint who does not covet. The bishop, going along with the *propheta*'s account,
sets the boaster up by suggesting that John may be a tippler. The liar is unaware
of the trap and, in fact, grows in confidence and makes a blunder.

In the lacuna that follows, the *propheta* makes the mistake of calling Saint
Peter the head cook ("magister cocorum"), for in the next extant strophe, Heriger
takes the storyteller to task for casting the saint in such a role:

8. "Mendax probaris,   cum Petrum dicis
   illic magistrum   esse cocorum,
   est quia summi   ianitor celi."
("You have proven yourself a liar when you said that Peter is the head
cook there, for he is the doorkeeper of those highest gates.")

Heriger, suspicious from the beginning, is now certain that the *propheta*'s
account is false. The verbal duel pitting liar and tester reaches a climax with
Heriger's inquiry: "Ubi sedisti?/Volo, ut narres, quid manducasses" ("Where
did you sit?/I want you to tell me what you ate").

10.   Respondit homo: "Angulo uno;
   partem pulmonis   furabar cocis.
   Hoc manducavi   atque recessi."
(The man responded.   "[I sat] in a corner; I stole a piece of lung from
the cook. I ate that, and then I returned [to earth].")

Once Heriger catches the *propheta* in a mistake, Heriger's mood changes to anger, and when he finally discovers that the boaster is a thief, he knows he is dealing with a liar and he therefore punishes the *propheta* with a flogging. But of course the *propheta* is not really a thief, for his story is untrue, so he is punished for something he did not do. The liar, stupid and naive, is unaware that his fiction has an inner logic, for his theft of lung spurs his sudden return to earth. The bishop's last words, spoken sternly, again show his sound knowledge of the Bible and his propensity for ironic understatement, in this final instance providing a "moral" to the story:[21]

12.   "Si te ad suum   invitet pastum
       Christus, ut secum   capias cibum,
       cave ne furtum facias!"
("The next time Christ invites you to dinner to share his food with you, make sure that you do not steal!")

Interpretations regarding the parody of this poem vary greatly. Friedrich von der Leyen sees "mockery of the belief in the miraculous" (131), and Paul Lehmann, modifying von der Leyen's view, finds "eine Parodie der sich haufenden ernstgemeintem Visionen" (*Parodie* 33). Gustav Ehrismann, perceiving comedy in the theft alone, which, he contends, has origins in Aesop's fables, does not see any parody in the poem, but rather, "the intervention of the Church against false stories" (371), and Jürgen Beyer, similarly rejecting parodic intent, finds comedy in the "Witzstruktur" of the poem (*Schwank* 80). Peter Dronke, finally, locates comedy in both the parody and the characterization: heaven "becomes a world of farce, as full of pranks and amusing deceptions as the world below. The fake visionary tries to trick the bishop, and is out-tricked by him" ("Medieval Fabliau" 284).

Certainly the comedy of this poem depends upon character and structure, and any religious parody, as in the *Modus Liebinc*, remains potential, unexploited. We have seen that both central characters, the admirable Heriger and the stupid *propheta*, are responsible for the poem's comic effect, the first through his ready repartees, the second through his mental inferiority. Further, Heriger's sudden mention of his swineherd has the same effect as the reduction of John the Baptist to a tippler, of Peter to a cook—socially inferior characters are generally comic ones. This reduction is, in a loose sense, a parody of serious notions about august saints, but just as the story of the snowchild avoids direct parody of the Immaculate Conception, the scene depicting John the Baptist serving wine to the gathered saints and the lost strophe presenting Peter as cook probably do not parody the Last Supper. Like the ninth-century *Cena Cypriani*, in which Biblical figures get drunk and sing, or the thirteenth-century *De Saint Piere et du jonglere*, in which Saint Peter is accused of cheating at dice, this poem belongs to a comic tradition that gently ridicules divine figures without parodying any portions of the Bible directly.[22] On the contrary, Heriger's allusions to the Bible are orthodox and serious.

Like many *ridicula*, this one centers upon the belief in the miraculous, and the kitchen humor of the tale is quite like that of the fabliau *Du provost a l'aumuche*, in which a provost, having stolen "lart" from a table, receives the same punishment as the lying *propheta*—he is beaten. Indeed, the subject matter of this poem, though thoroughly medieval, may still appeal to a modern reader's sense of humor. Unlike the three sequences, whose formal structures seem at odds with their mundane subject matter, Heriger's structure and matter are in harmony, and the rhythm's wit is pointed and effective.

Another rhythmic *ridiculum* that seems to parody religious institutions but does not is the shortest of these poems, appropriately titled *Rithmus de abbate Iohanne brevis stature* or, more simply, *De Iohanne abbate*. The poem has been attributed to Fulbert of Chartres, as it is found in several manuscripts containing his work, but such authorship remains dubious.[23] It is only the *ridiculum* having a definite written source: the sixth-century *Vitae patrum*.[24] "What the poet . . . found in *Vitae Patrum*," explains Dronke, "was indeed nothing more than a brief moral anecdote, told without humor, a warning against hubris for the over-ambitious contemplative. He transforms this into a *ridiculum* (lightening rather than forfeiting the moral) by the lively development of the *prank* that the one holy man plays on the other, in pretending not to recognize him" ("Medieval Fabliau" 284-85). Though the poem has a strong moral frame, it is critical of human presumption rather than physical weakness, and it probably does not offer a critique of "exaggerated monastic asceticism" (Lehmann, *Parodie* 34).

The composer supplies a prologue—lacking in the prose original—that, like the *Modus Liebinc*'s, leaps "from the solemn to the comic." After a narrative strophe identifying John as "parvulus stature, non virtutibus" ("short in stature but not in virtues"), the little hero informs his superior of his holy intentions.

3. "Volo," dicebat, "vivere   secure sicut angelus,
   nec veste nec cibo frui,   qui laboretur manibus."
("I want to live like an angel, free from cares, enjoying neither clothing
nor food, the products of manual labor.")

John's rejection of the physical necessities that only humans, not angels, require is missing in the original, which nonetheless contains the key word "securus": "Volebam esse securus sicut angeli sunt securi nil operantes, sed sine intermissione collaudantes Deum." The following two strophes, presenting the superior's warning and John's flippant response, have no counterpart in the *Vitae patrum*:

4. Respondit maior: "Moneo,   ne sis incepti properus,
   frater, quod tibi postmodum   sit non cepisse sacius."

5. At minor: "Qui non dimicat,   non cadit neque superat!"
    ait et nudus heremum   interiorem penetrat.
(4. The superior replied, "I warn you, brother, do not be o'er hasty
beginning something that had sooner not been undertaken."
5. But the lesser brother retorted, "Nothing lost, nothing gained!" and
naked, he enters the inner recesses of the monastery.)

The original, which merely states, "Et mox spolians se, quo vestitus erat, abiit
in eremum," lacks the sharp contrast between the monk's words and deeds.

    Presumption, which is a form of self-delusion and therefore a lie unto oneself,
leads John to speak of himself in the third person once he realizes that his
resolve has superseded his abilities:

6. Septem dies gramineo   vix ibi durat pabulo;
    octava fames imperat,   ut ad sodalem redeat.
7. Qui sero clausa ianua   tutus sedet in cellula,
    cum minor voce debili   "Frater," appellat, "aperi!
8. "Iohannes opis indigus   notis assistit foribus;
    ne spernat tua pietas,   quem redigit necessitas."
(6. He hardly lasts seven days there subsisting on a diet of herbs; on
the eighth day hunger overcomes him, so he returns to his cellmate.
7. His cellmate, meanwhile, sits comfortably in the little cell after
closing the door late at night, and John, with a weak voice, calls,
"Brother, please open!"
8. "John, needing your help, stands outside the well-known door; may
your pity not scorn him whom necessity drives back.")

With vivid speech and concrete detail (the cell is tiny—"cellula"), the poet vastly
improves upon his mundane source: ". . . et facta ibi hebdomada una reversus
est ad fratrem suum. Et dum pulsaret ostium, respondit ei, antequam aperiret,
dicens: 'Quis es tu?' Et ille dixit: 'Ego sum Joannes.'" The cellmate's
mischievous response in the *Vitae patrum*—"'Ioannes angelus factus est et ultra
inter homines non est'"—is slightly but significantly altered by the poet:

9. Respondit ille deintus: "Iohannes factus angelus
    miratur celi cardines,   ultra non curat homines."
("John has become an angel," the monk inside replied. "He gazes at
heaven's gates, no longer thinking about men.")

The cellmate's pretense of not recognizing John parodies the hero's earlier
resolve to live "secure sicut angelus," and his comment that John "ultra non curat
homines" suggests that John, by rejecting his own human nature, has rejected all
mankind. Indeed, John has lost his identity: by speaking of himself in the third
person, he leads his cellmate to refer to him as an entity no longer of this world.

The confusion about John's identity is explained rather obviously in the *Vitae patrum*. After spending the night outdoors, John receives the following clarification from his cellmate: "Si homo es, opus habes iterum operari, ut vivas. Si autem angelus es, quid quaeris intrare in cellam?" John, doing penance, confesses his sin: "Et ille poenitentiam agens dixit: 'Ignosce mihi, frater, quia peccavi.'" In the *ridiculum*, John's night outdoors is his penance, a rather humorous, though cruel, punishment for his presumption:

> 10.   Iohannes foris excubat   malamque noctem tolerat
>   et preter voluntariam   hanc agit penitentiam.
> (So John must sleep outdoors and endure the harsh night; most unwillingly he undergoes this penance.)

In the morning "crustula" ("little crumbs"), the unappealing diet of monks, becomes a delicacy for the starved ascetic:

> 11.   Facto mane recipitur   satisque verbis uritur,
>   sed intentus ad crustula   fert patienter omnia.
> 12.   Refocillatus Domino   grates agit ac socio,
>   dehinc rastellum brachiis   temptat movere languidis.
> (11. In the morning he is let in and is criticized by words enough, but intent upon little crumbs, he patiently endures everything.
> 12.   Revived, he gives thanks to the Lord—and to his comrade; immediately he endeavors to move a hoe with his weakened limbs.)

The "-ula" diminutive dominates the poem, to the point that John's hoe ("rastellum") sounds like a little one. The syntax of the line describing John's gratitude implies that the monk has begrudgingly acknowledged his fellow man's benevolence: "Refocillatus Domino grates agit...ac socio." His cellmate's abstract statement in the *Vitae patrum* ("'Si homo es, opus habes iterum operari, ut vivas'") is concretized as John "endeavors to move a hoe with his weakened limbs."

The "moral" tag of the poem reiterates the theme of John's rejection of his human nature:

> 13:   Castigatus angustia   de levitate nimia,
>   cum angelus non potuit,   vir bonus esse didicit.
> (Checked by necessity, reproved for caprice, John decides, since he could not become an angel, to be a good man.)

The change in theme reflects a changed attitude toward human nature: instead of attacking an individual's weakness, his lack of mettle for the rigorous ascetic life, the *ridiculum* criticizes John's failure to recognize his human nature and its limitations. Like the *Modus Liebinc* and *Heriger*, this poem lacks overt religious parody. Lehmann's suggestion that it may be a critique of "exaggerated monastic asthenicism . . . [which] . . . at the time may have found particular approval by the Cluniacs" (*Parodie* 34) remains only a possibility. The humor arises from the cellmate's prank, his feigned confusion of the starving man outside his door with the angel that does not exist, and the situation certainly appeals to our modern sense of humor. But humor also derives from John's penance outside the cell, and that is a cruel humor, like the *Modus Liebinc*'s, in which a boy is sold into slavery, like *Heriger*'s, in which the liar is flogged. Yet the theme of the poem, the ridicule of human presumption, the acceptance of one's human nature, hints at a humanism not found in the sixth-century source.

Two of the *ridicula* present animals as characters, yet unlike the fables, the Latin poems present humanistic themes differentiating man from beast. *Sacerdos et Lupus*, which draws its content from folklore,[25] demonstrates, like the *Modus Liebinc*, how one gets caught in his own trap—in this instance literally. It is the only *ridiculum* other than the *Modus Liebinc* that has direct parallels in Old French literature: the episode of "Isengrin et le pretre Martin" belonging to the *Roman de Renart*, which Mario Roques calls a "transposition" of the Latin poem.[26] A comparison of the two poems offers a rare opportunity to distinguish *ridiculum* from beast-epic.

The Old French poet expands and condenses the Latin original, often at the expense of the humanistic theme, the superiority of intellectual cunning over brute strength. The *ridiculum* begins typically with self-identification, and "with light irony the poet adds the minstrel's adage: 'It's truth, not fiction!'" (Dronke, "Medieval Fabliau" 283). The beast-epic begins by acknowledging its written source and supplying a proverb having little thematic relevance to the story:

> Seignor, ce dïent li devin:
> Il est escrit en parchemin
> que cil a sovent mau matin
> qui pres de lui a mau voisin.
> (Lords, this is what wise men say: it is written in books that he who has a wicked neighbor often has a bad morning.) (branch 15, lines 14843-46)

In the Latin poem, the priest is a low character and therefore a likely butt of humor, but the priest's social inferiority in no way implies intellectual deficiencies. This point is apparently lost by the French poet, who first calls *dant* Martin unlettered ("ne fu onques de lestre mestre," 15, 14850) and then describes him as "very wise" ("mout sages," 15, 14853). The overtly stated theme of the Latin poem is omitted by the later poet:

5.   Qui dolens sui fieri   detrimentum peculii,
       quia diffidit viribus,   vindictam querit artibus.
(Afraid that he would lose his entire flock, he seeks vengeance by his
cunning, for he had no confidence in his strength.)

This is a common theme in the comic literature of the High Middle Ages. In
Le vilain qui conquist paradis par plait, for instance, the theme is almost
identical to that of *Sacerdos et Lupus*: "Mielz valt engiens que ne fait force."[27]
This theme also occurs in other branches of the *Roman de Renart*,[28] but it is
omitted in this episode because it distinguishes man from animal and therefore
threatens the fictional reality in which a wolf can talk and reason.

As the theme develops in the *ridiculum*, the center of attention is on the
priest, while in the beast-epic the spotlight is on the wolf. In *Sacerdos et Lupus*,
the aged cleric first wisely trusts in his *ars* rather than his *vires*, and after he digs
a pit to trap his enemy, the poet breaks out in praise of human genius, "Humano
datum commodo nil maius est ingenio!" ("Nothing greater is given to man than
his genius!") Though the French poet greatly expands the description of the
priest's activities, he again overlooks the theme, and significantly, he gives the
wolf a speech, a lament on how greed has caught him ("com covoitise m'a
sorpris," 15, 14898).   In the *ridiculum*, the priest's presumption, his
overconfidence in his physical strength once the wolf is captured, accounts for
the failure of his scheme and the deflation of his character.

8.   Accurrit mane presbiter,   gaudet vicisse taliter;
        intus protento baculo   lupi minatur oculo.
9.   "Iam," inquit, "fera pessima,   tibi rependam debita.
        Aut hic frangetur baculus,   aut hic crepabit oculus."
10.   Hoc dicto simul impulit,   verbo sed factum defuit,
        nam lupus servans oculum   morsu retentat baculum.
11.   At ille miser vetulus,   dum sese trahit firmius,
        ripa cedente corruit   et lupo comes extitit.
(8. In the morning the priest runs to the hole and rejoices that he has
conquered his enemy.
9. "Now," he says, "worst of all beasts, I shall repay you what I owe
you. Either this stick will break, or your eye will rattle."
10. After saying this, he strikes, but the deed fails the word, for the
wolf, preserving his eye, holds the stick in his teeth.
11. The old wretch, drawing himself up firmly, falls into the hole
when the bank breaks, and he becomes the wolf's companion.)

The contrast between word and deed ("verbo sed factum defuit") is the same as
that of *ars* and *vires*. Cunning, genius, and language are qualities the priest
possesses, and his mistake is trusting in something he does not have: physical

strength. The result is that the priest becomes the wolf's equal, an outcome that the French poet perceives acutely:

12.   Hinc stat lupus, hinc presbiter,   timent, sed dispariliter,
    Nam, ut fidenter arbitror,   lupus stabat securior.

(Here stands the wolf, there the priest. Each is afraid, but unequally, for I am quite sure that the wolf was the more secure.)

    Or a Isengrin conpaignon;
    l'uns fu deça, l'autre dela,
    de paor l'un l'autre esgarda:
    mout ot Isangrin grant paor,
    mais le prestre ot asez graignor. . .

(Now Isengrin has a companion. One was here, the other there, and each looked at the other in fear. Isengrin was very afraid, but the priest was even more so . . .) (15, 14950-54)

The high point of the *ridiculum*, with the priest singing the Psalms and the wolf taking the opportunity to escape, possesses a comic cause-and-effect as the priest's plea to the Lord, "And deliver us from evil," is followed immediately by the wolf's departure:

17.   Nam cum acclinis presbiter   perfiniret "Pater noster"
    atque clamaret Domino   "Sed libera nos a malo,"
18.   Hic dorso eius insilit   et saltu liber effugit,
    et cuius arte captus est,   illo pro scala usus est.

(17. For while the priest, bent over, was finishing the "Pater noster" and exclaiming to God, "And deliver us from evil,"
18. The wolf leaps on his back and, with a jump, escapes free. Thus he used the old man, by whose cunning he was captured, as a ladder.)

The man who once used cunning to capture the animal is now reduced to a staircase used by that animal. Such a reversal does not occur in the fable, in which the wolf possesses human characteristics from the outset. Further, the dramatic irony that the priest's prayer, "Sed libera nos a malo," leads to the wolf's escape is also missing from the French poem, which greatly reduces the priest's spiritual plight.

The priest's sudden devotion, taking the form of prayer, develops the central theme of language: "The language of prayer, which had become insulated from reality in an autonomous verbal realm, cut off from feeling and action, is transported into a context which gives it real sincerity and real significance" (*Ysengrimus*, Mann 60). This theme is a common one in the fabliaux: in *Du prestre qui fu mis au lardier*, a priest imprisoned in a meatlocker addresses his brother in terms reminiscent of those in the *ridiculum*:

"Frater, pro Deo
Me delibera;
Reddam tam cito
Ce qu'il coustera."
Quant l'oy, en haut s'escria:
"Çavetiers me doivent amer de cuer fin
Quant à mon lardier fais parler latin."
(*"Frater, pro Deo/Me delivera;/Reddam tam cito* no matter what it
costs." When he heard it he cried out loud: "Cobblers should love
me dearly since I know how to make my locker speak Latin.")

The theme also occurs in the beast-epic *Ysengrimus*: when the priest catches
sight of the fox making off with his hen, he "immediately transposes his
mechanical recitation of the hymn 'Salue, festa dies [toto uenerabilis euo],' into
the anguished cry 'Ve tibi, mesta dies, toto miserabilis euo' (I 741-46); the ritual
formulae of liturgy are transformed by a reality which creates a pressing urge to
register their meaning" (*Ysengrimus*, Mann 61).

Both the *ridiculum* and the beast-epic conclude by criticizing the priest for
being less than devout:

20.   Hinc a vicinis queritur   et inventus extrahitur,
        sed nunquam post devotius   oravit nec fidelius.
(His neighbors look for him and, once they find him, draw him out [of
the pit]. But never again did he pray with more devotion and faith.)

Si sergent l'en orent tost trait,
puis se rïent de ce qu'a fait.
Bien vos puis dire et aconter
c'onques puis mese ne sautier
ne chanta puis de bon entent
ne par si bon entendement,
com il fist ovec Ysangrin
tant con il fu en son enging.
(His men have soon drawn him out [of the pit] and then laugh at what
he did. I can easily tell you that he never again sang mass or his
psalter with better intent or better understanding then he did with
Ysengrin, when he was in his trap.) (15, 14973-80)

This jab at the priest's lack of devotion accords with the earlier assertion by
the priest, in the Latin poem, that he has fallen into his predicament because of
"the prayers of the unfortunate people whose souls I have neglected, whose tithes
I have eaten" ("Hoc," inquid, "infortunii dant mihi vota populi,/quorum neglexi
animas, quorum comedi decimas," st. 14). The cleric's materialism, his neglect
of his parishioners, and his lack of devotion prohibit an allegorical interpretation

of the *ridiculum*, for the priest is first described as loving his flock ("vivebat amans pecudis"), which, if interpreted allegorically, would represent those unfortunate people whom he has robbed. The beast-epic, in contrast, does not mention the priest's negligence of the poor and thus does not disturb the potential allegory of the sheep representing Christian souls. While fables, beast-epics, and even fabliaux often sustain allegorical interpretation easily,[29] the *ridicula* generally resist allegorical treatment, just as they frustrate attempts to locate definite Christian parody. This failure to maintain overt moral allegory and to present unambiguous parody is consistent with the emphasis on theme rather than moral in the conclusions of these poems.

The fable writer, in transforming the Latin poem into an episode of the Old French beast-epic, suppresses the humanistic theme not because it is foreign to his genre—the theme does occur in both Latin and vernacular beast-epics—but because in this particular scene it disrupts the fictional reality, for a human being, appearing with an animal that similarly possesses the higher faculties of reason and speech, must not be shown to benefit from uniquely human qualities. If the main character of this episode were Renart instead of the priest, then the fable writer could have easily applied the theme "Mielz valt engiens que ne fait force" to the fox. But the Latin writer's insistence on *human* genius, his demonstration that relying on one's brute strength instead of intellectual cunning may spell disaster, leads the French "transposer" to omit the humanistic theme altogether. The *ridicula*, then, like the fabliaux, are a popular genre akin to fables and beast-epics, sharing certain themes and linguistic commonplaces, yet differing in their emphasis upon human motivations and emotions.

A second *ridiculum* presenting animal characters is the odd story about Alfrad and her she-ass, a narrative whose lack of any apparent point has led Dronke to surmise that a topical allegory may explain it.[30] The mock heroic language is striking: the animal is "strong in body and faithful" ("viribus fortem atque fidelem"); she enters the "full field" ("amplum exiret campum"), and when she loses the battle against the wolf, "she let out a great shout, wailing and calling her lady as she is dying" ("protulit grandem plangendo vocem/vocansque suam moritur domnam"). When the nuns and men attack, they do so "to lay low the strong host" ("ut fortem sternerent hostem"), but the wolf devours a "river of blood" ("sanguinis undam") before escaping into the forest. The tone becomes ludicrous when the sisters bewail the death of the ass:

10. Illud videntes   cuncte sorores
     crines scindebant,   pectus tundebant,
     flentes insontem   asine mortem.
(Seeing that, all of the sisters tore their hair and beat their breasts, bewailing the death of the innocent ass.)

The wealth of epithets drawn from Germanic epic literature suggests that the composer had great familiarity with that tradition, and his descriptions of the battle and lament are similar in tone, if not in language, to scenes in Apuleius' *Golden Ass*.[31]

But besides the comedy of the mock heroics, the story seems to have no point, and its childlike cruelty threatens its humorous potential. Because of the proper names and the provocative ending of the poem, some critics have suggested that the humor of *Alfrad* derives from its topical allusions. Alfrad's desire to have a "progeny" and the sisters' sentimental consolation may have sexual connotations:

> 11. Denique parvum   portabat pullum;
>   illum plorabat   maxime Alfrad,
>   sperans exinde   prolem crevisse.
> 12. Adela mitis,   Fritherun dulcis
>   venerunt ambe,   ut Alverade
>   cor confirmarent   atque sanarent:
> 13. "Delinque mestas,   soror, querelas!
>   Lupus amarum   non curat fletum:
>   Dominus aliam   dabit tibi asinam."

(11. Finally they bore the small animal away. Alfrad wept for her the most, for she hoped to have a distinguished progeny from her.
12. Gentle Adela and sweet Fritherun both came to comfort Adela and to cheer her.
13. "Stop your sad complaining, sister! The wolf doesn't care about your bitter tears, and the Lord will give you another ass.")

Quoting Hrabanus Maurus, Dronke furnishes possible allegorical meanings of she-ass and wolf: "'asses and she-asses sometimes signify the lasciviousness of sensual people,' and 'the first born of the ass means the beginnings of sensual life.' The wolf, predictably enough, means 'the devil . . . or heretics, or deceitful men'" ("Medieval Fabliau" 86). Hence "the foal Alfrad has hoped for from her *asina* (st. 11) could, in Hrabanus' terms, suggest her longing to embark on a life of sexual pleasure. And though the wolf in the episode has left again for the woods, the consolation offered by the other nuns, 'gentle Adela and sweet Fritherun,' could also be an unseemly jest: 'The Lord will give you another ass'—'the convent will renew your sensual impulses, will give you other opportunities.'" The fact that men and women are in the cloister is a surprising detail that may indicate the nuns lead a less than holy existence:

> 7. Clamor sororum   venit in claustrum,
>   turbe virorum   ac mulierum
>   assunt, cruentum   ut captent lupum.

(The shouting of the sisters reaches the cloister. A crowd of men and women gather to capture the bloodthirsty wolf.)

"Once the hint has been given, many phrases immediately gain the possibility of a double meaning (e.g., *levavit crura*, st. 3), so that the joke is there even though a perfect parallelism of *double entendre* has not been worked out" (Dronke, "Medieval Fabliau" 86).

Such an interpretation cannot be proven, for *Alfrad* does not offer any explicit allegorical referents, and analogues of the story in the beast-epic and fable traditions suggest that this *ridiculum* is not a topical allegory, a satire directed at a particular group of nuns with sentimental attachments to material things. In fact, *Alfrad* may be te prototype of an episode in *Ysengrimus*, the twelfth-century beast-epic composed by Nivard of Ghent, and it may be another instance of a *ridiculum* being converted into an animal fable.[32]   In Nivard's poem, Aldrada, lamenting the deaths of her gander and hen, threatens to kill the wolf, whose tail is caught in the ice.   Her humorous confusion of the popular mass—she thinks Osanna, Excelsis, Alleluja, and Celebrant are saints—reveals the same kind of humor found in *Sacerdos et Lupus*.   But Aldrada's concerns in *Ysengrimus* are quite different from Alfrad's: she is much more intent upon killing the wolf than lamenting her dead fowl.   Also, the allegorical significance of the wolf is clearly stated,[33] whereas in *Alfrad*, topical or moral allegory is a matter of interpretation.

An allegorical interpretation of *Alfrad* is tenuous, for the fable *De sacerdote horribiliter cantante*, contained in a fifteenth-century Göttingen manuscript, indicates that the story is still popular at the end of the Middle Ages.[34]   A woman in the priest's congregation weeps when he sings, and as he sings louder, the louder she weeps.   When he asks her the cause of her sorrow, she replies:

O domine, ego sum illa infelix mulier huius, cuius asinum lupus heri in campum abstulit et devoravit, cui ego non poteram resistere, quamvis asinus maxime clamaret.   Quando ergo audio vos cantare, statim ad memoriam reduco qualiter asinus meus resonabat propter similitudinem vocis vestre.

(O lord, I am the unhappy wife of that man whose ass the wolf led away into the field yesterday and devoured; I could not oppose the wolf, although the ass cried out most loudly.   When therefore I hear you sing, at once I am led back to the memory of how my ass resounded, because of the similarity of your voice and his.)

The poet's use of the genitive ("mulier huius, cuius asinum") suggests that the story is well known and popular, and the moral application is unambiguous: "Quo audito, sacerdos erubuit maxime, et unde quesivit gloriam et placentiam hominum, scilicet in cantu suo, inde tulit confusionem et ignominiam" ("When he heard this, the priest reddened a great deal, and where he sought glory and the suavity of men—namely, in his singing—there he obtained shame and disgrace"). In both this fable and in the beast-epic, allegory is explicit and unambiguous, whereas the "moral" of *Alfrad*, if it has any allegorical basis at all, is obscure: "Lupus amarum non curat fletum:/Dominus aliam dabit tibi asinam." The ambiguity of *Alfrad* makes this *ridiculum* an unusual one, for the other *ridicula* excel in clarity, both narrative and thematic.

If for no other reason than its sheer bulk, 215 rhythmic strophes, *Unibos* should have elicited more critical interest from admirers of Old French and Chaucerian fabliaux.[35] Unlike the short *ridicula*, which, with the exception of the *Modus Liebinc*, consist of single, tightly knit episodes, *Unibos* is composed of four extended episodes arranged in symmetrical order; like *De Iohanne abbate* and *Sacerdos et Lupus*, this poem is constructed in Ambrosian rhymed couplets. The themes of the other *ridicula*—falsity, presumption, craftiness—all flavor *Unibos*, which praises a peasant's ability to hoodwink his social superiors. The characters and situations in *Unibos* are those of the world of fabliaux; in short, *Unibos* is a full-length Latin fabliau of the eleventh century or perhaps before.

Superficially, *Unibos* appears to consist of six episodes: Unibos' discovery of treasure (st. 4-29); the sale of the ox-skins (st. 30-67); the murder of the wives (st. 68-114); the sale of the mare (st. 115-58); Unibos' fake death (st. 159-96); and the antagonists' deaths (st. 197-215). But close attention to narrative structure reveals that the first two scenes and the last two scenes constitute single episodes in which the hero performs an action and the antagonists imitate him with disastrous results. Hence the poem's structure is symmetrical, with lengthy episodes framing briefer ones at the center. Each episode, except for the first, begins with the antagonists bent upon killing Unibos, and each time they are tricked by the hero. A tendency toward greater brevity eliminates excessive repetitiousness in each episode: the priest is always the first to follow Unibos' advice, and his foolish behavior receives the greatest attention of the poet; the provost and the mayor, whose actions always follow the priest's, are treated more briefly. Despite Beyer's contention that only Unibos' character unites the poem (*Schwank* 74), many details reveal that the composer had a fine sense of narrative unity.

In each episode Unibos tricks his opponents by appealing to their vices, greed and lust. In the prologue the poet emphasizes the workings of fortune: "Natura fecit hominum, sed fortuna mirabilem" ("Nature made the man, but fortune produced wonders, " st. 4). Although Unibos' social position may be fixed at birth, through his cunning he may attain fortune and create wonders. This emphasis on fate, fortune, and destiny colors the first episode. Unibos buys oxen as "cruel fate's lot":

7. Frustra fortunam vincere   sua certat pauperie;
   Duro fatorum stamine   boves perdit assidue.

(Vainly he struggles to conquer his destined poverty; he continually loses oxen, thanks to the coarse thread of the Fates.)

"Bitter destiny deprives him of his last lowing ox" ("Tristis sors mugientium bovem rapit novissimum," st. 9), and when Unibos is at his most inferior position—defecating—he discovers the treasure that will change his fortune:

> 18. Anum dum certat tergere,   herbam festinat rumpere,
>   Sed herbam vellens repperit,   quod gens avara diligit.
> (In fact, as he seeks to wipe himself, tearing handfuls of grass, under a tuft he finds what greedy people love.)

After this discovery, fate and fortune disappear until the end of the poem, for Unibos, having received a fortune, himself becomes the maker of wonders.

The first episode, with its lengthy account of Unibos' loss of his remaining ox and his sale of the ox-skin at a market "beyond the border," permits the poet to delineate the protagonist's character. Like the priest in *Sacerdos et Lupus*, whose "life was simple" ("mos est rusticis"), Unibos is "rusticus de rusticis" ("a peasant from peasants," st. 4); like the lying Swabian, he is a socially inferior character who manipulates his betters. Though Unibos is called "stultus" for sending his boy to the provost (st. 21), his doing so stupefies the provost: "Unibovem pauperrimum stupet factum ditissimum" ("he is amazed that the destitute Unibos is now extremely wealthy," st. 23). Unibos constantly surprises his adversaries: what he tells them is always a "miraculum," "prodigium," and they are always rendered "stupidi." Like Heriger, Unibos is an admirable character who is capable of generating comedy.

The three fools who blindly follow Unibos' advice are unrealistically stupid, yet they are the kind of simpletons found in Old French fabliaux. To avenge himself upon the provost, who has roused the hero's anger by accusing him of theft, Unibos claims that ox-skins may be sold for a good price at a foreign market. The lengthy council scene, in which the provost informs his two comrades of Unibos' success, is a tedious exposition of the provost's pompous character, and it ends with the priest swearing he would kill his wife—foreshadowing the subsequent scene, in which the priest indeed kills his wife—and with the mayor pledging to slaughter all of his oxen, if only they could acquire wealth equal to Unibos'. The following market scene, in which the three fools wrangle with a group of shoemakers, is vividly drawn in the manner of the fabliaux:

> 54. Dicit sutor: "Quantum dabo   hoc pro bovino corio?"
>   Respondet maior subito: "Tres libras da continuo!"
> 55. Sutor inquit: "Es ebrius!"   Maior ait: "Sim fatuus.
>   De tribus libris minimum   non dimittam denarium."

56.   Tunc infit sutor setifer: "Dicis ioculariter."
      Econtra maior somnifer: "Tres libras!" clamat firmiter.
57.   Vulgaris ammiratio   sonoro mox fit in foro;
      Est vulgus in spectaculis   relictis mercimoniis.

(54. One of the shoemakers asks, "How much do I have to pay for this
ox-hide?" The mayor replies quickly, "Three pounds at once!"
55. The shoemaker replies, "You must be crazy." "Maybe I am,"
replies the mayor, "but I will not budge a penny under three pounds."
56. Then the surly shoemaker says, "You're joking," and in reply the
mayor, still sleepy, says steadily, "Three pounds."
57. Filled with surprise, the people in the crowded marketplace soon
leave their goods aside to attend the show.)

When the priest steps in to show his colleagues how to make a business deal,
his undiplomatic insistence that the shoemakers open their purses leads one of the
buyers to make a joke:

61.   "De qua sint hi provincia,   dicant tres in praesentia,
      Qui putant boum tergora   divitiarum maxima!
62.   "Decem nummorum corium   ad magnum levant precium.
      Nudis plantis incedite   huius coloni patriae!"

(61. "Let these three men, who think ox-hides are the greatest riches,
tell us here and now what country they are from.
62. "They value ten-cent hides at the highest price. People from that
country must walk barefoot!")

When the scene turns into near-riot, the law must intervene, and the fools end
up being fined the value of their ox-skins for dishonest business practices. This
intervention of the law, a motif absent in other *ridicula*, is common enough in
the fabliaux and *nugae*, and the marketplace is the setting of many a comic scene
in Apuleius and Boccaccio. [36]
    In the second scene Unibos appeals to another vice, lust, and he plays upon
the credulity of the three fools. The hero performs a magical ceremony that
supposedly resurrects his apparently dead wife, and hence he relies on the fools'
readiness to believe in the supernatural. His actions are not parodic of Christian
ritual; rather, they are pseudo-magic rites, much like those found in versions of
Querolus. When the priest imitates Unibos by first killing his wife and later
attempting to resurrect her, the humor is sardonic (st. 101-04); the provost's
attempt to revivify his wife is pathetic, the irony pointed (st. 110-11).
    Unibos again appeals to the threesome's greed in the third episode, which
begins, like *Alfrad*, with a mock heroic description of the conflict between the
hero and his foes: "They rush forth and gather arms" ("Ad arma corrunt
protinus," st. 118), but Unibos "succeeds in tricking the armed host" ("Armatos

hostes decipit," st. 120). Earlier the poet had commented on the extraordinary nature of Unibos' manipulation of the three men:

> 68. Infra caeli tentoria   non sunt audita talia,
>   Quae perpetravit Unibos,   ut sedaret stultissimos.
>
> (Never has such a deed as Unibos performed to soothe the stupid threesome been seen under heaven.)

Now the poet calls him a "master of stratagem" ("Artificem versutiae," st. 118) and breaks out in admiration of Unibos' cleverness:

> 119. Calliditas Unibovis   plena multis ingeniis
>   Superavit iactantiam   trium virorum fervidam.
>
> (But Unibos' cleverness, brimming ever with new tricks, again overcomes the angry threats of the three men.)

Like the priest in *Sacerdos et Lupus*, whose reliance on cunning (*ars*) leads the poet to praise human genius, Unibos' cleverness (*calliditas*) gains the poet's admiration. The hero's intellectual talents again create a "causam mirabilem" that astonishes the three fools:

> 124. Tres stant in domus limine   volentes interficere
>   Unibovem, sed non valent,   de novo facto dum stupent.
>
> (Standing on the threshold, they want to kill Unibos, but they are stunned into inaction by the new event.)

After the fools purchase the money-producing mare, the priest discovers a small coin in the mare's dung; again money and excrement are linked, as they were in the beginning of the poem when Unibos found the buried treasure. This episode concludes, like the second one, ironically, as the provost follows the priest's lead with even less success (st. 156).

   In the final episode of the poem, the three men's resolve to kill Unibos is again told in mock heroic terms ("Conveniunt cum turbine ferrata tres in acie" ["These three assemble like a whirlwind, assume proper battle formation"], st. 160), and Unibos, instead of providing a spectacle for the fools, offers a ruse that is his tour de force: he asks that he may choose how to die. The hero thus appeals to the pity of the three men, who drink wine after Unibos is enclosed in a barrel. By chance an unlucky swineherd passes by, and Unibos, appealing to his greed, creates a fiction that is his salvation:

> 182. "Pro quo clausus es crimine   in apotheca, perdite?"
>   Prompte respondet Unibos: "Honores nolo maximos.
> 183. "Huius coloni patriae   me compellunt cotidie
>   Me volentes efficere   praepositum potentiae.

184. "Ergo nunquam praepositus   ero meis aetatibus,
Nam sufficit, quod habeo;   honores regni renuo."
(182. "For what crime, O lost soul, are you enclosed in this barrel?"
Unibos replies readily: "I refused the highest honors.
183. "The people of this country urge me daily to become their leading
provost.
184. "But never in my life will I become their provost, for what I have
suffices me, and I reject the honors of this world.")

Unibos certainly does not appear to be a master of his fate, nor does his initial
ruse of being enclosed in a barrel seem a sound one, since he relies upon the
unlikely chance that a passing fool would be willing to change his unenviable
position. The poet reintroduces the theme of fate, not mentioned since the
opening scene of the poem, when the swineherd thinks he is compelled by fate
("Compulsus sum fataliter," st. 186) to take Unibos' place. The swineherd's
position leads to a comedy of errors, like that of *De Iohanne abbate*, when he
insists that he will accept the office of provost:

192. "Fiam, fiam praepositus   sub vestris voluntatibus;
Maris ne iacter fluctibus   a vobis iam edomitus."
193. Plenus vino praepositus   in indignationibus
Subulco dixit simplici: "Non est haec vox dulcis mihi.
194. "Tonnam certate volvere,   o socii, certissime.
Fit fluctuum praepositus   hic Unibos nequissimus."
(192. "All right, I'll be your provost. I give in to your wishes. So
don't throw me into the sea! I am ruled by your desires."
193. The provost, full of wine, replies indignantly to the swineherd,
"I don't find those words very amusing.
194. "Let's roll this barrel, comrades, with strong hands. Let this
Unibos become provost of the waves.")

Like the slaughter of the oxen and the murder of the wives, the death of the
innocent, forgotten swineherd is incidental and does not detract from the humor
of the story.
   When Unibos returns from the realm of the dead in the role of a swineherd,
his self-resurrection parodies the earlier resurrection of his wife.
Characteristically, the three fools are "stunned" by the news of the existence of
Unibos, who they think is a ghost (st. 202), and the hero's last lie appeals once
more to their greed: he convinces them that he has acquired his herd of pigs
from a miraculous realm below the sea—one is reminded of Heriger, who would
not send his swineherd to the forest girding hell. Unibos interrupts his account
of this otherworld with an explanation of their wives' deaths.

207. "Non fuit culpa bucinae,   sed bucinantis pessime,
    Omnes si vestrae feminae   modo sternunt sub pulvere."
("It wasn't the fault of the flute if your wives now snore under the
dust—it was your bad playing that is to blame.")

Only Unibos, then, plays the flute well enough to resuscitate the dead, and the
fact that he plays the flute while leading the pigs (st. 199) suggests that the hero
has brought the animals back from the realm of death, that he has resurrected
even himself.

Within the fiction, the narrator is generally approving of Unibos, whose
consistent character lends unity to the work. But at the end of the work, the
poet steps away from his creation, the character and the story, as he apparently
rejects both:

216. Inimici consilia   non sunt credenda subdola,
    Ostendit ista fabula   per seculorum secula.
(As this story reveals, the deceitful counsel of the wicked should never
be believed.)

This retraction is sudden, unexpected, much like the poet's unequivocal rejection
of his fiction in the eleventh-century *Gallus et Vulpes*.[37] Within the story,
Unibos is certainly the admirable hero; in fact, he is like the poet, for he is a
performer who creates fictions. He plays the swineherd at the town's crossroad
("quadruvium") as a mime would,[38] and he does so successfully, in contrast to
the fools, who perform poorly at the marketplace, where "the people soon leave
their goods aside and attend the show" (st. 57). Playing the magician, Unibos
performs mock ceremonies, and perhaps the poet, like Unibos, ends his poem
with an ironic play on the traditional fable's moral or the formula of prayer.[39]
But it is also possible that the poet ultimately judges his hero from a Christian
perspective, viewing him, like the three fools, as the "confusionis trux faber"
("wicked sower of confusion," st. 75). Unibos' greatest skill—his ability to trick
his stupid enemies—may be the very quality that makes him inimical, for he is
"magis seducens" (st. 172) and "dolosus" (st. 71).

Although there may be minor inconsistencies in characterization and theme,
the unity of this poem is impressive. The poet is particularly adroit at thematic
foreshadowing. The shoemaker's accusation, for instance, that the priest must
be drunk (st. 55)—which is a cliché found in the fabliaux and beast-
epics[40]—foreshadows the drinking scene of the last episode (st. 176-78); the
priest's statement that he would skin his own wife (st. 43) anticipates the next
scene, in which he actually kills her (st. 99-102); and Unibos' resurrection of his
"dead" wife with a magical flute (st. 80-83) foreshadows his resurrection of the
pigs and of himself with such an instrument (st. 199, 206-8). The themes of
greed, lust, and fortune control the poem, and the simple, repetitious structure
complements its childlike humor and adds to its rigid unity. *Unibos'*

symmetrical order, with extended episodes framing the shorter scenes at the center, with the formal "frame" enclosing the whole, constitutes a magnificent medieval structure, like a huge Gothic cathedral towering over the shorter, chapel-sized *ridicula*.

Unibos is the earliest version of a folktale that has had worldwide popularity, and later medieval analogues reveal generic distinctions among three types of short comic narrative: *ridiculum*, *Schwank*, and fabliau. The twelfth-century *Rapularius*, a Latin *Schwank* written in elegiac couplets, consists of two episodes, the second one paralleling the fourth episode of *Unibos*, when the hero convinces a dupe to enter a barrel. But it is the first episode of *Rapularius* that, though thematically comparable to the opening scene of *Unibos*, reveals a marked change in sense of humor: a giant turnip grows in the garden of a poor man, whose wife convinces him to give it to the king as an unusual present, for he will make no money selling the oddity and the king may reward him well. After he returns home wealthy, his rich brother burns with envy, and he decides to give the king all his money, hoping to reap hundredfold profits by imitating, in a grandiose way, his once-poor brother. The king, at odds what to do, receives timely advice from the queen: give this great citizen the giant turnip as a token of royal appreciation. This neat inversion of roles is rare among the primitive *ridicula*; only the *Modus Liebinc* and *Sacerdos et Lupus* contain a comparable twist. And the amusing subject matter of *Rapularius*, the giant turnip, is much more attractive, despite its childishness, to a modern audience than the sale of a child into slavery. In the second episode of *Rapularius*, less humorous than the first, the main character has been enclosed in a bag and placed hanging from a tree; a student passes by, and the hero, speaking from the bag, convinces the foolish *scholasticus* that he will gain all the knowledge of the world if he changes places with him. Rapularius, freed, steals the student's horse. This poem is flavored by a scholasticism foreign to the *ridicula* and fabliaux: a *scholasticus* replaces the lowly swineherd, and the hero's appeal is not for worldly power, but for worldly knowledge. *Schwänke* like *Rapularius*, *Asinarius*, and *De uxore Cerdonis* may well be considered Latin fabliaux, yet they differ from *ridicula* in form, characterization, and humor.[41]

Another version of the Unibos folktale is the German fairytale *Das Bürle* ("The Little Peasant"), containing two of the episodes of the Latin *Unibos* and introducing an entirely new scene at a miller's house.[42] This story is apparently a conflation of the *ridiculum* and the fabliau *Le povre clerc*, providing the fairytale's added scene. Here is a rare instance of a direct relationship between the kindred genres of *ridiculum* and fabliau, which become fused and eventually emerge as a later fairytale. Although no exact analogue to *Unibos* exists among the extant fabliaux, this story shares obvious commonplaces with the Old French narratives. The peasant farmer who has only one animal is a stock comic character of the fable tradition, and he appears in *Brunin ou La vache au prestre*.[43] The structure and characterization of *Des trois boçus* recall those of *Unibos*: a "porteur" repeatedly disposes of dead hunchbacks' corpses, and when he finally meets a live hunchback, he thinks it is "enchanté." This character is as dense as the three fools when they believe Unibos has been resurrected. An even more extreme case of repetition and stupidity, *Du sot chevalier*, acquires humor from sexual naïveté and threatened perversion. Thus elements of theme, structure, and characterization are shared by *ridicula* and fabliaux, yet the later narratives are generally more overtly sexual, and their comic inversions are more pointed. Such differences are readily apparent in *Du bouchier d'Abeville*: the butcher, after going to market, is denied lodging at a wealthy priest's abode; to avenge himself, he steals one of the priest's sheep, offers the sheepskin to the priest as payment for lodging, and also offers it to the priest's wife and maid for sexual favors. The poet's amoral stance at the end of the story is far bolder than the amoral "morals" concluding the *ridicula*:

> Bien et a droit et leaument,
> chascuns en die son voloir:
> liquels doit miex la pel avoir,
> ou li prestres or la prestresse,
> ou la meschine piprenesse?
> (Which of these by law and right should have the fleece, the pastor or
> the pastoress or the saucy little servant lass?)

The likely ancestors of the *ridicula* are the comic Carolingian rhythms of the ninth century and before, few of which are extant. The account of the tippling monk from Angers, found in a ninth-century Verona manuscript, is no story at all; it is merely the amusing description of a monk who drinks immense quantities of wine.[44] A fragmentary poem in hexameters, one of the *Carmina Sangallensis*, is the brief tale of three brothers who must outdo each other in eloquence in order to claim the inheritance of their father, a single goat.[45] The orderly presentation of speeches, with the eldest brother always speaking first, resembles the tedious council scenes in *Unibos*, when the priest is always first to speak. The poem ends with an address to the audience similar to the close of *Du boucher d'Abeville* and other late medieval narratives:

> At quicumque sibi sapiens quicumque videtur,
> Decernat horum quis victor iure putetur
> Et teneat hircum felici munere pulchrum.
> (Let the reader judge who is the wisest of the three, let him decide
> which one is considered the victor and let the winner have the pretty
> goat as a fortunate prize.)

The longest of the Carolingian rhythms is the ninth-century *Cena Cypriani*, which has the same formal structure as the Parisian version of *De Lantfrido et Cobbone*. The prologue, like that of *Unibos*, claims oral performance:

> Quique cupitis saltantem   me Iohannem cernere,
> Nunc cantantem auditote,   iocantem attendite. . .
> (Whoever desires to see me, John, dancing,
> Listen to me sing, listen to me tell stories . . .)

But the *Cena Cypriani*, consisting of 324 lines, has the thinnest of storylines: personages from the Old and New Testaments, invited to the wedding feast of King Johel, perform various activities according to their roles in the Bible. All the saints get drunk on a multitude of wines except John the Baptist, who drinks water (lines 165-88). As Raby points out, "the catalogue continues interminably with variations, relieved only by a few crude jokes and a grain of obscenity" (*SLP* 1:220). The poem is still popular during the eleventh century, for Alphanus of Salerno (flourished 1058-85), suggestively stating that he had "often re-read about the zeal of Cyprian" in his *Prologue* (col. 1221), writes a hymn "more comicorum" that demonstrates familiarity with the earlier poem:

> Sanctorum omnis concinit exercitus:
> Jubal est primus in choro canentium;
> Pulsat Maria soror Aron tympanum,
> Rex autem David personat psaltarium,
> Et Benedictus regulare praemium.
> (The entire group of saints sing together: Jubal is first in the band of
> singers; Mary, sister of Aaron, beats the drum while King David sings
> the Psalter and Benedict distributes the prizes) (col. 1234)

Alphanus must have re-read—and altered—the following passage from *Cena*:

> David citharam percussit   et Maria tympana,
> Choreas Iudith ducebat   et Iubal psalterium . . .
> (David struck the harp and Mary the drums, Judith was guiding the
> dances and Jubal [was singing] the Psalter . . .) (198-99)

Both the Carolingian rhythms and the *ridicula* probably have a common source: popular stories circulated orally. The only *ridiculum* with a definite written source, *De Iohanne abbate*, draws upon a particularly "popular" Latin work, the *Vitae patrum*. The other *ridicula* have no identifiable sources, but a look at Stith Thompson's *Motif-Index of Folk-Literature* should convince any skeptic about likely origins. Later analogues, such as the *Roman de Renart*, *Ysengrimus*, *Rapularius*, and *Das Bürle*, are generally "popular" works, as opposed to scholarly productions, such as the *comediae elegiacae*, which are heavily influenced by the classical literary tradition. The prologues of several *ridicula* reinforce the likelihood of popular origins. Only one of these poems, the *Modus Liebinc*, has analogues in all genres of late medieval comic narrative, and this phenomenon is evidence that even the scholarly Latin writers are at times inspired by the storehouse of folkloric themes.

The humor of the *ridicula* is strikingly different from that of later comic narratives, though these stories do possess universal techniques of comedy. Irony and mock heroics are elements found in the late Antique novels as well as in the Old French fabliaux; other universal aspects, such as unification, inversion, repetition, and comic characterization, are excessively simplified in the *ridicula*. The grim basis of humor is most peculiar: slavery, death, fraud, and various forms of cruelty are treated lightly, for such subjects, intimately familiar to tenth- and eleventh-century audiences, are not as abhorrent to them as to twentieth-century readers. Sexuality is a latent or discreetly handled theme in these poems: the lying Swabian's success in the suitor's contest yields him the princess, but she does not appear; the three fools desire beautiful, young wives, but their wives die. Only in two poems, the *Modus Liebinc* and *De Lantfrido et Cobbone*, does the theme appear openly, yet these stories treat the theme far more discreetly than the ribald fabliaux.

Despite their simplicity and cruelty, the *ridicula* present a humanistic concern with man's ingenuity, a theme that may reflect the poets' own moral dilemmas about the profitability of their art. The fiction is a playground where a liar, if he or she is good enough, can become a hero, but outside the fiction, the lying hero is often rejected, the story qualified "yet useful as a moral tale." The criticism of human presumption rather than physical ineptitude in *De Iohanne abbate* and the strange sentimentality of *Alfrad* indicate a strong interest in human motivation, human emotion. The celebration of *ars* and *ingenium* gives these poems not moralistic value, but humanistic value: "Humano datum commodo nil maius est ingenio!"

NOTES

1. The *ridicula* presenting liars (Poems 6, 14, 15, and 24 and *Unibos*) have more speech and less narration than the other *ridicula* (Poems 20, 35, 42) and may be classified as *ridicula dicta* as opposed to *ridicula facta*. See Beyer (*Schwank* 68-79), who considers *Unibos* a *ridiculum factum*.

2. See Thiener 122: "It is as vain to ask whether the fabliau audience was actually drawn into faith in the authenticating levels of its tales as it is to suppose that the modern comedian's audience believes that the anecdote he relates deals with an event that actually happened 'on the way to the studio.'"

3. Schupp (29-41) argues unconvincingly that Heribert is a composer of this poem.

4. See Thompson 109, 132 (J.1532.1. "Snow Child").

5. See *Cambridger Lieder* 42: "Die Strophe weist sich durch Inhalt und Reim als zugedichtet aus." But the content of the interpolation is not necessarily at odds with the account of the *Modus Liebinc*, as I explain below.

6. See Müllenhoff and Scherer 115; Meyer 176; *Cambridge Songs* 83.

7. See Bergson 71-72; Freud 231.

8. Notably Paul Winterfeld and Karl Strecker. See *Cambridger Lieder* 43.

9. The Cambridge manuscript, a *florilegium* containing Prudentius' *Psychomachia*, various *enigmata*, Cato's *Distichs*, and other miscellaneous verses, has copious interlinear glosses giving synonyms and even, sometimes, Anglo-Saxon equivalents, suggesting that the collection was some sort of primer or Latin textbook. In Vat. Palatinus 1710, the *Modus Liebinc* occupies the first leaf of the eleventh-century section of the manuscript; the poem was written on a blank page of this collection of Persius' *Satires*.

10. Dronke comments that "miraculous conception through eating or drinking is so common a folktale motif that it would not necessarily have specific religious connotations at all" ("Medieval Fabliau" 281, n. 14). Curiously enough, the folktale motif of the snowchild appears in the Middle English mystery *The Trial of Joseph and Mary*, belonging to the *Ludus Coventriae*, when details of the story are recalled by Mary's prosecutors "in ironic explanation of her pregnancy" (Pearcy 745).

11. Cf. *De l'oue au chapelein* (Montaiglon and Raynaud 6:46-49) and *Du prestre crucifie* (Montaiglon and Raynaud 1:194-97), in which parody of religion is obvious.

12. See Röhrich 1:297-98 for later German versions of the story.

13. In addition to constructing an elaborate form, the composer of the *Modus Liebinc* demonstrates a superficial knowledge of Horace's poetry. Compare "vix remige/triste secat mare" (st. 2a) and "ratim quassam reficit" (st. 4a) with the following lines of Horace, *Odes 1.1.11-18*:

Gaudentem patrios findere sarculo
Agros Attalicis condicionibus
Numquam dimoveas, ut trabe Cypria
Myrtoum pavidus *nauta secet mare.*
Luctantem Icariis fluctibus Africum
Mercator metuens otium et oppidi
Laudat rura sui; mox *reficit ratis*
Quassas, indocilis pauperiem pati.

14. See *Cambridger Lieder* 20. Not every line maintains the fifteen-syllable count. Strecker, along with Kögel, speculates there is a common origin for both versions of *De Lantfrido et Cobbone.*

15. Cf. Isadore, *Etymologia* 3:19 f. (quoted by Strecker in *Cambridger Lieder* 17): "Ad omnem sonum, quae materies cantilenarum est, triformem constat esse naturam. Prima est harmonica, quae ex vocum cantibus constat. Secunda organica, quae ex flatu consistit. Tertia rhythmica, quae pulsu digitorum numeros recipit. Nam aut voce editur sonus sicut per fauces, aut flatu sicut per tubam vel tibiam, aut pulsu sicut per citharam aut per quodlibet aliud, quod percutiendo canorum est."

16. See *Cambridger Lieder* 14-15 for these Biblical allusions.

17. The theme also occurs in the legend of Ami and Amile, first appearing in Radulfus Tortarius' *Epistola II*, which Francis Bar (58-108) tries unsuccessfully to link with the story of Lantfrid and Cobbo.

18. Ehrismann 370 translates *propheta* as "Aufschneider" (boaster), but also as "Fahrender" (vagrant). Cf. Kögel 263.

19. See Freud 11-14; also see Nichols 16-29, who analyzes three songs of William IX of Aquitaine in terms of dissimulation and revelation.

20. Cf. Luke 1:15: "Et vinum et siceram non bibet."

21. Cf. Matthew 19:18: "non facies furtum." The last strophe is corrupt; see *Cambridger Lieder* 66.

22. See Dronke, "Medieval Fabliau" 284: "While in general fabliaux shun the supernatural sphere, just as they tend to shun motifs of enchantment or *féerie*, the supernatural and the enchanted can also be given an earthly, comic twist." Cf. *La cour de paradis* (Barbazon and Méon 2:128-48); the *Apocalypse of Golias*, described by Raby, *SLP* 2:214 f.

23. This popular *ridiculum* is located in a number of manuscripts, including the Vatican's Reg. lat. 278 (in which it occurs in the middle of Fulbert's poems), Reg. lat. 61 (located at the end of Reginald of Canterbury's poems), and Reg. lat. 1762 (in which it is written on the last folio after Fulbert's poems). In BN lat. 2872, stanzas 1-5 of the poem are found in a collection of rhythms that themselves are situated in the middle of Fulbert's poems. See *Cambridger Lieder* 100-1.

24. The text is printed by Strecker in *Cambridger Lieder* 100: "Dicebant de abbate Joanne brevi statura, quia dixerit aliquando fratri suo maiori: 'Volebam esse securus sicut angeli sunt securi nil operantes, sed sine intermissione collaudantes Deum.' Et mox spolians se, quo vestitus erat, abiit in eremum; et facta ibi hebdomada una reversus est ad fratrem suum. Et dum pulsaret ostium, respondit ei, antequam aperiret, dicens: 'Quis es tu?' Et ille dixit: 'Ego sum Joannes.' Et respondens frater eius dixit ei: 'Ioannes angelus factus est et ultra inter homines non est.' Ille autem pulsabat dicens: 'Ego sum,' et non aperuit ei, sed [di]misit eum affligi usque mane. Postea aperiens dixit ei: 'Si homo es, opus habes iterum operari, ut vivas. Si autem angelus es, quid quaeris intrare in cellam?' Et ille poententiam agens dixit: 'Ignosce mihi, frater, quia peccavi.'"

25. See Sudre 329-31 for a plausible evolution of the folktale.

26. Cf. *Roman de Renart* branch 15, lines 14843-980. Close analogues also occur among the fabliaux (cf. *Du prestre et du leu*, Montaiglon and Raynaud 6:51-52) and among the learned Latin poets (cf. *Parabola de fraude a lupo opilioni facta*, erroneously attributed to Marbod, in Migne et al., *Patrologiae cursus completus* 171: col. 1728-30). Also compare the following unpublished poem, located in a Parisian manuscript (BN lat. 3705, f. 146v) containing Hildebert's *De quodam servo* and *De Milone mercatore*:

> Parvus erat limes quo presbiter ire solebat
> Et lupus hic ad oves presbiter ad dominam;
> Rusticus hoc sensit foveam facit; ecce sub acta

Nocte lupus veniens corruit in foveam.
Sicut erat solitus et presbiter ibat eodem
  Quoque lupus cecidit presbiter ipse cadit.
Cumque moram faceret ancillam rustica misit.
  Quid tunc? haec etiam corruit in foveam.
Ad foveam vir mane redit tres invenit intus
  Hanc fugat hunc jugulat huicque pudenda secat.

(A priest and a wolf used to travel down a narrow path, the wolf [to visit] sheep, the priest [to visit] his mistress. The woman's peasant husband was aware of this, so he made a pit. When night had fallen, the wolf, approaching [the sheep], tumbled into the pit. And as he was wont, the priest went to the same place and he himself falls where the wolf fell. When he is delayed, the peasant woman sent her maid [after him]. What happened then? She also tumbled in the pit. The husband returned to the pit in the morning and discovered the three within. He chases the maid away and kills the wolf; let him cut off the priest's private parts.) This poem is also contained in BN lat. 8433, f. 118r.

27. See Muscatine, *Old French Fabliaux* 98.

28. See *Roman de Renart* branch 3a; lines 4607-8 ("Paor a de perdre l'escorce,/se plus n'i vaut engin que force'); 7a, 6012-14 ("enging et art/si vaut a la chose bornir/c'on ne puet par force fornir"); 8, 8109 ("engingneus est, mes n'est pas fort," speaking of Renart).

29. See, for instance, Helsinger's allegorical interpretation of the fabliau *Du prestre et du leu*: "the priest who has dug a pit for the wolf that is preying on his flock finds that he has also caught the priest who is his wife's lover"; the beast and priest are "analogous predators upon the innocent" (97-98).

30. Dronke, "Medieval Fabliau" 285. Müllenhoff and Scherer (128) call the poem "eine Magdeburger Klostergeschichte aus dem Jahre 1017"; they believe the ass represents Alfrad's sister (!). Strecker (*Cambridger Lieder* 61) and Kögel (263) do not see an allegorical basis.

31. Kögel 261-62 gives German and Old English parallels from epic literature. Cf. Apuleius 4. 148-49.

32. Cf *Ysengrimus* 2:1-158. Wallner (174 f.) conjectures that *Alfrad* is based on an "Isengrinschwank" composed c.1000. But as Mann (*Ysengrimus* 4) notes, Voigt has shown that the *Ysengrimus abbreviatus* is later than the twelfth-century poem by Nivard of Ghent.

33. The wolf is called *diaconus* (2:121), *presul* (2:129), and *pontifex* (2:36, 136), and Aldrada threatens to shave the wolf's head "so that your tonsure . . . doesn't need the frequent ministrations of a barber." See Raby *SLP* 2:151: "The wolf is throughout the monk, and it is against monasticism that the bitter satire of the work is directed."

34. Hervieux, ed. 3: 350-51. The same story is located in Jacques de Vitry's *Exempla ex sermonibus vulgaribus* (22; *exemplum* 56) and in Poggio Bracciolini's *Facezie* (358-59).

35. Only German critics have given *Unibos* significant attention: Ehrismann 373-74 and Kögel 272-73 give plot summaries of *Unibos*; more recently, Beyer and Suchomski have given the work more analytical attention. Neither Dronke nor Raby mentions the poem.

36. See Apuleius 7.382-86; 9.448-50; 10.494-96; Boccaccio, *Decameron*, Second Day, Fifth Story.

37. The first half of *Gallus et Vulpes* is a straightforward narration about the cock and the fox; the second half is a lengthy moral diatribe condemning indulgence in such worthless storytelling.

38. See Ogilvy 614: "mimi cantant et saltant in triviis." *Trivium* is synonymous with *quadrivium*. Note that the three fools have their first council "in trivio" (st. 30).

39. See Beyer, *Schwank* 78; Suchomski (107 f.) does not see the irony.

40. The shoemaker's insult, "es ebrius," meaning "you're a fool," is a turn of phrase also occurring in the fabliaux. Cf. *Du chevalier qui fit les cons parler* (Harrison 226): "ne soiez ivres"; *Des tresces* (298, in Montaiglon and Raynaud 4:77): :"Ne me tenroiz pas si por ivre"; *Jouglet* (302, in Eichmann and DuVal 1:130): "Robert . . . estes vous yvres?" The cliché is also found in the *Roman de Thèbes* 3501: "Es tu fous u ivre?" and in the *Roman de Renart* branch 11, line 11822; 11, 11856; 11, 11936-37; 11, 12173; 11, 12293.

41. *Rapularius* and *Asinarius* are edited by Langosch (*Waltharius* 307-31, 333-57). *Rapularius*, composed c. 1200 in metrical verse, is the basis of "The Turnip," one of Grimm's fairytales; see Grimm 637-40.

42. For "The Little Peasant," see Grimm 311-16 and Bolte and Polívka 2:1-18. Also see Hart (343-74), who is unaware of *Unibos*.

43. See Hervieux 2:596-97 (*De agricola qui habuit equum unum*); Montaiglon and Raynaud 1:132-34; Wright, *Selection of Latin Stories* 108;114.

44. *Poetae Latini aevi Carolini*, *MGH* 4:591. Raby (*SLP* 1:217-18) also publishes the poem.

45. Theodulf of Orléans, *MGH*, *Poetae Latini aevi Carolini*, 2:474-75. The theme of inheritance is a widespread one in the Middle Ages. Cf. Hervieux 2:291; *Gesta Romanorum* (417-18, *Caput* 90; 466-70, *Caput* 120).

Chapter 2

Nugae: The Trifles of Learned Latin Poets

Unlike the *ridicula*, which consist of a small but homogenous group of poems, the metrical *nugae* include a variety of sub-genres: school exercises, amatory verses, comic narratives. The *exempla* of Egbert of Liège, the epigrams of Hildebert of Lavardin, the epistles of Fulcoius of Beauvais, and the anonymous comic narratives of the late eleventh century all belong to distinct literary traditions, yet all may be grouped in the broad category of *nugae*, trifles of learned members of the Church. The simplest poems, briefest in their structure, are not far different from the short narratives of Theodulf of Orléans (d.821), employing puns to elicit humor. The comic narratives of early eleventh century poets are terse, obscure, and moralistic, but by the end of the century, partly because of the revival of classical studies at the schools, brief narratives attain great lucidity as epigrams in the manner of Martial. Both Egbert and Hildebert draw upon popular tradition and cast their stories, with differing success, in the mold of classical rhetoric and style. As the century progresses, comic narratives tend to increase in length, and these longer poems anticipate, in structure and theme, the great narratives of the twelfth century, notably elegiac comedy and romance. The most prolific writer of such poems is Fulcoius of Beauvais, whose *epistola frivola* are both pedantic and moralistic.[1] Other poems, such as the anonymous *Res mea* and the sixth epistle of Radulfus Tortarius, are clear in style and ribald in theme. As with the short comic narratives, these works often disregard the frontiers of satire and romance, comedy and tragedy.

Whereas the *ridicula*, for all their slow-witted, clumsy humor, are nonetheless identifiably comic poems, the *nugae* often present serious problems regarding the nature of their comedy. On the one hand, their frequent obscurity, resulting from a delight in rhetorical play rather than narrative clarity, demonstrates a humor that can scarcely be appreciated by the modern audience; on the other hand, heavy moralizing about inherently comic themes and situations jeopardizes the stories' comic potential. Only in a few poems, such as Hildebert's epigrams and Radulfus' epistles, does rhetoric rise above obscurity, while the moralizing tendency is suppressed. More typically the comic tale, whether obscurely or clearly written, conveys a strong moral point, and at times the didactic impulse is so strong that the poet finally abandons the comic realm. This desire to draw serious morals from comic stories reflects the dilemmas of orthodox churchmen trifling with amoral themes.

Eleventh-century poets typically approached a theme in two ways: either by reducing it through the technique of abbreviation or by expanding it through amplification. Both methodologies are explained and illustrated by Geoffrey of Vinsauf in his early thirteenth-century rhetorical handbook, the *Poetria Nova*. Geoffrey says much less about abbreviation than he does about amplification, for Latin and vernacular writers of the twelfth and thirteenth centuries, unlike eleventh-century writers, preferred above all to expand a given theme. The seven techniques of abbreviation include several used by the most skilled abbreviator of the eleventh century, Hildebert of Lavardin:[2]

Let *emphasis* be spokesman, saying much in few words. Let *articulus*, with staccato speech, cut short a lengthy account. The *ablative*, when it appears alone without a pilot, effects a certain compression. Give no quarter to *repetition*. Let skillful *implication* convey the unsaid in the said. Introduce no *conjunction* as a link between clauses—let them proceed uncoupled. Let the craftsman's skill effect a *fusion of many concepts in one*, so that many may be seen in a single glance of the mind.

Geoffrey's model exercise, an abbreviation of the snowchild theme, reflects the whole technique:

Rebus in augendis longe distante marito,
Uxor moecha parit puerum. Post multa reverso
De nive conceptum fingit. Fraus mutua. Caute
Sustinet. Asportat, vendit matrique reportans
Ridiculum simile liquefactum sole refingit.
(Her husband abroad improving his fortunes, an adulterous wife bears a child. On his return after long delay, she pretends it begotten of snow. Deceit is mutual. Slyly he waits. He whisks off, sells, and—reporting to the mother a like ridiculous tale—pretends the child melted by sun. (lines 713-17)

The poet is like a metalworker, and "the glory of the brief work consists in this: it says nothing either more or less than is fitting" (730-31). Geoffrey's second *exemplum* of abbreviation shows how "the exercise of an unusual brevity may be yet more pointed":

De nive conceptum quem mater adultera fingit
Sponsus eum vendens liquefactum sole refingit.
(A husband selling him whom the adulterous mother feigns begotten of
snow in turn feigns him melted by sun. (733-34)

Without full knowledge of the story, the reader would be left with an enigmatic
tale like several of Egbert's insoluble *exempla*.   But Egbert's obscurity is
compounded by his arcane style; further, he writes *exempla*, not epigrams. The
epigrammatists strive for terseness and lack the didacticism of *exemplum* writers.
    The eight techniques of amplification illustrate the methodology of such
writers as Fulcoius of Beauvais and Radulfus Tortarius. Geoffrey spends much
time   explaining   and   exemplifying   repetition,   periphrasis,   comparison,
apostrophe, personification, digression, description, and opposition. Eleventh-
century writers use most of these techniques, but the most conventionalized
rhetorical figure of the twelfth century, the *descriptio* of the beautiful lady, has
not achieved the formal order, prescribed by Geoffrey, during the eleventh-
century. Most eleventh-century poets prefer one method over the other; only
Fulcoius tends to abbreviate and amplify.   While the epigrammatic tradition
becomes more and more widespread by the end of the century, narratives also
grow longer as the century progresses.
    Geoffrey's explanation of comic style shows how different the eleventh-
century perception of comedy, in the broad, generic sense of the term, was from
his own.   Twelfth- and thirteenth-century theorists agree with late classical
writers that there are three basic styles: *sermo humilis*, *sermo mediocris*, *sermo
gravis*, each demanding appropriate characterization and vocabulary. Geoffrey's
precepts for comic style clearly indicate that it demands the use of the *sermo
humilis*:

> Yet there are times when adornment consists in avoiding ornaments,
> except such as ordinary speech employs and colloquial use allows. A
> comic subject rejects diction that has been artfully labored over; it
> demands plain words only . . . A comic discourse is marked with the
> character of lightness in the following ways: levity of spirit is the
> source of comedy; comedy is an immature form, attractive to green
> years. Moreover, the subject of comedy is light; to such a subject the
> sportive period of youth readily devotes itself . . . Let all aspects, then,
> be light: the whole is in perfect harmony if the spirit is light, and the
> subject is light, and the expression light. (1883-87, 1910-16)

But Geoffrey also states that "easy ornament" requires the poet "to have recourse
to means that are simple, but of a simplicity that does not shock the ear by its
rudeness," and he proceeds to give thirty-five rhetorical colors that may be used
for easy ornament (1095 f.). His examples of the "res comica," *De tribus sociis*
and *De clericis et rustico*, do not lack rhetoric and scholastic vocabulary, though

they are considerably more toned down than Egbert's *exempla* or Fulcoius' *epistolae*.

Geoffrey's definition of comic style is quite inapplicable to eleventh-century literature, for the earlier poets employ a high style, especially in their emphasis on rhetoric, to describe a low subject matter. In the course of the century, poets gain control over style, but Hildebert's epigrams and Radulfus' epistles are still formal compositions whose primary source of interest is rhetoric. Even the *comediae elegiacae* of the twelfth century tend toward rhetorical excesses that are at odds with the subject matter, so Geoffrey's theories may offer advice rather than describe contemporary practices. Yet the elegiac "comedies" have a clarity and simplicity profoundly different from the obscurity and complexity of many of the eleventh-century *nugae*. Both genres use similar motifs and even similar subject matter, but the success of the *comediae* lies in the better harmony of style and subject.

German scholars consider two short narratives by the Carolingian satirist Theodulf of Orléans as the first extant *Schwank* material of the later Middle Ages.[3] But Jürgen Beyer errs when he places Theodulf's poems in the context of the *ridicula*; the Spanish poet's *Delusa expectatio* and *De quodam equo* clearly belong to the learned tradition of metrical poetry, as the two poems rely heavily upon rhetorical punning for their humor. Beyer himself acknowledges that *Delusa expectatio* is a parody of the high style (*Schwank* 69):

> Grande habet initium cum res vilissima dictu,
> > Tunc gignis murem, magne elephante, brevem.
> (When matter most paltry to speak of has a great beginning,
> Then, great elephant, you beget a little mouse.)

The "matter most paltry to speak of" is introduced with a rhetorical flourish, the "formel-logischen Cum-tum-Satz" and the apostrophe to the great elephant, an allusion to a proverb made famous by Horace in his *Ars Poetica*—"parturient montes, nascetur ridiculus mus" ("mountains will labor, to birth will come a laughter-rousing mouse")—and forming the basis of a popular medieval fable.[4] The opening of the poem, then, contains a metaphor found in both classical literature and the medieval popular tradition.

The teacher-pupil relationship characteristic of the *exemplum* tradition is slightly altered by Theodulf to a father-son relationship, and the "sic" that begins the narrative, a catchword of the same tradition, further reveals that Theodulf has that genre in mind:

> Sic patri quidam retulit sua somnia natus,
> > Depromens animo frivola dicta suo . . .
> (Once a boy described his dream to his father
> And fetched trifling words from his memory . . .)

The "frivola dicta" are both the son's words to his father and the poem itself.
The wit of the son's story hinges on the rhetorical play of the *genus dicendi*:

> "O pater, in somnis dicam quae mira videbam,
>   Moverunt animum talia visa meum.
> Bos dabat humanas nostras hac nocte loquelas,
>   Ille loquebatur, nos stupebamus," ait.
> ("O Father, I will tell you about wonders I saw in my sleep;
> Such great sights disturbed my mind.
> An ox produced our own human speech last night.
> He spoke; I was stunned," he says.)

The son begins in the high style with an "affektischen Vokativ," "O pater,"
utilizing the *genus grande*. The story itself centers upon the ox's speech, the
"humanas nostras . . . loquelas," and this emphasis returns one's attention to the
"res vilissima dictu" and the "frivola dicta" earlier in the poem. When the father
asks the son what the ox said, the answer is a pun, and the story's punch line is
like a joke's:

> Tum pater attonitus rem sic inquirit ab illo:
>   "Dic, quod dicebat," intulit ille: "Nihil."
> (Then the astonished father asked his son for facts:
> "Tell me what it said." The son concluded: "Nothing.")

The ox said nothing, or it said, "Nothing." This deflation of the poem's
rhetorical balloon, like that of Fulcoius of Beauvais' *Epistola* XV or William
IX's *Farai un vers de dreyt nien* almost 300 years later, underscores the poem's
parodic basis. But Theodulf is parodying more than the classical high style; he
is also ironically inverting the teacher-pupil relation of the *exempla*, for in this
poem the son tells the father a story, while in the *exempla* it is always the older
teacher delivering moral tales for the young student's edification. Also, unlike
the fables, this poem does not present a speaking animal, for even if the ox says,
"Nothing," this human speech is limited to the son's dream, which is removed
two steps from reality, since it occurs in a fiction. The rhetorical nature of the
story's humor reveals Theodulf's pedantic bent, yet by pitting low and high
styles, the poet draws upon popular genres, the *exemplum* and fable traditions.

Theodulf's second comic narrative, *De equo perdito*, is less rhetorical than
Delusa expectatio and derives its humor from the prank pulled by the main
character. The prologue introduces the theme of *Sacerdos et Lupus*:

> Saepe dat ingenium quod vis conferre negabat,
>   Compos et arte est, qui viribus impos erat.
> (Often wit yields what strength has refused to give;
> He who is weak in strength is powerful in cunning.)

The theme of cunning, *ars*—most common among eleventh-century *ridicula* and *nugae*—is again mentioned as the story begins:

> Ereptum furto castrensi in turbine quidam,
>   Accipe, qua miles arte recepit equum.
> Orbus equo fit, preco ciet hac compita voce:
>   "Quisquis habet nostrum, reddere certet equum.
> Sin alias, tanta faciam ratione coactus,
>   Quod noster Roma fecit in urbe pater."
> (A thief snatched a horse from a soldier in a crowd;
> Listen by what cunning the soldier got it back.
> Deprived of his horse, he launches a threat with appropriate tone:
> "Whoever has my horse, he'd better try returning it.
> Otherwise, in this affair I shall be forced to do
> What my father did in the city of Rome.")

This threat convinces the thief to let the horse go—a rather unrealistic result, since if he did not fear stealing the horse, he certainly would not fear mere words. The soldier's second speech, answering the inquiries of onlookers, explains what his father did when he once lost a horse:

> "Sellae," ait, "adiunctis collo revehendo lupatis
>   Sarcinulisque aliis ibat onustus inops.
> Nil quod pungat habens, calcaria calce reportans,
>   Olim eques, inde redit ad sua tecta pedes.
> Hunc imitatus ego fecissem talia tristis,
>   Ni foret iste mihi, crede, repertus equus."
> ("He attached hooks to his saddle and carried it on his back,
> And loaded with other smaller bundles, he returned poor.
> Having nothing to spur, wearing spurs on his heel,
> Once a knight, now he returned to his abode a foot soldier.
> Imitating him, I sadly would have done the same,
> Believe me, if I hadn't recovered my horse.")

In other words, the soldier would have done nothing. His elaborate description of his father's actions, like the son's description of the ox's language in his dream, constitutes so many words to express nothing. Language which allows the son to trick his father, the soldier to outtrick the thief, replaces action as the motivating force behind these mini-narratives.

In the late tenth and early eleventh centuries, German and Italian writers developed a tradition of comic narrative poetry, but much of this production is lost, and the little that remains is exceedingly obscure in style and meaning. An exceptional writer with a substantial output is Egbert of Liège (born c. 972), whose *Fecunda ratis* ("The Well-laden Ship"), like the *Delicie Cleri* of Arnulf, the *Disciplina Clericalis* of Petrus Alfonsi, and the epigrams of Geoffrey of Winchester, begins with short pieces and gradually expands into full-length narratives. Much of what Egbert himself says about the origins and purpose of his work anticipates the prologue of the early twelfth-century *Disciplina Clericalis*: Egbert says that he mingles a "few new and popular fables with a few holy tales" ("novis atque vulgaribus fabellis aliquot divinisque paucis interserens"); moreover, he composes the work for the instruction of "fearful boys" ("formidolosis adhuc sub disciplina pueris operam dedi").[5] In *Fecunda ratis*, Egbert dresses proverbs, fables, and popular tales in classical and patristic garb, drawing upon Horace, Juvenal, Virgil, the Bible, and the Church fathers for his language, which is often more important to him than his meaning.

Egbert's methodology is well illustrated by his two poems about bald men. The first is a three-line narrative drawn directly from the fable tradition:

> Gaudebat super invento sat pectine calvus;
> Quam melior foret inventus sibi pilleus unus,
> Calvitiem unde suam recrearet sole geluque!
> (A baldheaded man rejoiced enough over finding a comb.
> How much better had he found a felt cap—
> He could have protected his baldness from sun and cold!) (163; pt. 1,
> lines 1018-20)

Egbert's story is a condensation of Phaedrus' fable about the two bald men who find a comb:

> Invenit Calvus forte in trivio pectinem.
> Accessit alter, aeque defectus pilis.
> "Heia!" inquit, "[in] commune quodcumque est lucri."
> Ostendit ille predam et adiecit simul:
> "Superum voluntas favit; sed fato invido
> Carbonem, ut aiunt, pro thesauro invenimus."
> (By chance a bald man found a comb on the road.
> Another arrived, equally wanting in hair.
> "Aha!" he cried. "Whatever we find is ours in common."
> He showed him the prize and added at once:
> "The will of the gods is favorable, but because of envious fate
> We have found, as they say, a piece of coal instead of treasure.") (5.6)

Egbert uses only the first line of the fable, and then he creates a unique mini-narrative whose humor is not overshadowed by the abstract moral. Such extreme abbreviation or condensation, however, reduces narration to a mere point in time, so that character and plot are lacking.

In his second poem about bald men, more typically Egbertian in its obscurity, he expects his reader to have intimate knowledge of the proverb tradition:

Quattuor ut calvi Calvo puto Monte creati
Occurrere mihi, fatie cum nomine noti,
Mirabar sic conflatos que flabra tulissent,
Ridebam frontes levi quoque pelle glabellas;
Cuiusdam subiit quinti mihi mentio calvi:
Is plane curruca foret, si quintus adesset.
(As four bald men, created, I believe, on Mount Baldy,
Ran toward me, known by their appearance as by name,
I wondered what breeze had brought them together in this way.
I also laughed at their balding brows with scant hair.
I've read of a fifth baldy—
A fifth would clearly be a cuckold if he were nearby.) (191; pt. 1,
1481-86)

This odd narrative presents serious problems of interpretation. The Mount Baldy on which the four men are begotten is an obvious pun adding to the alliteration of the line, and the reference is probably not a topical allusion, since no mountain with such a name, as Egbert's editor points out, exists in the environs of Liège.[6] The punch line of the poem, where the humor resides, raises the greatest difficulty in our understanding Egbert's point. Ernst Voigt proposes a possible, though tenuous, solution in the proverb tradition: he conjectures that Egbert is alluding to the French proverb "il y avait trois pelés et un tondu," which is used "en parlant d'une réunion peu nombreuse, où il n'y avait que des gens de peu de considération."[7] The English translation is: "There was nothing but the ragtag and the bobtail" or "the riffraff and the rabble." Voigt further explains "curruca," a word taken from Juvenal's sixth satire, as "Hahnrei, und als solcher überflüssig" ("cuckold, and as such superfluous").[8] In short, Egbert may be implying that a fifth bald man, since four already constitute a party not worthy of notice, would be utterly superfluous; he would be like a cuckold, whose role, unlike his wife's and the lover's, is sexually meaningless. This rather circuitous path to an understanding of Egbert's point makes Voigt's interpretation a tentative one, yet Egbert does employ one-, two-, and three-line proverbs frequently in the *Fecunda ratis*, so it is not farfetched that Egbert had this proverb in mind. In any case, the narrative reveals Egbert's delight in purposeful obscurity, as the story's climax is a riddle whose solution no doubt amused and delighted his students.

Not all of Egbert's narrative poems are so enigmatic, and several of them present characters and themes found in the *ridicula* and the fabliaux. The short *De pretio medico negato*, for instance, with its unstated theme of "sic fraus fraudem vicerat," is about an astute doctor who outtricks his stingy patient:

Ringeris archiatro non solvens debita digno;
Qua re letargum patieris, ut ante solebas.
Respondit medicus forsan commotus in iram:
"Cardiacum te faxo indignum vivere sanum,
Utere nunc pretio nostro cum fine maligno!"
(You snarl at a worthy physician and don't pay your bill.
For this reason you suffer lethargy, as before you were wont.
The doctor replied, perhaps moved by anger:
"Since you're unworthy of leading a healthy life, I'll make you a stomach case—
Now use the money you owe me to meet a bad end!") (169; pt. 1, 1088-92)

Egbert's narrative has epigrammatic qualities, such as the address to a second person and the theme of greed, and it has incidental relations with a satire by Horace, in which a rich man, beleaguered by an impatient heir, refuses his doctor's advice:[9]

"Deficient inopem venae te, ni cibus atque
ingens accedit stomacho fultura ruenti.
tu cessas? agedum, sume hoc tisanarium oryzae."
"quanti emptae?" "parvo." "quanti ergo?" "octussibus." "eheu!
quid refert, morbo an furtis pereamque rapinis?"
("You are weak, and your veins will fail you unless food and strong support be given your sinking stomach. Do you hold back? Come now, take this drop of rice gruel." "What's the cost?" "Oh, a trifle." "How much, I say!" "Eight pence." "Alack! what matters it, whether I die by sickness or by theft and robbery?")

Another of Egbert's poems having a stock comic character and a familiar theme is *De duobus venatoribus inique partientibus*:

Cum sotio gnarus venator foedera sanxit,
Quicquid cepissent, dirimendum partibus equis:
De lepore accepto pellem dedit et sibi carnem,
Pellem vero sibi, carnem de vulpe sodali.
Qui nequit obscure, deceptor fallit aperte.
(A skillful hunter confirmed a pact with his companion:
Whatever they should capture would be divided into equal parts.
From a hare he gives the skin to the recipient and keeps the flesh for himself,
But from a fox he keeps the skin for himself and gives the flesh to his friend.

The deceiver who cannot deceive covertly does so openly.) (201; pt.
1, 1664-68)

This little story closely resembles Petrus Alfonsi's *De duobus burgensibus et rustico*: in a contest for a bit of bread, two city men describe miraculous dreams they have had of heaven and hell; the countryman who accompanies them says he dreamed that neither of them returned, so he ate the bread.[10] The theme of *fraus* is a central one in the *exempla* of both Egbert and Petrus, yet the two writers have different aims. Egbert is above all concerned with rhetoric, as his chiasmatic lines about rabbit and fox illustrate; Petrus, drawing upon Arabic lore and directly influencing the elegiac comedies and Old French fabliaux, is interested in clear storytelling. Both writers make moral points, Petrus' being "sic fraus fraudem vicerat": "sic evenit eis qui socium decipere voluerunt, quia suo ingenio decepti fuerunt" ("this is what happened to those who wished to deceive their fellow traveler, and who were themselves deceived by the sharpness of wit," 137).

Four of Egbert's short narratives depict husband and wife, and one of these, so short that it is a maxim rather than a developed narrative, has adultery as its theme:

> Zelotipam curruca suam devinctius ardet,
> Suspectam excusat, prior offensacula donat.
> (The cuckold burns more devotedly for his adulterous wife.
> He excuses the suspected woman; first he forgives her little offenses.)
> (124; pt. 1, 659-60)

This miniature narrative is not very well constructed, as the second line, drawn from Prudentius' *Psychomachia* (line 781), makes no effort at maintaining chronology. The real inspiration of the poem, both thematically and verbally, is probably Juvenal's sixth satire:[11]

> tu credis amorem,
> tu tibi tunc, curruca, places fletumque labellis
> exorbes, quae scripta et quot lecture tabellas,
> si tibi zelotypae retegantur scrinia moechae!
> (You, poor cuckold, are delighted, believing them to be tears of love,
> and kiss them away, but what notes, what love letters would you find
> if you opened the desk of your green-eyed adulterous wife!) (6.275-
> 78)

Contemporary analogues presenting doting cuckolds who overlook their wives' sexual transgressions are found in the fable tradition: in the eleventh-century *Romulus*, for instance, a *rusticus* catches his wife with her lover and her ruse consists of concocting a false prophecy about how she would die if ever she were

seen with another man; the husband then swears he did not see the *leccator*.[12]
Stories of cheated husbands who are reconciled with their clever wives abound
in the later Middle Ages: the tale of the wife who pulls her husband's tooth in
order to prove her devotion to her lover is the basis of the elegiac comedy *Lydia*
and one of Boccaccio's tales.[13]   May's deception of January in Chaucer's
Merchant's Tale is another example, having Latin analogues belonging to the
exemplum and fable traditions.[14] Egbert, inspired by Prudentius and Juvenal,
may have had any of these stories in mind when he composed his mini-
narrative.

Egbert's second narrative depicting marital problems, *De uxore infensa
marito*, illustrates best how this poet expects his audience to be familiar with a
popular story and then to appreciate an odd twist to it. This narrative is merely
the conclusion of a widespread tale:

> Lite procax mulier fluvio submersa profundo,
> Que stolido vixit verbis infesta marito;
> Quam cum labenti quesissent amne deorsum,
> Vir suus adiecit: "Non id de coniuge novi,
> Has imas tenuisse vias, at compotis ira
> Indefessa adeo superas obtenderat undas."
> Inportuna fidem non prebent iurgia rectam.
> (An argumentative woman, who was hostile toward her
> Husband when she was alive, sank in a deep river.
> When they sought her in vain downstream,
> Her husband commented, "I have not known such behavior of my wife—
> That she would have mastery of the downstream current—but the unweary
> Wrath of this powerful woman carried her upstream."
> Bothersome quarrels do not lead to strong faith.) (185; pt. 1, 1378-84)

Again Egbert's density makes the story obscure, but fortunately, analogues in
contemporary popular literature present the beginning of the story, which Egbert
has chosen to suppress. In one of the fables of the *Romulus*, a husband has his
servants induce his quarrelsome wife to lunch on a riverbank and, as he sits next
to his wife, the cantankerous woman withdraws toward the edge. This maneuver
continues until she falls into the river.   When the servants search for her
downstream, the husband checks them:[15]

> Frustra eam in decurrentibus aquis queritis;
> expectate eam ad ortum fluminis, et illuc properate,
> quia, ut solebat vivens contra me niti, sic mortua
> contra impetum nititur fluvii.
> (In vain do you search for her in waters flowing downstream. Look for
> her at the river's source; hasten there, for just as she used to contend

against me while alive, while dying she contends against the river's current.)

This conclusion is considerably more straightforward than Egbert's account, in which it is unclear whether the drowning wife is upstream, downstream, at the bottom of the river, or near the river's surface. At first it appears that "they," perhaps the husband's servants or neighbors, are searching for the wife downstream ("labenti . . . amne deorsum"), but the husband's words complicate matters: he has never known her to have mastery of the "bottommost ways" ("imas . . . vias"), but this woman's unweary wrath overcame the "uppermost waves" ("superas . . . undas"). A late medieval version of the tale, in which the husband himself searches for his wife, is verbally close to Egbert's account and further clarifies the meaning of "bottommost ways" and "uppermost waves":[16]

At ille tristitiam simulans, intravit in navim, et navigans contra impetum fluvii cum magna pertica quaerebat uxorem suam in aquis. Cumque vicini ejus quaererent quare in parte superiori quaereret eam, cum deberet eam quaerere in parte inferiori, respondit, "Nonne novistis uxorem meam, quae semper contrariam faciebat, et nunquam recta via incedebat? Credo pro certo quod contra impetum fluvii ascendit, et sicut alii consueverunt non descendit."

(But he, feigning sadness, entered a boat, and sailing against the river's current, with a long staff he was seeking his wife in the water. And when his neighbors asked why he was searching for her in the upper region when he ought to search for her in the lower areas, he replied, "Didn't you know my wife, who would always do the opposite and never took the right way? I think for certain that she ascended against the river's current and did not descend as others are wont to do.")

This clear prose account depicts the husband sailing upstream, "contra impetum fluvii," and his neighbors' description of upstream ("in parte superiori") and downstream ("in parte inferiori") must be equivalent to Egbert's "superas undas" and "imas vias." This woman's impudence is as great as that of the contentious wife in a similar story who, when her tongue has been cut out by her husband, manages to show her disagreement through signs with her hands.[17] Thus Egbert, poeticizing a popular story, reduces narrative to the climactic scene at the expense of a faulty pronoun reference. He demands knowledge of the full story, and he delights in a curious rendition.

The strong moral ending of this poem, "bothersome quarrels do not lead to strong faith," demonstrates a didactic tendency characterizing Egbert's two other stories about wily wives. But in *Quomodo ploravit gravem sibi virum uxor defunctum*, the moral application is not quite logical:

Vir gravis uxori ius morti solvit avitum;
Post obitum multos lacrimarum fuderat imbres
Tamquam mesta viri multum de funere coniunx.
Cur in flagra gravem ploret, rogantibus addit:
"Non queror excessisse animam de luce malignam,
Ingemo plus adeo superantem tempora longa."
Letitie interdum simulatur causa doloris.
(A man who was cruel to his wife paid the due of death.
After his passing, she poured forth showers of tears
As if she were most distraught over her husband's burial.
She tells her inquirers why she must lament him,
who was savage when he used the whip:
"I don't lament him because his wicked soul has
departed from the world of light;
I mourn because he lived for such a long time."
Grief is sometimes the counterfeit of joy.)   (185-186; pt. 1, 1385-91)

The humorous potential of the supposedly faithful wife at her husband's grave
has its most famous application in the episode about the matron of Ephesus in
Petronius' *Satyricon*, which is the basis of several fables and an Old French
fabliau.[18]   Structurally and thematically, Egbert's narrative is closer to an
epigram by Martial:[19]

Amissum non flet cum sola est Gellia patrem,
    si quis adest, iussae prosiliunt lacrimae.
non luget quisquis laudari, Gellia, quaerit:
    ille dolet vere qui sine teste dolet.
(Gellia weeps for her lost father not while she is alone; if anyone is
present, her tears leap forth at her bidding. He does not lament who
looks for praise, Gellia; he truly sorrows who sorrows unseen.)

Martial's moral is simple and clear. Egbert's, however, is illogical, for the
hypocritical wife informs her inquirers that the true cause of her sorrow is her
husband's longevity, but then the poet concludes that grief can be a counterfeit
of joy, though the wife has nothing left to hide. The poet mindlessly and
inappropriately attaches a moral to the story.
    Egbert's last narrative presenting married types, *De muliere quae vidit iurgare
virum et natos*, is coherent, but it no doubt alludes to a longer story familiar to
Egbert's intended audience:

Olim cum proprio natos iurgare marito
Ut vidit mulier, sic fari protinus orsa:
"Absque meis pugna est, pugiles, miscete capillos,
Non mea res agitur neque rerum cura mearum."

Qui simulat non esse suum, fert sepe dolorem.
(Once when a wife saw her sons quarrel with her own husband,
She immediately began to speak thus:
"This fight is not my affair—fighters, tear your hair—
This is none of my business, nor is it my concern."
One who pretends no interest in a situation often bears the pain of it.)
(190; pt. 1, 1466-70)

As characteristic of Egbert, excessively formal rhetoric ("pugiles, miscete capillos") contrasts with the mundane theme. Unlike Theodulf, who parodies high style by creating a tension between high and low, Egbert intends simply to elevate common stories for the purpose of moral edification.

While some of Egbert's narratives, such as *De uxore infensa marito*, can be fully understood only with the assistance of analogues and others, like *De pretio medico negato*, remain comprehensible in and of themselves, there are still a handful of stories whose meaning is so enigmatic that their humor is nearly impossible to appreciate. *De insipiente magistro et discipulis eius*, for instance, bases its wit on etymological play with the name Drogo:

Presbiteri insulsi super hoc responsa parabant:
"Nos docuit sapiens multorum Drogo magister,
Nobis iudicibus quo non sapientior alter."
Consultus nescit, "Sabaoth" et "Osanna" quid esset,
Ac "Dominus vobiscum" se nescire professus!
Credo, quod docuit, proprio de nomine traxit:
Deceptus decepit, fraus in fraude pependit.
(Some foolish priests furnished these answers on this subject:
"The teacher Drogo, wise in many things, has taught us;
In our judgment there is no one wiser."
When he is consulted, he does not know what "Sabaoth" and "Osanna"
mean
And confesses that he doesn't understand "Dominus vobiscum"!
I believe what he taught he extracted from his own name:
Deception has deceived, fraud has dealt out fraud.) (173; pt. 1, 1145-
51)

The basic meaning of the story is clear: Drogo, whom his followers esteem highly, does not know the significance of Hebraisms in ecclesiastical Latin; moreover, he does not know the meaning of even the most rudimentary Latin.[20] The crux lies in the punch line, as it so often does in Egbert's stories: obviously what Drogo has taught is a deception, a fraud, but how does he extract this teaching from his name? Evidently Egbert is punning on the Germanic *trügen*, "to deceive," whose past tense is *trogen*; the theoretical form of this word is *dragan-*, whose past tense is *drog*.[21] Everything in the poem gains its humor from word meaning and wordplay: Drogo does not understanding the meaning of Hebraisms and Latin expressions, and what he teaches he "has drawn" (*traxit*, derived from the same Indo-European root as *trügen*) from his own name, which means "deception."

Perhaps Egbert's most obscure tale is *De viro qui lunam fecit de pane seliginis*, the story of a fool who hopes to make a magical orb out of white bread:

> Quidam inpune ratus vanissimus et male sanus
> Sese posse aliquid furve succurrere nocti,
> Doctor ut is prudens tanta incrementa dedisset
> Preter opinatum, quotiens se Cinthia condat,
> Quendam formavit de pane seliginis orbem,
> Ut foris expositus lumen diffunderet amplum;
> Cumque moras ageret, quas fixas semper habebat,
> Inventor probulus iurat per Castoris aedem:
> "Si deberet," ait, "lucere aliquid, patuisset."
> Inconcessa gemat qui stultus vota ministrat.
> (A most empty-headed and irrational man
> Believed that he could somehow relieve the darkness of night,
> So in order to provide additional light,
> Contrary to expectations, whenever the moon was hidden
> This clever genius molded a ball of white bread
> To scatter full light when he was outside.
> And when he encountered continual delays in his project,
> The worthy inventor swears by Castor:
> "If there was going to be any light, it would have appeared by now."
> Let fools who entertain impossible desires complain.) (186-87; pt. 1, 1404-13)

Again the basic plot is clear, yet we feel we are missing the point—if there is one. The protagonist's motivations for molding this breadball are unstated: does he fear robbery, or is he merely a *stultus* with an absurd theory? He appropriately swears at the temple of Castor, a star that casts light—hence he is "swearing by the stars"—but the "continual delays" are vague and the climax is flat. An analogue to the story may explain such details and reveal the poem's humor, but no analogue exists.[22]

Egbert's longest narrative, *De Waltero monacho brachas defendente*, has direct analogues in the eleventh-century *Chronicon Novaliciense* and in the Old French *Moniage Guillaume*, and not surprisingly, it contains irresolvable ambiguities.[23] The humor resides in involuntary nudity, and the high point of the narrative, Walter's crude speech to his attackers, is confusing:

Mandant Waltero fratres non tradere brachas,
Omnibus ablatis tacito defendere solas,
Dum contingat iter fortes transire per hostes.
Interea datur experientia militis huius:
Mittitur imperiis ad certa negotia fratrum.
Fors fuit, ignorans in prorumpentibus hesit
Hostibus et faleras et equum tollentibus una,
Mastigiam, cunctos habitus iuxtaque cucullam;
Non renuit neque contendit, facere omnia sivit.
Tandem de bracis solvendis tendere coepit,
Usus militia viguit, que nota, sub armis:
Dissipat assultus macta virtute repressos,
Omnes disiectos ab equis sine sanguine stravit,
Dicens, "Omne quidem spolium, de podice nullum
Fratres his tolerant, qui fratrum nuntia portant,
Tales exuvias avido vetuere latroni."
Collectis spoliis et equis ad sacra meavit
Psallentum sub laude dei collegia fratrum,
Tantam militiam mirantum et fortia facta
Vergentis vetulique hominis nova bella moventis.
(The brothers command Walter not to give up his trousers,
To protect his only pair in silence when everything else has been taken
away,
Whenever it should happen to him to make a journey through strong
enemies.
Soon a chance is given the former soldier to test this advice:
He is sent by his brothers' orders to conduct a certain business.
It chanced that the unaware monk fell into trouble when the enemy
broke forth
And took both his horse and its equipment at the same time,
His whip, all his clothes along with his cap.
He neither refused them nor fought; he allowed them to do all.
At last he began to struggle when his trousers were about to be drawn
off.
Experience in warfare made him vigorous, as was known, in arms.
He routs the checked attacks with noble strength.
Bloodless, he lays all low, driven asunder their horses,
And he says, "The brothers will allow anything to be taken from their
Messengers, except from their bottoms—
Such spoils have been prohibited the greedy thief."
When the spoils and the horses are collected, he went to the holy
Company of his brother, sang psalms in praise of God,
And his brother marveled at such warfare and strong acts
Of the bent old man inflicting new exploits.) (203-4; pt. 1, 1717-36)

In the *Chronicon Novaliciense*, the Walter of this story is confused with the famous Walter of Aquitaine.[24] The hero must rout a group of thieves in the neighborhood of the monastery, and by no means must he give up his *femoralia* ("thigh coverings").[25] When he is attacked, he first slays his foe with a single blow of his fist, thus revealing his true identity as Walter, Strong of Hand; he kills the remaining robbers with the shoulder ripped off a nearby calf. This story constitutes a major episode of the *Moniage Guillaume*, in which the hero must not give up his *braies* ("breeches"): "C'est une chose c'on claime famulaires" (75; lines 686-87). As in Egbert's poem, much emphasis is laid, by the hero himself, on his military exploits before his *moniage*. Also, concrete motivations for Guillaume's trip are given: the monks are angry that he eats too much, so they compel him to traverse a forest haunted by thieves in order to purchase fish by the sea. Guillaume manages to buy the fish, but on his return he is attacked by the rogues. He fights them with the leg of a horse, and his boast is as indecent as Walter's in Egbert's account:

> "Fil a putain, vous aves tout perdu,
> Mar m'i aves si vilment desvestu,
> Por mon braiel estes hui mal venu."
> ("Sons of bitches, [now] you've lost everything;
> Wrongly have you wickedly undressed me.
> Because of my breeches you have had a bad day.") (117; lines 1596-98)

In neither Egbert's version nor the *Chronicon* is it clear why Walter must keep his trousers yet allow the robbers to take everything else, while in the *Moniage* the monks are plainly tricking the ex-soldier into enduring this torment. Walter's odd speech to the defeated thieves contains a vulgarity unusual for Egbert: literally he says, "Indeed, of all this spoil, nothing from the anus/Do brothers who carry brothers' messages allow to these," the "these" being explained by a manuscript notation as the "enemies."[26] My paraphrase, benefiting from the known analogue, makes some sense of Walter's words: "The brothers will allow anything to be taken from their messagers, except from their bottoms." This poem is a final instance of Egbert's density and ambiguity and of an extreme condensation that can be deciphered only through extant analogues.

These analogues to Egbert's stories are essential to understanding his production, and they provide insight into his methodology and purpose. The contents of his narratives have identifiable parallels in popular literature, while his style, laced with borrowings from classical and patristic writers, seeks an elevation that is usually excessive and awkward. This preoccupation with rhetorical effect contributes most to his obscurity. Obtrusive formalities like "ius morti . . . avitum" and "pugiles, miscete capillos" and the use of rare words such as *curruca* are the unhappy results of his attempts at a high style. His play on words (Drogo) and allusions to proverbs ("Is plane curruca foret, si quintus adesset") make his humor difficult to appreciate, as does his elliptical style, when he reduces a story to a two-line moral application. When an analogue to a narrative exists, one may, perhaps, appreciate an abbreviated, witty rendition of a story, but without analogues, Egbert's meaning and humor are often lost. The worst result of Egbert's rhetorical style is utter sacrifice of meaning to style, as revealed by the inappropriate moral conclusion of *Quomodo ploravit gravem sibi virum uxor defunctum.*

But despite Egbert's manneristic style, his comic narratives do present universal comic characters and themes, and his rhetoric occasionally contributes to comic effect. His conclusion to the poem about Drogo, "Deceptus decepit, fraus in fraude pependit," echoes the dominate theme of the *ridicula*, "sic fraus fraudem vicerat." Irony, reversals, and inversions remind us that we are reading comic stories, though we may find the humor difficult to fathom. Sometimes Egbert's rhetoric creates a pointed twist: the tricky hunter's division of spoils, described in chiasmatic lines, is all the more amusing because of the rhetoric. Similarly, the wife's struggle first with the "imas vias" and later with the "superas undas," though confusing, contains a pointed inversion. But universal comic structures and occasionally successful rhetoric do not redeem Egbert's narrative art. Only the most sensitive twentieth-century reader can find his stories amusing, and one is most struck by the poet's mindless retelling of better-told tales, his utter neglect of good storytelling, his self-abandonment to words.

Other learned Latin poets of the late tenth and early eleventh centuries, such as Fulbert of Chartres (c. 960-1028) and Leo of Vercelli (c. 965-1026), may have written trifles during their youth, but apart from a fragmentary fable by Leo, there is no proof that they composed narratives that may be considered comic.[27] Two of the Cambridge Songs, including the *ridiculum* about little John, have been attributed to Fulbert, but these attributions, as Strecker points out, are questionable, and there is no certain evidence that Fulbert wrote *nugae*, much less *ridicula*, during his poetic career.[28] Toward the middle of the eleventh century, comic narratives are still scant, but one story, the episode about the redhead in *Ruodlieb*, is a masterpiece anticipating the vernacular narratives of the twelfth and thirteenth centuries.[29] Dronke calls the tale a fabliau, emphasizing "the dramatic unity underlying the comic and the serious halves . . . it is not a ribald tale followed by an *exemplum* of Christian repentance, but a single story, in which sexual deception is seen in a new light when the three characters—cuckold, wife, and lover—are suddenly brought face to face with death" (*Poetic Individuality* 48). But the story does have a strong moral frame: before the episode, Ruodlieb's lord gives him various bits of advice, such as avoiding redheads, taking the broad road, avoiding an older man who has a young wife, but visiting a young man who has an old widow as wife (fragment 5, lines 449 f.). Soon after, Ruodlieb meets *rufus*, and while the hero visits a young man and his old wife, the redhead seduces the young wife of an old man.

Like Unibos, the redhead is a master of stratagems, a creator of fictions. The poet forewarns his reader that *rufus* will trick his host by pretending the young wife is his cousin, but his reward will be death: "Currit et ad neptem, nil nacturus nisi mortem" ("and [he] runs to his 'cousin' to find nothing but death," 7, 34). *Rufus* beats the house gate and insists that the old man recognize him ("pande, rogitas quasi nescieris me" ["Open! You act as though you didn't know me"], 7, 41), and once inside, he behaves like a madman:

Rufus proterve nimis incursando superbe
In curtem mitram non deponebat et ensem
(Desiliens ab equo, freni loro sude iacto)
Strinxit ut insanus, prae se stetit utque profanus.
(The redhead stormed very impetuously and haughtily into the court,
did not leave his hat, and like a maniac drew his sword [leaping from
his horse and slinging the strap of the bit around a post] and stood
there like a demon.) (7, 44-47)

When the old man repeats that he does not know the redhead, the latter explains, "Est uxor vestra mea neptis valde propinqua;/Hanc ut conveniam solus permittite solam" ("Your wife is my cousin, very close of kin,/Permit me to meet with her alone," 7, 52-53). The old man believes this lie all too readily, and *rufus*, chatting with the woman at the gate, creates a second fiction about a young man in love with her. She reveals her true nature when the redhead requests a reward for his role as go-between:

"Ter mihi succumbas in mercedem volo laudes."
"Si decies possis, fac," inquit, "vel quotiens vis."
("As reward I wish that you will promise to submit to me three times."
"Do it ten times if you can," she said, "or as often as you wish.") (7,
85-86)

In the seduction scene, emphasis is shifted to the old man, who becomes a Peeping Tom, witnessing his own wife's seduction. Whereas the two lovers are characterized by play, the old man is a representative of seriousness, and the poet's *descriptio* of ugliness is a very early occurrence of a topos found in later comic and romance literature.[30]

Ingreditur senior, quo non seriosior alter,
Hispidus in facie, poterat quod nemo videre,
Eius quid vultus fuerat, quia valde pilosus,
Ni solus nasus curvus fuit et varicosus.
Stant oculi gemini velut effosi tenebrosi,
Hosque retortorum superumbrat silva pilorum
Neve foramen ubi sit in os, quit quisque videre,

Sic se barbicia praetendunt longa ve spissa.
(The old man, who is more serious than anyone, comes in, shaggy of face, so that no one could see what his countenance was, since it was very hairy, except the nose alone, which was crooked and many-colored. The two eyes were dark as though they had been gouged, and a forest of bushy hair shaded them above, nor can anyone see where the opening of his mouth is. His long and heavy beard projects from his face.) (7, 98-105)

The husband interrupts the play with a warning: "Non debet mulier sic esse procax, neque sed vir,/Et praesente viro ludat decet haut alieno" ("A woman should not be so brazen, not even a man,/and when the husband is present she should not play with another," 7, 113-14). The climactic scene occurs when the husband, pretending to use the privy, spies on the lovers "like a thief":

Respiciebat eo terebelli perque foramen.
Rufus et in solium salit infeliciter ipsum,
Una manus mammas tractabat et altera gambas,
Quod celabat ea super expandendo crusenna.
Hoc totum ceu fur rimans senior speculatur.
Quando redit, sibi non cedit, nam non ea sivit.
(But he looked back through a hole made by a borer. Unhappily the redhead leaped to the old man's chair; one hand took hold of her breasts, the other her legs, which she concealed with a fur garment by spreading it out over her. Like a thief spying, the old man watches all that. When he returned, the redhead did not withdraw before him, for she did not permit it.) (7, 116-21)

The scene concludes with the husband's ironic statement to his wife: "You have made him tired enough; now let him rest" ("Satque fatigastis hunc, nunc pausare sinatis," 7, 129).

The tragic outcome of this story has already been hinted at by the poet's mention of death, and in the fragment that follows, depicting a judgment scene, it is clear that the lovers have murdered the old man. The wife weeps blood and offers various punishments for herself, one of which is identical with Unibos' proposed punishment: "Inclusam vase vultis submergere si me,/Deforis in vase quod feci notificate" ("If you wish to enclose me in a keg and submerge me,/record on the outside of it what I did," 8, 52-53). Excused by the pitying onlookers, she settles upon simply mutilating herself, and her pious behavior afterward underscores the shift from comic to tragic: "Haec nunquam risit, cum nemine postea lusit" ("She never laughed and never again jested with anyone," 8, 114).

This conclusion of the story, lacking the overt moral of an *exemplum*, is nonetheless antithetical in mood to the comic scene of seduction. The true counterpiece to the *rufus* story is the shepherd's tale of the young man and the old wife, a romance contained in a fragment preceding the two fragments about *rufus*. This idyll begins with a miser whose servants "never saw him laughing or joking" ("Nunquam ridentem viderunt neve iocantem," 6, 36). When the scoundrel dies, the young servant who has ingratiated himself into the household becomes the widow's lover:

Nemo vetat, vidua iuveni tunc fiat amica
Corde tenus, sed ad ecclesiam simul ire videmus,
Ad mensam resident simul, ad lectum simul ibunt.
(No one forbids the widow to become friendly with all her heart toward the young man, and we see them going to church at the same time; at table they are together, and to bed they go at the same time.) (6, 105-7)

Thus the poet juxtaposes romance, comedy, and tragedy, all three fragments illustrating the king's maxims to Ruodlieb. While the strong frame may reflect the poet's moral sensibilities, his immediate attention within the tales is focused on vivid, dramatic presentation. His balance of genres reveals more than simple awareness of generic distinctions; it also shows great skill in integrating the three genres into a coherent work.

Another mid-eleventh-century work balancing playful and serious moods is *De octo vitiis principalibus*, composed by Herimannus Contractus (1013-54) sometime between 1044 and 1046.[31] The poem is not only a mixture of genres, but also a mixture of styles, for Herimannus experiments with a number of metrical and rhythmic verses. The poet sends his muse to his sisters, "dominellae," who accuse the muse of being sexually promiscuous with the poet. The goddess, resentful at this slur, launches a lengthy dissertation on sexual misconduct and the horrors of hell. When she returns to Herimannus, he asks her why she is late; again the muse is insulted, while the poet is upset that she played a *satyra* to the girls instead of a love song. "Ludis insanisne, quid ista dicis?" ("Are you joking or are you mad? What is this you are saying?," line 302) shouts the muse. Herimannus then turns about:

ludicra respue, seria prome,
concine vani noxia mundi
gaudia, nugas, plures naenias,
pestes, mortes, mille labores.
(Reject games, produce serious poems,
Sing of the harmful joys of this empty world,
Of the trifles and the many lamentations,
The diseases, deaths, the thousand labors.) (lines 389-92)

When the muse is with the girls later, she bids them not to dismiss her with a joke ("non mox despicias ridiculo me neque despuas," line 464), and she then delivers a *Carmen de contemptu mundi* consisting of nearly 16 hundred lines of poetry. Thus the poem begins as a two-act comic drama in which the muse, because she is misunderstood, is the butt of humor. But once the muse's virtues are accepted by the mortal characters, the tenor of the poem shifts from playful and trifling to serious and religious.

While the comic narratives of the early eleventh century are largely German productions, those of the latter half of the century are predominantly French. The most skilled craftsman of epigrams is Hildebert of Lavardin (1056-1133), whose compact, lucid narratives are so imbued with the spirit of Antiquity that many of them have been erroneously attributed to Martial.[32] His two most important epigrams are about Milo, "le plus trompé des maris" (Hauréau, *Notice sur les mélanges poétiques* 48). *De Milone mercatore* extends a metaphor equating wife with field:

Milo domi non est. Peregre Milone profecto
Arva vacant, uxor non minus inde parit.
Cur sit ager sterilis, cur uxor lactitet edam:
Quo fodiatur ager non habet, uxor habet.
(Milo is not home. When Milo has set out on a journey
The fields lie fallow; his wife, nonetheless, is fertile.
Why the soil is sterile, why the wife milky, I shall declare:
His soil has no cultivator; his wife does.) (*Carmina Minora* 3; poem 7)

The spun metaphor lacks the crudity of similar equations by Martial and William IX, yet the manner in which it is extended and realized recalls the structure of Martial's epigrams (1.10; 4.41; 9.21). Like Egbert, Hildebert is concerned with rhetoric, yet the meaning of this little poem, whose narrative lacks significant development, is unambiguous. Peter von Moos, classifying the poem among Hildebert's satirical "Kleinkunstwerke," comments on its unity: "die Vorliebe für den pointierten Satzbau, der die Hauptsache bis zuletzt aufspart, um sie dort in gedrängtem Wort, oft in seinem Gedankenblitz aufleuchten zu lassen" (45). Von Moos places the second poem about Milo in the category of *nugae* (211):

Thura piper vestes argentum pallis gemmas
Vendere, Milo, soles, cum quibus emptor abit.
Coniugis utilior merx est, que vendita sepe,
Numquam vendentem deserit aut minuit.
(Incense, pepper, garments, silver plate, cloaks, jewels
You are wont to sell, Milo, and the buyer goes off with them.

Your wife is as merchandise more useful to you; she, though often
sold,
Never leaves the seller or diminishes his estate.) (*Carmina Minora* 3;
poem 9)

Employing asyndeton effectively, Hildebert again develops a metaphor in witty
fashion, "aber der Ton fällt nicht auf diese herkömmliche antike Vorstellung,
sondern auf das ironische Paradox, das an den Witz Martials erinnert: Die Frau
ist das, was der Mann gleichzeitig hat and nicht hat" (Van Moos 211).

These two epigrams about Milo, like Egbert's epigrams having analogues in
popular literary traditions, occupy an important place in the medieval comic
tradition, for they are very early abridgments of a theme later amplified by
Matthew of Vendôme in the elegiac comedy *Milo*. Matthew's poem tells how
this merchant becomes a cuckold while on a voyage; when Milo returns home,
he faces the king, who is his wife's lover, and through allegorical wit he traps
the king and compels him to end the adulterous relationship with Afra.
Matthew's rhetorical play as he describes Milo's absence recalls Hildebert's
laconic "Milo domi non est":

Afra favet, Milo nescit; Milone remoto
   Rex humilis coitus sustinet esse comes;
....
Absens Milo facit ad votum regis, amicat
   Sponsa sibi mechum, sponsus adauget opes.
Sponsus abest, sponsa regi consentit amorem
   At sponse sponsi gracia victa iacet.
(Afra gives her favors; Milo knows nothing. As soon as Milo is away
The king does not blush at being a partner of a humble love.
....
Milo's absence suits the king's desires. The wife
Befriends an adulterer; the husband works at increasing his goods.
The husband is absent; the wife shares the love of the king,
And the love of wife and husband lies vanquished.) (lines 63-64, 67-
70)

Also, Hildebert's figure equating wife and field is implicit in Matthew's contrast
of laboring husband, loving wife:

Sponsus arat, mecho blanditur sponsa, frequentat
   Sponsus agros, sponsus predia, sponsa ducem.
(The husband labors; the wife is caressed by her seducer.
The husband visits his fields, the husband his lands, the wife the ruler.)
(71-72)

The common names of the protagonists, the similar situations, and the linguistic parallels suggest that Hildebert's Milo and Matthew's Milo are the same character. Hildebert, long before Matthew of Vendôme composed *Milo*, is using the rhetorical process of abbreviation to recount in compact form a well-known story.

Variations of the theme of traveling husband, faithless wife abound in the late Middle Ages. Marcel Abraham, the editor of *Milo*, and Edmond Faral, in "Le fabliau latin au moyen âge," suggest the possible influence of the *Historia septem sapientum* on this *comedia*, but in the *Historia* the outcome is quite different: the wife saves her virtue, the king gives up, and the husband's suspicions are unjustified. A similar resolution terminates a pair of metrical declamations wrongly ascribed to Hildebert, the *Versus de sponso adversus sponsam suam* and the accompanying *Responsio sponsae* ("Carmina Miscellanea" col. 1453-55). These exercises are neither comic nor tragic, but are legalistic in tone. The husband's speech juxtaposes husband on the seas, wife at home:

> O res mira! dolo caret unda, fide caret uxor,
>   In pelago tutus, naufragus exsto domi.
> (Marvelous indeed! The wave lacks deceit; the wife lacks faith.
> On the deep I am safe; at home I seem drowned.)

Like Milo, the husband likens his wife's activity to a field being plowed:

> Sed scio quod juvenis lectum, non littus aravit,
>   Sparsit, et in campo messuit ille meo.
> (But I know that the adulterer plowed the bed of my young wife, not the shore;
> He scattered seed, and he reaped plenty in my field.)

The wife's *responsio* reveals a situation similar to that concluding Chaucer's *Franklin's Tale*: she resists her suitor, who, when he dies from grief, wills her his fortune because he was so impressed by her heroic chastity.

Hildebert's methodology in constructing epigrams is similar to Egbert's, but his style has classical clarity, and his condensation of popular tales suggests a sense of formal abbreviation, like that explained in Geoffrey of Vinsauf's *Poetria Nova*. Both Egbert's and Hildebert's epigrams are means of detecting the early proliferation of tales later finding embodiment as *comediae elegiacae*, courtly romances, and fabliaux. Hildebert's mini-narratives form part of his juvenilia and, according to Von Moos, may be called *nugae* (238-39). Though they are much more easily understood than Egbert's obscure *exempla*, Hildebert's epigrams obviously lack detail and often present only the kernel of a longer story. Such is the case of *De virgine seni nupta*, a story so brief that it is generic:

Virgo seni, generosa novo, prelarga tenaci
  Iungitur, et differt tempore, gente, manu.
(Virgin to old man, noble to upstart, abundant to stingy
Is joined, and differs in age, rank, hand.) (*Carmina Minora* 44; poem
52)

The noble maiden who marries a stingy old man differs from the *ancilla* who
marries an old man in *Ruodlieb*, but the essential elements of the January and
May theme are here. A longer poem, *Quid sit vita pudica*, contains the bare
outline of a story about a man whose name lends itself more easily to punning
than Egbert's Drogo:[33]

In noctem prandes, in lucem, Turgide, cenas,
  Multimodoque mades nocte dieque mero.
Cumque cuti studeas, uxorem ducere non vis.
  Cur nolis? Dicis, "Vita pudica placet."
Turgide, mentiris, non est hec vita pudica.
  Vis dicam quid sit vita pudica? Modus.
(Till nightfall you lunch, till dawn, Turgidus, you dine,
And you reek day and night with all sorts of wine.
And although you are careful with your person, you are unwilling to
take a wife.
Why don't you? You say, "A chaste life pleases me."
Turgidus, you lie—this is not a chaste life.
Would you have me tell you what is a chaste life? Moderation.)

Martial's style pervades this poem, and as in *De Milone mercatore*, this epigram
reveals Hildebert's "Vorliebe für den pointierten Satzbau," ending as it does with
the single word "Modus" qualifying the entire poem.[34] Hildebert's description
of Turgidus' care for his own person provides further punning, for "cumque cuti
studeas" may also mean "since you're partial to flesh." Von Moos sees in this
Spottgedicht a healthy and moderate stance against sexual asceticism, a viewpoint
not differing greatly from that of *De Iohanne abbate* (226).

  Hildebert's most interesting *Spottgedicht*, *De quodam servo*, is a succinct
story with the unusual love triangle of lord-lady-servant:[35]

Servus ait domino, "Gratis famulabor in annum,
  Si facis ut famula qualibet arte fruar."
Poscit herus coitum, sibi ponit servula noctem.
  Ille thoro famulum collocat, hec dominam.
Res patuit casu; vir nuptam provocat in ius.
  Facta refert; risum facta relata movent.
Uxor et ancilla laudantur, virque monetur
  Ne messem famuli sic emat ulterius.

(A servant says to his lord, "I will serve you for a year without pay
If you can arrange, by some stratagem, that I may enjoy a female
servant."
The master demands sex with a servant girl, and she tells him what
night to come.
He places the male servant in bed, and she places her mistress there.
The deed is made known by accident; the husband summons his wife
to a court of law.
The deeds are recounted; the recounted deeds cause laughter.
The wife and the female servant are praised, and the man
Is warned not to make these kinds of annual contracts with servants.)

The adulterous triangle, lord-lady-servant, rarely occurs in the fabliaux and the
courtly romances. While it is true that the troubadour Marcabru often laments
the bastardization of the nobility by servants who seduce the ladies they are
guarding, Marcabru's social criticism seems to attack a real problem in the real
world.[36] Hildebert's fiction is structurally close to the fable, *ridiculum*, and
exemplum traditions, which also end with "morals" preceded by "sic." But
Hildebert's legalistic conclusion indicates the influence of the metrical
declamations and anticipates the *iudicia amoris* of Andreas Capellanus and the
questione d'amore of Boccaccio.[37] While the content of Hildebert's epigram
could certainly use further detail—just how the "deed is made known by
accident," for instance, is unexplained—the poem nonetheless has clear structural
development and thematic integrity. It may be a school exercise, but unlike
Egbert's, it does not rely upon knowledge of the full story for proper
understanding.

A large number of anonymous epigrams, some of which may be the works of
Hildebert and Marbod, reveal the diversity of comic narration during the late
eleventh and early twelfth centuries. In addition to drawing on contemporary
mores and popular literature, the epigrammatic tradition often condenses well-
known stories from the Bible and from Antiquity. An anonymous epigram
located in the British Library's Additional Manuscript 24199, a twelfth-century
collection of poetry including the broadest representation of Marbod's and
Hildebert's works, portrays the trick Aristotle plays on Alexander:

Magnus Alexander bellum mandavit Athenis,
    Infestus populo tocius urbis erat.
Ibat Aristotiles caute temptare tyrannum,
    Si prece vir tantus flectere posset eum.
Quem procul intuitus, sceptrum capitisque coronam
    Testans, "Non faciam si qua rogabis," ait.
Mutat Aristotiles causam subtiliter: urbem
    Obsideat, frangat moenia Marte petit.

Penituit iurasse ducem bellumque roganti
    Dat pacem, lusus calliditate viri.
(Alexander the Great declared war on Athens,
Hostile toward the people of the entire city.
Aristotle went cautiously to test the tyrant,
To see if, by entreaty, he could bend his will.
Seeing Aristotle from afar, Alexander invokes his scepter and the crown
on his head,
Swearing, "I will not do whatever it is you ask."
Aristotle perceptively changes the situation for the better:
May the tyrant besiege the city, may he shatter the walls with warfare,
he asks.
He makes the leader sorry for what he had sworn, and to one who
asked for war
Alexander, tricked by his cunning, grants peace.)

Aristotle's ruse depends on words, not actions, and in this respect it resembles the ploys of the clever knight in *De equo perdito*, who says he will do what his father did—which was nothing—and the boy in *Deluso expectatio*, who says the ox in his dream said nothing—or said, "Nothing." In this anonymous epigram, Aristotle would like to beg Alexander to do nothing, but instead he says, "Do everything," which, in the context of Alexander's oath, means "Do nothing"! Unlike the fraud of the Swabian merchant in the *Modus Liebinc* or the lie of the Swabian suitor in the *Modus Florum*, Aristotle's cunning relies on the meaning of words and the perversion of meaning. The poem's humor thus derives from a scholarly interest in rhetoric, as in the *comediae elegiacae*.

Alexander and Aristotle, of course, are characters in numerous comic tales from late Antiquity to the early Renaissance. In one of the *Gesta Romanorum*, several philosophers counsel Alexander to erect a mirror in order to kill a basilisk with its own glare (493-94; *Caput* 139); in another one, Aristotle advises Alexander not to marry a girl whose kiss is poisonous (288; *Caput* 11). Perhaps the most famous account of the pair is the *Lai d'Aristote*, in which the philosopher, representing the *clergie*, is the butt of ridicule. In the *Roman d'Alexandre*, the hero promises the killers of Daire various rewards, but the killers fail to recognize that these rewards actually lead to their deaths.

The closest analogue to the anonymous *Magnus Alexander* is the variant offered by Geoffrey of Vinsauf in the *Poetria Nova*:[38]

Magnus Alexander, cum bella moveret Athenis,
Nulla reformandae placuerunt foedera pacis,
In pignus nisi forte datis sapientibus urbis.
Unus prudentum respondit ad istud et istis:
"Forte lupus bellum pastori movit. Utrimque
Tractatum de pace fuit; sed formula pacis

Nulla lupo placuit nisi pignus et obses amoris
Traditus esset ei custos gregis. Hoc ita facto,
Ante fuit timidus, sed post securior hostis."
Substitit hoc dicto.
(When Alexander the Great declared war on Athens, no terms for
restoration of peace were acceptable unless perchance the sages of the
city were surrendered as pledge. One of the wise men replied to the
proposal in these words: "It happened that a wolf declared war on a
shepherd. Terms of peace were discussed between them, but no
covenant of peace was agreeable to the wolf unless as pledge and
warrant of amity the guardian of the flock was handed over to him.
When this was done, the enemy who before had been cautious then
became more assured." After saying this much, he ceased.)

Geoffrey uses this story to illustrate the rhetorical figure of analogy, which is a
variety of *significatio*. While the anonymous epigram, with its emphasis on
human confrontation and trickery, is more humanistic than Geoffrey's rendition
and certainly has a wittier punch line, both epigrams present nearly identical
situations and begin in almost the same way. Also, both epigrams are clearly
school exercises designed to develop rhetorical skills.

Some of the rhetorical epigrams present situations that are inherently
comic—that is, later writers of fabliaux and *novellini* would exploit them for their
comic potential—but the anonymous poets temper the comic impulse with strong
moralism. Two poems, both contained on the same folio of a British Library
manuscript housing a large number of Marbod's poems (Cotton Vitellius A XII,
f. 131r), may be described as having toilet humor. The first, *De marito ab
uxore turpiter interempto*, once attributed to Hildebert, describes how a wife, in
order to enjoy her lover, murders her husband and sticks him in a latrine:

Federe nupta viri nolebat sene potiri.
    Cum jugulum diro rumperet ense viro,
Posset ut electo secura recumbere lecto
    Et corruptori nubere lege thori,
Clausum latrina, transfixum plus vice trina,
    Corpus, digna quidem quae pateretur idem,
Ad turpem ritum sepelivit nupta maritum.
    O facinus dirum sic tumulare virum!
(A married woman did not want to be ruled by an old man.
When she cut her husband's neck with a sharp sword
So she could recline on a bed of her choice
And marry a lover in a legal ceremony,
The body, pierced more than three times, was shut up in a latrine—
Certainly a fine woman carried him there!—

The wife buried her husband in a dirty ceremony.
Oh, cruel crime, thus to entomb a man!)

The strong moral context of the little story, much more pronounced than Egbert's in *De uxore infesta marito* and *Quomodo ploravit gravem sibi virum uxor*, undermines its humorous potential and makes it more of a tragedy than a comedy.

Similar moral application occurs in *De Judeo in latrinam lapso*, when a Jew insists upon waiting until the day after Sabbath before being drawn from the pit into which he fell:[39]

Cum de latrina lapsum salomona ruina
   Extraherent, laqueis "Non trahar!" inquit eis,
"Sabbata sunt!" plaudit populus, plausum comes audit.
   Plaudit et ipse iubet, cras ut ibi recubet.
(When men try to draw a Jew who has slipped and fallen
From a latrine, the Jew calls out from his trap: "Don't move me!
It's the Sabbath!" The people applaud him, and a count hears their applause.
He also applauds and orders the Jew to lie there tomorrow [as well].)

In a Zurich manuscript, a moral tag concludes the poem:

Sicut in omne quod est mensuram ponere prodest,
   Sic sine mensura vix stabit regia cura.
(In all things of this world, it is best to set a measure,
For without moderation the state's affairs will hardly remain stable.)

This epigram is so compact and the political allegory so distant from the narrative that it is difficult to appreciate it fully without an analogue. Such an analogue exists in the *Gesta Romanorum* (633; *Caput* 229):

Legitur de quodam judeo quod cecidit in cloacam die sabbati et voluit die sequenti extrahi, hoc est die dominico; sed rex terre illius ipsum etrahi non permisit dicens: "heri servavit sabbatum suum, hodie custodiet meum." Per judicem quilibet peccator qui non vult exire in die vite sue presenti foveam viciorum in quam sentinam et immundiciam cecidit cum peccatum commisit, et hic in die future non permittitur exire de peccatis si in eis mortuus fuerit, et tunc a rege celesti condempnabitur.
(We read about a certain Jew who fell into a sewer on a Saturday and wanted to be drawn out on the next day—that is, Sunday. But the king of that country did not permit him to be withdrawn [on Sunday], saying, "Yesterday he observed his Sabbath; today he will observe

mine." It is just that any sinner who does not want to abandon immediately the pit of vices, into which dregs and filth he has fallen when he committed a sin, is not allowed at a future time to leave behind his sins if he dies with them, and then he will be damned by the King of heaven.)

The *comes* of the metrical epigram is equivalent to the king who orders the Jew to remain in the latrine on Sunday as well as Saturday, and in both accounts the moral applications transform an inherently comic situation into a serious *exemplum*.

A number of early epigrams associated with the name of Hildebert are little more than fables elevated by rhetoric. The fable about the man with two wives, for instance, demonstrates an interest in rhetoric like other school exercises:[40]

> Fertur, erat binis meretricibus unus amator.
> > Haec aetate fuit marcida, floruit haec.
> Ille vero senior, junior sene, mixtus utroque,
> > Nec bene non canus, nec bene canus erat.
> Hunc miserum dum quaeque sibi cupit assimilari,
> > Fit neutri similis dissimilisque sibi.
> Alterutrum quia dum gremiis incumbit earum,
> > Huic junior canos, vellit anus reliquos.
> Sic deformatum, depilem ridiculumque
> > Exponunt populo. Ridet eum populus.
> (Once upon a time, a single lover had two mistresses.
> One was decayed with age while the other bloomed.
> He truly was the older—or was he the younger?—differing from both.
> It was not good that he was hoary, nor was it good that he was not hoary.
> While each desires to make the wretch similar to herself,
> He becomes similar to neither and dissimilar to himself,
> Because while he lies upon the bosom of either of the two,
> His junior plucks the white hairs, the old lady the rest.
> Thus, the deformed, hairless, and ridiculous man
> Is exposed to the public, who laugh at him.)

The man has become "ridiculous" or "comical" and is thus open to public disgrace, like the knight in Hildebert's *De quodam servo*. Another epigram associated with Hildebert also uses the word *ridiculum* to qualify the actions of a character:[41]

> Concilium domino papa Romae celebrante,
> Rusticus irrupit clamando: "Tacete, tacete!"
> Concio tota silet quasi grande quid afferat ille.

Uxor erat quam perdiderat, turba rapiente.
Hanc vocat, illa venit. Gavisus ea veniente:
"Uxor adest," inquit, "fundite, turba, valete."
Rident pontifices; pudet hos tamen et piget aeque
Tali ridiculo sua seria postposuisse.
(When our Lord the Pope was holding a council in Rome,
A peasant interrupted, crying, "Everybody be quiet!"
The entire assembly grows silent as if what he was going to say was important.
He had lost his wife when the crowd carried her off.
He calls her name and she arises. He rejoices at her arrival.
"Here's my wife," he says. "Now you can go, you people—goodbye."
The bishops laughed, but they are ashamed and annoyed
That they have postponed their serious matters for such a trifle.)

The text, as Hauréau points out, is corrupt, but its construction, with each verse ending with the same sound, indicates its nature: "Le poète s'est évidemment proposé la difficulté de raconter cet accident burlesque en huit vers finissant par la même voyelle . . . Ce sont là des amusements d'écolier."[42] The meaning is not entirely clear: apparently the peasant loses his wife during a large celebration and, by silencing the crowd, he finds his wife by simply calling her name. The humor of the story resides in the reduction of socially superior characters, the diversion from "serious matters" to "jest." Neither in this poem nor in the epigram about the man with two mistresses is the word *ridiculum* used generically; the epigrams, in style and structure, differ profoundly from the *ridicula*.[43]

In the late eleventh and early twelfth centuries, a narrative tradition closely related to the epigrammatic tradition emerges, but this literary development, sharing rhetorical interests with the short *nugae*, differs from the epigrams in two fundamental ways: the simple narratives are expanded significantly; the humor is often replaced by moral judgment, even tragedy. Metrical declamations like the *Versus de sponso adversus sponsam suam/Responsio sponsae* are not comic narratives, though they certainly have an important place in the evolution of the twelfth-century *comediae elegiacae*. At least one extended narrative, however, does belong to the world of comedy: in the British Library's Additional Manuscript 24199, just two folios before the epigram beginning "Magnus Alexander" is a narrative poem, commencing "Res mea, dum noctem vocat aurea luna," that depicts a situation very much like that of Hildebert's *De quodam servo*.[44] The poem apparently lacks a beginning: a knight is commanding his wife to "go forth" and choose her companions, a command that seems to be a ploy, for later the knight indulges in debauchery and drunkenness and is finally defeated by his own cunning ("lusumque sua se comperit arte," line

31). By beginning in the middle of the story, the poet may be using the order
of art, instead of the order of nature, as Geoffrey of Vinsauf puts it (*Poetria
Nova*, lines 87 f.). The poet's rhetorical bent is revealed by the apostrophe at
the beginning of the poem:

> Nil agis, infelix, non haec custodia salva est,
>> Quae tibi perpetui causa doloris erit.
> Dum licet et nondum pudor est violatus in illa,
>> Vxorem nulli crede, marite, tuam.
> (Do not go, unlucky one, this custody is not safe,
> It will be cause of everlasting pain for you.
> While it is possible, while her honor has not yet been violated,
> Entrust your wife to no one, husband.) (5-8)

The writer progresses in the opposite direction of the epigrammatists: instead of
abbreviating, he amplifies. The apostrophe is one means suggested by Geoffrey
for doing so; repetition and exclamation are other ways of amplifying a given
theme (*Poetria Nova* 219 f.). Hence the lady is twice described as burdened
with wine and sleep (13, 24), and when she is seduced by the servant, the poet
breaks out:

> Frangitur ecce pudor, pudor integritatis honeste,
>> Et servata federa rumpit amans.
> (See how honor is shattered, the honor of respectable uprightness,
> And a lover breaks the prescribed laws!) (27-28)

Other indications that this poem is a school exercise include the presence of
pagan gods to describe concrete actions: while Bacchus accompanies the lady
and two servants, the knight "places hope for his salvation in Venus" ("In
venerem ponit spem sibi," 22). The judgment ending the poem is literally a
questione d'amore:

> Quis pocius reus est? Domini mandata peregit
>> Servus, at illa stuprum victa sopore tulit.
> Ergo sopor dominam, domini violencia servum
>> Defendit, solus miles adulter erit.
> (Who is the guiltier? A servant performed the commands
> Of his lord, yet she, overcome by sleep, endured violation.
> Therefore sleep excuses the lady, the lord's impetuosity
> Excuses the servant, and only the knight will remain an adulterer.)
> (35-38)

As in Hildebert's *De quodam servo*, the clerical writer condemns the knight for the scandalous affair, whereas the troubadour Marcabru, describing similar love triangles, blames the servants for corrupting households.

The first editor of this poem, André Boutémy, calls it "une sorte de fabliau" and explains that "il s'apparante aux paraphrases métriques de déclamations et controverses antiques si fréquentes au XIIe siècle et dans lesquelles excella le Rémois Pierre Riga" ("Manuscrit Additional" 35, n. 1). The seduction of a sleeping woman is a common occurrence in both fabliaux and romances: in *De la demoisele qui sonjoit* a "bachelers" seduces a sleeping maiden repeatedly, and when she awakens, she seduces him.[45] In the romance *Richars le biaus*, Clarisse, suffering a fever, drinks too much wine in an effort to alleviate her fever; having fallen unconscious in a garden, she is seduced by a passing knight.[46] This second story is very close to *Res mea*, but the important difference is the social status of the lady's seducer, who is a knight in the romance but a servant in the Latin poem.

Not only does characterization differ, but the mood of *Res mea* is less playful, more serious, than that of the French fabliaux and romances. Boutémy is more accurate when he relates this poem to the tradition of metrical paraphrases of Antique declamations and *controversiae*, and indeed, like Andreas Capellanus and Boccaccio, the writer of *Res mea* is strongly influenced by this legalistic rhetorical tradition. Yet *Res mea* differs from contemporary paraphrases in its lack of explicit legal judgment and in its lack of moralizing. Also, the metrical declamations have distinct structures differing from that of *Res mea*: they are typically speeches made by a plaintiff or defendant in court. Hence the *Versus de sponso adversus sponsam suam* and the accompanying *Responsio sponsae* are like a debate, as is the *Disputatio inter Pontificem Romanum et Ulgerium*.[47] The *Versus de quodam paupere* is a single speech in which a peasant accuses a rich man in court.[48] The *Versus de geminis languentibus*, however, possesses a true narrative structure, beginning with an assertion that the story is true ("res est, non fabula vana") and ending with a judgment for the father.[49] In all of these poems, including *Res mea*, the nature of humor is ambiguous, yet in *Res mea* the poet is concerned not with law, but with proper storytelling, with rhetoric. The comic potential of the poem is thus undisturbed by serious legal wrangling; instead, it is tempered by the poet's moral sensibilities.

Res mea, like Boccacio's *questioni d'amore* in *Il Filocolo*, is a fiction influenced by the tradition of metrical paraphrases. Wesley Trimpi's distinction between the *iudicia amoris* of Andrea Capellanus and the *questioni d'amore* of Boccaccio sheds light on the narrative processes of *Res mea*:

> The *tema* . . . of a *questione d'amore*, as of a declamation, is a "proposed hypothesis" consisting of a brief outline of events and of one or more general rules or "laws" in the light of which the given actions may be interpreted. . . The *questioni d'amore* in Book IV of Boccaccio's *Il Filocolo* stand midway between the *iudicia amoris* of

Andreas and the *novelle* of the *Decamerone* . . . From the ingenious debate *about* the question in *De Amore* [by Andreas Capellanus], the emphasis has been shifted to the detailed presentation *of* the question by means of fiction in the *Filocolo*. (331, 336, 339)

In one of the most famous *questioni* of *Il Filocolo* (82-95; book 4, question 4), the analogue of Chaucer's *Franklin's Tale*, a husband requires his wife to honor her word by sleeping with a wooer—consciously imposing what the drunken knight of *Res mea* unconsciously demands. Chaucer's rendition, like *Res mea*, ends with a literal question:

> Lordyings, this question, thanne, wol I aske now,
> Which was the mooste fre, as thynketh you?
> Now telleth me, er that ye ferther wende.
> I kan namoore; my tale is at an ende. (5, 1621-24)

While *Res mea* obviously lacks the narrative development of the later stories and loses much of its effectiveness because of the poet's moral outrage, the creator of this poem employs a methodology later used by Boccaccio. In addition to being a school exercise utilizing various rhetorical figures, this poem makes use of the declamatory tradition to create a non-legalistic fiction.

A few extended narratives composed in the late eleventh century belong to literary traditions that allow a sedate humor to flavor otherwise serious poems. The friendship tradition perhaps demands the most widespread creative energy of the time, and it consists of fictional and nonfictional epistles exchanged by men and women. Some of the fictional letters of Baudry of Bourgueil (1046-1130)—the exchanges between Ovid and Florus, Paris and Helen, and Baudry and Constance—are labeled school exercises by Raby and probably would have been called *nugae* by Baudry, who uses the word and its cognates more than any other eleventh-century poet.[50] Baudry's *musa jocosa*, like Ovid's, is harmless; his life is chaste.[51] The poet invites others to share *nugae* with him, and in his epistle to Constance he calls his exercises on the theme of the *Tristia nugae* (127; poem 150, line 5 and 192; poem 191, line 35). But twice, like Froumond and Marbod, Baudry counsels against indulgence in *nugae* (129; 151, 20 and 248; 200, 34). None of Baudry's extant corpus contains a true comic narrative; Baudry's trifling poetry is above all love poetry, amorous exchanges among men and women. Only one of Baudry's secular poems, his *Somnium et expositio somni*, has any sustained narration, and his obliviousness to the sexual implications of a column that blocks him in a river creates a certain humor at his expense (19-23; 37). Baudry's only other narratives are saints' lives, which he contrasts to his *nugae*, composed at night or while traveling ("Talia dictabat noctibus aut equitans," 14; 36, 64). Similarly, William IX of Aquitaine composes his "vers de dreyt nien" while he is "sleeping on a horse" and thus reveals a like attitude about trifling poetry, "quod nichil est," as Fulcoius of Beauvais puts it.[52]

Other narrative works of this time that are not comic nonetheless are the trifles of church poets indulging in irreligious activities. *De molesta recreatione* by Marbod of Rennes (1035-1123), for instance, is a lady's lament and may form part of a tragic romance, according to Dronke.[53]   An erotic poem by Marbod's friend, "Gautier," is a romance with a certain humor:

> Aeole, rex fortis, ventosae cura cohortis,
> De vento nequam si rem mihi feceris aequam,
> Thus et aroma dabo, vitulum tibi sacrificabo.
> Unde querar dicam: jam complexabar amicam;
> Ecce furens ventus, quem non amet ulla juventus;
> Dum sumus in latebris, ferit ictibus ostia crebris;
> Credidimus flantem fore quemlibet insidiantem,
> Qui complexantes deprendere vellet amantes.
> Res erat in tactu, modicum distabat ab actu.
> Surgimus haud lente, mutantur cuncta repente;
> Oscula rumpuntur, quae nuda fuere teguntur.
> Hunc igitur ventum claudas per secula centum;
> Carcere claudatur, ne, si foris egrediatur,
> Quaslibet in partes similes exerceat artes.
> (Aeolus, strong king, caretaker of the windy enclosure,
> The winds would mean nothing to you if only you would do something favorable for me.
> I will give you incense and spice; I will sacrifice a small calf for you.
> So I shall say what I seek: Now may I embrace my love.
> Behold the raging wind, which no young girl loves.
> While we are in a cozy place, it strikes the doors with thick blows;
> We thought the wind was some kind of ambush,
> Somebody who wanted to catch embracing lovers.
> Indeed we only touched—we were far from the act.
> We rise by no means slowly; everything is changed quickly.
> Kisses are broken; what was naked is covered.
> Therefore shut up this wind for a hundred centuries.
> Let it be shut up in prison, lest, if it should ever escape,
> It would use similar cunning wherever it pleases.) (222)

Within the prayer to Aeolus is woven a thin comic narrative about the wind's disruption of the lover's play; like a tricky protagonist, the winds use "cunning" ("artes") to accomplish their misdeed. Gautier's interest is in love as a passion, and both he and Peter the Painter compose delicate narratives about how they encounter dancing ladies unexpectedly.[54] Such poems, like the late eleventh-century Italian *Versus Eporedienses*, properly belong to the world of romance.

The most important and most neglected writer of narrative epistles is Fulcoius of Beauvais, whom André Boutémy describes as "un précurseur trop méconnu de cette renaissance des lettres latines classiques qui dominera tout le XIIe siècle. Une place, bien plus importante que celle qu'on lui a accordée, lui revenait dans l'histoire de la poésie médiévale, puisqu'il fut, une génération avant Marbode et Hildebert, un écrivain de talent varié qui sut, à l'occasion, remonter aux meilleurs sources antiques" ("Foulcoie" 177). Virtually nothing is known about Fulcoius' life, but judging from the well-known recipients of his epistles, we may conclude that he composed roughly between the years 1050 and 1090.[55] His 26 *epistolae*, which, along with the epitaphs, form the extant portion of the *Uter*, are written in a more obtuse style than Baudry's friendship letters, and in nearly half of them a salutation frames a moral *exemplum* designed to give the recipient advice or warning. Eight of Fulcoius' letters draw upon classical, Biblical, patristic, and popular sources and recast these stories in a peculiar mold, moralistic in tone and elevated in style.

Fulcoius' eighth *epistola* is a scholarly rendition of the snowchild story, and it vividly demonstrates the contrast between the simple style of the *ridicula* and the rhetorical style of the pedantic trifles. The poem begins with a frame, an address to the letter's recipient, Fulco, who will learn from this *exemplum* what he may expect from the poet. Fulcoius provides classical names for the nameless characters of the *Modus Liebinc*, and his exposition, like the rest of the narrative, is highly rhetorical:

> Mercator quidam quandam sibi comparat Idam
> Corpore formosam varia sed mente dolosam,
> Custodem rerum quam deputat. Inde dierum
> Paucis expletis celer impatiensque quietis
> Visit nundinas estates atque pruinas.
> Qui labor est gratus; plures ad lucra moratus.
> Cum vasis vestes cumulat studiosus Acestes,
> Nec mercis quicquid monstratur ubique reliquit
> Vt sic placaret quam sic vehementer amaret.
> (A certain merchant married a woman named Ida,
> Whose body was beautiful but whose fickle mind was deceitful,
> And he placed her in charge of his possessions. Then,
> When a few days passed, overhasty and impatient with quiet,
> He visits markets for whole summers and winters on end.
> His work pleases him, and he awaits a greater profit.
> Eager Acestes accumulates garments along with vases;
> He does not overlook any gain wherever it appears
> In order to please her whom he loves so ardently.) (6-14)

Fulcoius develops his theme by establishing a series of dichotomies (the wife is beautiful in body but deceitful in mind; the husband visits markets "for whole summers and winters on end") and by employing *repetitio* (lines 11-13 restate the same idea in three different ways). Similar rhetoric colors his description of the wife's infidelity:

> Haec culpando moras dum menses odit et horas,
> Impatiens peperit. Quae det mendatia quaerit
> Quid commentetur dum vir lucrando moretur,
> Quo mitem faciat sponsum, quo credula fiat.
> Et sic indennis crescit puer estque triennis.
> (She, complaining of his absence and hating the days and months,
> Impatient, gave birth. She wonders what lies she should tell,
> What fictions she should invent while her husband is delayed by profits,
> So that she might make her husband mild and herself believable.
> Meanwhile, a blameless boy grows up, and three years pass.) (15-19)

Fulcoius again employs dichotomy (she will make "her husband mild and herself believable") and *repetitio* (she hates "the days and months"), and he uses an artistic rather than a natural ordering of events ("quae det mendatia" anticipates her future guile). Fulcoius creates a parallel between the husband's pleasure in business and the wife's pleasure in lovemaking with a single word, "impatiens" (16), which is earlier applied to the husband, "impatiensque quietis" (9). The narrative progresses with stunning rapidity (Fulcoius states that she gives birth without even mentioning her seduction or pregnancy), and chronological realism is absent—she begins planning her lie three years before her husband's return.

The wife's lie to her husband, lacking the clear expression of the *Modus Liebinc* and the lyricism of *Nam languens*, is utterly different from the corresponding passage in the sequence:

> Gaza, merce graves deducit navita naves.
> Occurrendo viro coniunx in robore miro,
> Audax figmenti, tendens puerum venienti,
> "En," ait, "hunc sine te tribuerunt numina de te.
> Sic sic egisti, pater, hunc absens genuisti.
> Coniugis oblitum dum quero nocte maritum,
> Dum iuvat insanos amplexus reddere, vanos
> Quaerere concubitus, vehemens hoc visito litus,
> Quem sic arderem tanquam te, sponse, viderem.
> Te non audivi, mea vota videre nequivi.
> Cum magis exarsi, nivis hoc in gutture sparsi.
> Pro te consumpsi, vice seminis ignea sumpsi.
> Hoc desiderio pregnans, hoc nomine fio.
> Hoc, pater, in nato tua, coniunx, ora notato."

(The sailor draws his ships, heavy with treasure, with goods, into port.
When her husband runs forth to meet her, the wife, with astonishing vigor,
Bold in her fiction, stretches the boy to the oncomer
And says, "Behold, the gods granted you this boy in your absence.
Yes, father, it is true: you produced this son; you engendered him when you were away.
When I was seeking my husband, forgetful of his wife, at night,
At the time when it is most pleasing to exchange heated embraces, to seek fruitless coition,
I was burning with passion, and I visited this shore;
I was burning for you as if I saw you, my husband.
I did not hear you, nor could I see my prayers.
When my passion blazed even more, I sprinkled snow in my throat.
I took it in place of you; burning, I took it in lieu of your semen.
Because of this desire, through this agency, I became pregnant.
Observe your features, husband [and father], in this son.") (20-33)

In the *Modus Liebinc* "the faithless wife/runs toward [her husband] dragging the little boy with her," while in Fulcoius' account the wife addresses her husband as *he* "runs forth to meet her." Also, the narrator of the sequence states that the wife was "inmemor/viri exulis," whereas Fulcoius' Ida accuses her husband of being "coniugis oblitum." Fulcoius changes the negative attitude about this progeny in the *Modus Liebinc* ("damnoso foetu/heu gignebam") into a miraculous conception favored by the gods. Finally, the setting of this insemination has been changed from the Alps to the seashore, where the wife seeks her husband much like the woman of the lyrical strophe intruding into the *Modus Liebinc*. Just why Fulcoius changes so many details is a matter of conjecture: perhaps, like Sextus Amarcius, he heard a mime's performance of a poem like the *Modus Liebinc* but forgot several of its details; perhaps Fulcoius heard an alternate version of the snowchild story, one in which the wife visits a seashore instead of the mountains. Certainly some of Fulcoius' alterations reveal his artistic concerns, his originality: his introduction of the "numina," for instance, reveals his characteristic interest in pagan gods. The wife's speech lacks the clarity of the comparable fiction in the *Modus Liebinc*, and she is "bold in her fiction," carefully using the words "pater" and "coniunx" (33), unlike the hesitating wife of the sequence, who bumbles through an impromptu lie. Generally Fulcoius' language is dense and difficult, and he seems to condense—that is, abbreviate—and amplify his theme at the same time.

The remainder of the narrative reveals Fulcoius' interests in rhetoric and classicism. Earlier in the poem Fulcoius contrasted Ida's beautiful body and fickle mind; now the contrast of exterior and interior applies to Acestes:

Fit sponsus letus sed non in corde quietus:
Quippe liquet puerum nive, grandine non fore verum.
Sponsae cum nato dat munus et oscula grato.
(The husband appears joyful but is unquiet in his heart.
Indeed, it does not appear likely that his son could be born from snow,
from hail.
He gives gifts and kisses to his wife and the dear child.) (34-36)

The narrative progresses quickly: instead of waiting five years, the husband immediately commands his wife to light "the altar of Neptune and of the sacred pit" ("Neptuni flagret ut ara/Fac prius et mundi"), for "it is time to go" ("'tempus vocat,' inquit, 'eundi'").

Preparet heredem iubet haec, res servet et edem.
"Quem non viderunt, quem fata deusque dederunt
Notis ostendam divis et vota rependam."
(He orders her to prepare the heir and to look after the property and the house.
"Him whom the fates and god have not seen, whom they granted,
I will show him to the known divinities and give them thanks.") (40-
42)

Fulcoius' classicism is esoteric: the "sacred pit" ("mundus") is, in the largest sense of the word, Olympus, the residence of the gods, the vault of the universe; the word also signifies the opening of the underworld, or hell, and Plutarch uses the Greek equivalent *bathros* when describing the sacred pit dug at the Palatine.[56] Apparently Acestes plans to show his son "to the known divinities"—that is, to Neptune and to the gods of the sacred pit—"and give them thanks."

The narrative progresses in fits and starts. Like Egbert, Fulcoius is unconcerned with tight chronology or character consistency, and events often follow upon each other without transition:

Est quoniam natus, non amplius incomitatus
Merces augebit sed et ipsum cuncta docebit.
Paruit ergo, parat sponsus quaecunque rogarat.
Fraudis plena nihil metuit de pignore fraudis.
Discedunt laeti. "Memor," addidit, "est niveti;
Nostros per fluctus serva, karissime, fructus."
Distracto puero facta pro fraude molesto.
It, redit. Ut mestus queritur sed pectore festus. . .
(Since he has a son, the merchant is no longer unaccompanied,
But he will expand his business and teach him everything.
Thus she obeyed him and she prepares whatever her husband had requested.

Full of fraud herself, she has no fear concerning the pledge [i.e., child] of fraud.
Joyful they depart. "Be careful," she added, "with the snowchild.
Protect our offspring in the open seas, dearest."
He sold the boy, who was irksome because of the committed fraud.
He leaves; he returns. He laments as if sad, but he is joyful in his heart.) (43-50)

The wife's lack of fear concerning her child (46) is contradicted by her farewell speech to her husband (47-48), and the important point that the husband sold the boy (49) occurs unexpectedly and without detail. Again Fulcoius brings up the theme of exterior-interior (the husband "laments as if sad, but he is joyful in his heart"), and he introduces the moral theme ("Fraudis plena nihil metuit de pignore fraudis").

After the husband's fiction about the snowchild's death (51-54), Fulcoius states the moral in very familiar terms:

Percussit simili percussus vulnere pili.
Sic fuit ars arti, fuit et fraus obvia fraudi.
(Having been cheated, he struck back with a similar blow of the javelin.
Thus cunning checked cunning and fraud fraud.) (55-56)

But the epistle does not end here: Fulcoius still has to narrate an enigmatic tale about a robber and to develop the theme of fraud so it is relevant to his recipient. In the transitional lines that separate the story of the snowchild and the obscure tale of the robber, Fulcoius indicates that there are popular origins to his story:

Sermo quidem gratus vulgi. Sum premeditatus
Quid velit, inque mera lunae quid nescio spera
Astruit. Apparet quod inumbrat cum mage claret
Vulgi simplicitas. Quae vix haec frivola vitas,
Quodque semel discis vix aut nunquam resipiscis.
(This is a pleasing popular tale. I have wondered
What the story means, and I don't know what on earth it shows.
What is in the dark becomes clear when
The simplicity of the common people becomes bright.
Such trifles you scarcely avoid,
And hardly ever do you recover what you have once learned.) (57-61)

The diction and syntax of this passage are difficult, as is the message. First Fulcoius says that he does not know what this popular story "shows" ("astruit");

then, in so many words, he states that simple stories have clear messages ("apparet quod inumbrat cum mage claret/Vulgi simplicitas"); finally, he implies that by learning such "trifles" ("frivola"), "hardly ever do you recover what you have once learned."

The difficulty does not end here. Fulcoius' brief story about the robber who conceals moonlight with two thorns, a tale serving as an *exemplum* of deception, is more of an allusion than a self-contained narrative:

> Dicis latronem sic permansisse peronem
> Dum radios binis, scandendo per ardua, spinis
> Obstruit in luna, quae furtis officit una.
> (You say that a robber awaited a leather boot
> When, scaling steep places, he obstructed the moon's rays,
> Which alone hindered his theft, with two thorns.) (62-64)

Notwithstanding the difficulty in understanding this curious Latin,[57] it seems, at first glance, that Fulcoius is referring to the medieval notion of the Man in the Moon, who, according to one version, is "a peasant who has been banished there because he has stolen thorns or brushwood, which he is still carrying on his fork" (Menner 3). A famous Middle English lyric depicts this figure vividly:

> Mon in the mone stond and strit;
> On his bot-forke his burthen he bereth;
> It is muche wonder that he n'adoun slit—
> For doute leste he falle, he shoddreth and shereth.
> When the forst freseth, muche chele he bid;
> The thornes beth kene, his hattren to-tereth.
> Nis no wight in the world that wot when he sit,
> Ne, bote it be the hegge, whet wedes he wereth. (Luria and Hoffman
> 131)

But Fulcoius' character is a robber, not a peasant, a hedge cutter, or even Dante's "Cain with his thorn-bush" (*Inferno* 20, 125). Further, Fulcoius explains at length why he has invented this story:

> Res est fallaci tibi ficta tuoque sequaci.
> Fur vult furari nec vult furando notari.
> Vult metuendo crucem spinis obducere lucem.
> Non vult monstrari quisquis male vult operari.
> Sed viciis fuscat si quis virtute choruscat,
> Et spinis pungit cum verbis verbera iungit.
> Sed caveat latro quia lux lucebit in atro.
> Nec poterunt tenebrae lucem convincere crebrae.

(This story is invented for your fallacious self and for your follower.
The robber wants to rob and does not want to be known for his
robbery.
In fear of the gallows, he wants to cover up the moon with thorns.
Whoever wants to commit evil does not want to be pointed out.
But he darkens with vices if anyone glitters with virtue,
And he pierces with thorns when he joins blows to words.
But let the robber beware, since light will light in darkness.
Nor can thick darkness overcome light.) (69-76)

The story is as enigmatic as Egbert's comparable *De viro qui lunam fecit de pane
seliginis*, in which a foolish man molds a sphere of white bread to scatter light
when the moon is but forming. The same theme is treated in intelligible fashion
by Petrus Alfonsi, who portrays a rich man tricking a thief into grasping a
moonbeam to descend into the house.[58]   Possibly Egbert and Fulcoius are
abbreviating popular stories well known to their readers.

In his lengthy moralistic conclusion to this epistle, Fulcoius indicates that he
did not read the story about the robber ("Hoc ego non legi," 65), but that the
story is "invented" ("Res est . . . ficta," 69).   Fulcoius has philosophical
concerns about the means by which "it may be possible to distinguish true things
from false,/If what is said to be false in fact were also false in appearance" (66-
67). This abstract consideration of the theme of exterior appearances and interior
reality is a concern of Fulcoius' in other works, in which he relates exterior and
interior "truths" to fiction and truth, *ludicra* and *seria*. This philosophizing
about the value of fiction reduces the comic impact of a poem already told in a
self-consciously elevated fashion, yet it is essentially not different from similar
concerns expressed in some of the *comediae elegiacae*.

A similar philosophizing tendency flavors the elusive story about seven men
who each lack a sense or bodily part. The poem is addressed to someone who
wants "to be called victor but [you] do not care to conquer./You want to be
called king but do not rule" (epistle 15, lines 2-3). So Fulcoius offers a "rustic
tale" that demonstrates "what is nothing, what is something" ("Quod nichil est,
aliquid quod, rustica fabula, cantas," 15, 12):

Senis officiis seni privantur et uno,
Vel nulli nullo coeunt lare nulla loquentes.
Qui cecus, "video"; qui surdus hic, "audio fures";
Qui mutus, "clamemus," ait; truncus, "fugiamus,"
Mancus, "pugnemus"; qui naris, "odoror," obesae;
Hic "dulces escas comedamus" qui sine gustu.
Ex aliquo nihil est, ex re privatio rursus.
Est aliquid tamen ex nichilo si fabula malit:
Sic nulli fures, sic nulli qui coiere;

Sic in re nulla sermonem collige nullum,
Sicut rem, sermo sermonem, res probat esse.
(Seven men are similarly deprived of seven senses,
And none of them, saying nothing, assembled in no house.
The blind one says, "I see thieves"; the deaf one says, "I hear them";
The mute cries, "Let's call for help"; the man missing a leg, "Let's flee";
The man missing an arm says, "Let's fight"; he whose nose is not quick, "I can smell them";
From something there is nothing, from something a nothing in return.
But from nothing there is something, if the story should have it:
Thus there are no thieves; thus there is none who assembles;
Thus in nothing you acquire a story,
Just as something proves that something is, a story a story.) (15, 16-25)

Fulcoius' epistemological interests not only reduce the comedy of this story, but also threaten the fiction's very existence, for he contends that since the seven men, each lacking something, in fact produce nothing, their story ("something") is not a story ("nothing"), for the event could have never taken place. Though the story is inherently amusing, being a variation of the common folktale about deformed individuals, Fulcoius' philosophizing, lacking the parody of Theodulf's *Deluso expectatio* and William IX's "vers de dreyt nien," removes the story from the world of fiction and places it in the realm of Platonic ideas.

Two of Fulcoius' narratives depict lovers who disguise themselves as gods in order to seduce women. The poet forges the *exemplum* about Mundus and Paulina, which he takes directly from Josephus (*Antiquities* 18.3.4), "for amusement, but it is not without weight" ("pro ludo sed non sine pondere cudo," 18, 7). He hardly changes the names and events of Josephus' account: Mundus, falling in love with Saturninus' wife, Paulina, fails to seduce her by offering money. His servant Ida serves as go-between, bribing the priests of Isis' temple and arranging for the meeting of the two lovers in the sanctuary, where Mundus disguises himself as Anubis. The chaste Paulina is flattered to become the god's lover, and after the seduction, she delights in the god while Mundus delights in his victory ("Haec quasi laeta deo, letus redit ille tropheo," 18, 73). But so long as Mundus hides the crime, he values it as "nothing" ("Dum facinus celat, nihil estimat," 18, 77), so he boasts of his deception, and the scandalized family brings him to court. Ida and the priests are executed, but Mundus, because of his passion, is merely exiled.

Fulcoius' only significant alteration of Josephus' account is the addition of two speeches: Mundus' offer to Paulina (18, 23-25) and Ida's encouragement of Mundus (18, 61-66). Fulcoius adds a frame to the story, informing Gervais, Archbishop of Reims (1055-67), that the *exemplum* illustrates the vices of greed and lust. These slight changes to the original tale reflect Fulcoius' preference for direct discourse and moral abstraction, but the fact that Fulcoius makes only minor changes to Josephus' story suggests that the original is particularly well adapted to eleventh-century storytelling. The supernatural disguise is a popular motif in twelfth-century narratives, such as the *comedia Geta*. The go-between Ida, though she is not an *anus* in either Josephus' or Fulcoius' account, is a stock character by the twelfth century. The judgment terminating the poem, finally, does not differ in detail from Josephus' account. An identical judgment terminates Hrotsvitha's *Callimachus*, in which the hero, "blinded by passion of the flesh," is excused, and such a legalistic turn is still a popular device in the late eleventh century, as we have seen in *De quodam servo* and *Res mea*.

A second poem by Fulcoius presents a nearly identical situation: a tyrant disguises himself as Saturn in order to seduce the "matronae" of his city. Through cunning, he conceals himself in a statue to accomplish his crime. When Venus intervenes, the deception is discovered ("sic fraude reperta," 20, 44) and the tyrant is tortured. Fulcoius ends the account with an amusing assessment of the seducer's victims: "Spuria stirps, pater est incertus, adultera mater" ("The offspring is spurious, the father uncertain, the mother adulterous," 20, 48). He almost answers the question of *Res mea*: "Quis pocius reus est?" Both this narrative and the story of Mundus and Paulina contain the most common theme of the eleventh-century comic narratives: fraud and cunning. The seducers' disguises as pagan gods demonstrate Fulcoius' interest in classicism; in vernacular stories by William IX and Boccaccio, tricksters disguise themselves as pilgrims or saints in order to seduce women.[59] But despite the inherent humor of Fulcoius' stories, his heavy moralistic frames make the tone of his narratives somber—marked, perhaps, by curiosity, but not by humor. As Fulcoius himself says, he composes these poems "for amusement," yet much of his amusement lies in rhetorical play.

Fulcoius uses classical writers and the Bible as sources for his other narratives. His "fabula" about Mars and Venus, for instance, is indebted to Ovid, Virgil, Horace, Juvenal, and other writers of Antiquity for its theme and language. Vulcan laments his misfortune in a lengthy monologue, and the Sun's discovery of the lovers introduces a common eleventh-century theme: "Et certum patuit quod dubium latuit" ("And he revealed as certain what was hidden as unlikely," 19, 62). Much of the poem is an attack upon Milo, possibly a real personage who became Archbishop of Benevento in 1074, but the nature of the attack is not clear: on the one hand Fulcoius criticizes Milo for "arming yourself with trifles" ("armaris nugis," 19, 82); on the other, Milo is reproached for seducing virgins and nuns ("Quid tibi cum tali, cum virgine, cum moniali?," 19, 95).

The poet's long epistle to Fulcrad (*Epistola* X) belongs to the history of eleventh-century pamphlet literature advocating the marriage of priests and tolerance toward priests who are already married, and he uses classical and Biblical *exempla* to illustrate his point: Jupiter and Io, Moses and Tharbis, David and Bathsheba, Ammon and Thamar are among the practitioners of acceptable heterosexual love. The latter tale receives great amplification through dialogue and internal debate, though Fulcoius does not mention that this love is incestuous.

Fulcoius' most impressive narrative, an amplification of the Biblical story about Joseph and Potiphar's wife, reveals the romantic inclinations of the poet, and though the poem's tone is serious rather than playful, this epistle shows Fulcoius' willingness to allow his curiosity freedom to explore human passion and moral dilemmas. The poem is modeled on a passage of Josephus (*Antiquities* 2.4), who himself greatly amplifies the Biblical account (Genesis 39). But unlike Josephus, Fulcoius employs much direct discourse to dramatize the story; he also adds a scene in which Potiphar's wife induces Joseph to give a sentimental account of his past life with his parents and brothers. Fulcoius no doubt has the affair of Aeneas and Dido in mind, for the central conflict, located within the lady's mind, contrasts *pudor* and burning passion. Her interior debate almost attains the personified conflict of Chrétien de Troyes' romances:

> At mulier lacrimis nimios quae paverat ignes
> Hebreo limphata mero consurgit et inde
> Interiore domo residens eliminat omnes
> Ex animo curas; in Ioseph pectore tota
> Disceptat, cudit, secum deliberat utrum
> "Illum conveniam, quod eum sic diligo dicam."
> Sed pudor est dominae si servum dicat amare,
> "Sanus, quod nollem, cum sit vivusque maritus."
> (But the woman, who has dreaded love's great flames with her tears,
> Distracted by Hebrew wine, stands up and, hence
> Abiding in the interior of the house, rids all cares
> From her mind; in her breast she debates about Joseph,
> Beats herself, deliberates with herself whether
> "I should call him, so I may tell him that I love him so."
> But the lady is ashamed to tell the servant she loves him,
> "While my husband is healthy and alive, though I don't care about
> him.") (9, 70-77)

Fulcoius is interested in love psychology, as he carefully delineates the lady's progress from sight to speech to touching.[60] Although the story ends with Joseph, falsely accused of rape, in prison, Fulcoius realizes that the tale is not really a tragedy: "Paucis vexatus post est, per multa beatus" ("He was later troubled by small problems; he was blessed on account of his many virtues," 9, 9). The poem is a *comedia* in the Dantesque sense, and Joseph's virtue makes him second to the king ("Post in muneribus virtutis delitiatur/Qui primo servus, post est a rege secundus," 9, 156-57). The Christian view of comedy, complicated by the medieval confusion of dramatic performance and public recitation—that is, the failure to distinguish drama and narrative—differs fundamentally from classical and modern concepts.[61] From our viewpoint, Fulcoius' ninth epistle belongs to the realm of serious romance, while Fulcoius himself may well have thought of the work as a *comedia*.

Even when Fulcoius narrates a story that has much comic potential, his rhetorical emphasis and moralistic frame detract from the comedy and make the story a neutral *conte*, neither predominantly tragic nor comic. The story of the brother and sister bloodletters is a final instance of Fulcoius' method. The pair treats patients of the opposite sex, and illicit favors bulge the horn of plenty: "Gaudebant quod erat tunc pleno Copia cornu" (21, 8). The judgment ending the poem is so cruel that the amusing story turns tragic: once they are discovered in their crime, the brother is castrated and the sister is burned. This is Fulcoius' only narrative lacking an opening salutation, yet the poem's conclusion moralizes at length about how girls should treat girls and boys should treat boys. Fulcoius could have easily exploited the brief narrative core of this epistle for its comic potential—indeed, the theme of the seducing bloodletter occurs in the fabliau *De la saineresse*[62]—but Fulcoius does not find it humorous. If we apply the term *comedy* to Fulcoius' narratives, we must do so as the writers of twelfth-century *comediae elegiacae* did: "ce titre, les hommes du moyen âge l'ont pris dans une acception très éloignée de l'antique, sans penser au théâtre, et simplement pour marquer l'intention plaisante de certaines oeuvres . . . En fait, les comédies latines médiévales appartiennent à la littérature narrative et sont proprement des contes" (Faral, "Fabliau latin" 381).

Radulfus Tortarius is another late eleventh-, early twelfth-century writer whose scholarly *epistolae* include several remarkable narratives. Like Baudry of Bourgueil's poetry, Radulfus' has survived in a single manuscript, "témoin sévère de son influence littéraire très limitée dans le temps et dans l'espace."[63] Of his eleven extant *epistolae*, four contain substantial narration, and one of these, a fictional letter to Sincopus, has been compared to twelfth-century *comediae elegiacae*. Its nineteenth-century commentator, refusing to discuss its prurient content, calls it "un conte grossier, un de ces fabliaux plus que libres que le goût peu épuré de l'époque laissait pénétrer dans les couvents aussi bien que dans les châteaux" (Certain 506-7). In the twentieth century, Francis Bar's evaluation hardly differs:

> Il est d'abord assez surprenant que le régulier irréprochable qui fut, selon toutes apparences, Raoul le Tourtier, le sage et prudent conseiller des jeunes gens, se soit complu à un badinage burlesque qui brave souvent l'honnêteté par les détails crus qu'il ne dissimule en aucune façon. (150-51)

Bar also compares Radulfus' sixth epistle to "les 'comédies' latines du XIIe siècle . . . que des clercs illustres se sont amusés à composer, souvent avec esprit, et qui seraient par leur caractère érotique (lequel est absent de notre 'épître') de nature à étonner plus encore un lecteur de nos jours" (151, n. 1). A better term than *fabliau* or *comedia* for this poem is probably *nugae*, for it is clearly the prurient excursion of an otherwise orthodox churchman. Unlike the moralistic, romantic comedies of Fulcoius, this narrative by Radulfus is predominantly satirical in tone.

Like other *nugae*, *Ad Sincopum* possesses a frame, an elaborate prologue revealing that the story is pure fiction. The poet addresses Sincopus, "cautious guard of beautiful Flora," and after seventy-four verses describing the rivalry of two brothers for the fair Flora, Sincopus himself recounts the lengthy tale of his castration. Like Fulcoius, Radulfus uses various methods of amplification, yet his style is lucid. He opens the poem with an apostrophe addressing Sincopus (epistle 6, lines 1-4), and to illustrate his point that this *custos* must beware of wily lovers, the poet introduces a classical *exemplum*, the rape of Danae by Zeus (lines 5-10). Radulfus applies the *exemplum* to Sincopus, who, unlike other men, strengthens his reason despite the temptation of "gilded metal," or gold (11-14). Employing the clichés of Ovid and elegiac comedy, the poet then describes the *anus*, the go-between of later comic and romantic genres:

> Crebro suadelis anus inportuna paratis
>> Pota venena cavis evomit auriculis;
> Tedia difficilem frangunt aliquando puellam,
>> Mollis enim durum gutta cavat lapidem.
> (Repeatedly the troublesome old woman vomits forth
> With ready persuasions drinkable potions in her hollowed lobes;
> Boredom sometimes subdues a difficult girl,
> For the gentle drop hollows the hard stone.) (15-18)

Though Radulfus draws upon Ovid for his language, the *anus* whom he criticizes is unlike the wine-tippling Dipsas or the *custos* Bagaos and also unlike Fulcoius' Ida, who is a freed slave but not an old woman. Indeed, she is very similar to the go-between in *Pamphilus* and to the *vieilles* Richeut and Auberée.[64] But Radulfus' moral stance sharply differs from the attitude of the later anonymous composers of *Pamphilus* and the fabliaux, who vividly depict the old woman's actual words, while Radulfus only tells about those words briefly.

After warning Sincopus of the old woman, the poet launches an extended description of two rival brothers, Artimises and Xanticus, who vie for Flora's love despite the jealous Panemos. The bizarre description of the two brothers (19-38) is explained by Francis Bar (151-52), who notes the following entry in the fifth-century *Kalendarium seu Laterculus* of Silvius Polemius:

> APRILIS: . . . Vocatur . . . apud Graecos Xanticos
> MAIUS: . . . Vocatur . . . apud Graecos Artemosios (sic)
> IULIUS: . . . Vocatur . . . apud Graecos Panemos

The goddess Flora, Bar points out, was honored at the end of April and beginning of May; hence it is logical that Artemesis and Xanticos have the best hopes of obtaining Flora's love, while Panemos, the jealous figure representing July, has no chance. This allegorical explanation accounts for the startling description of the brothers' hair and clothing and reveals that the entire situation is fictional. It also shows that Radulfus expects his reader to understand his narrative as a kind of puzzle or riddle that only the wise can appreciate: "If you are wise, you will be able to tell who they are by signs" ("Si calles, poteris qui sint cognoscere signis," 37).

A formal *descriptio* of the symbolic Flora follows the descriptions of the brothers:

Felix qui Florae iugi potiatur amore,
 Cuius sic facies nix veluti renitet,
Nec candor tantus perpenditur esse molestus,
 Cocci vernantis cum rubor insit ei.
At non parte viget color idem corporis omni
 Gratia neç membris omnibus est eadem:
Congruit ergo suo mire speties sua membro,
 Nil in ea fedum nil videas mutilum. . .
(Happy is he who may enjoy the perpetual love of Flora,
Whose beauty glitters just like the snow,
Nor is such dazzling white considered to be evil,
Since the redness of the spring oak berry is in her;
But the same color does not flourish in all of her body,
Nor is the same grace in all of her members:
Accordingly her beauty is wonderfully suited to her limbs,
Nor would you see in her any foul blemish. . .) (45-52)

This *descriptio* lacks the order, but not the elements, of Geoffrey of Vinsauf's model exercise using dawn as a metaphor for the mingling of white and red:[65]

Aemula sit facies Aurorae, nec rubicundae
Nec nitidae, sed utroque simul neutroque colore.
(Let her countenance emulate dawn: not red, nor yet white—but at once neither of those colors and both.)

Surprisingly, the poet admits that he too "would pine if her love captures me" (54), but he then rejects Sincopus' Flora, preferring another goddess:

At tua fors sodes non est mea, Sincope, Flora,
 Nam tua pulcra quidem sed mea pulcra magis.
Totius hec orbis, tua civis solius urbis.
 Est tua nota tibi, sed mea nota Iovi.

Iam tua nupta viro sed adhuc constat mea virgo.
   Inberbis Phebi quam trahit unus amor.
(But your Flora, Sincopus, is, if you please, not my lot,
For yours is indeed pretty, but mine is even prettier;
She is an inhabitant of the entire earth, yours the citizen of only a city,
Yours is distinguished for you, but mine is distinguished for Jove;
Now yours is married to a man, but mine still remains a virgin,
Whom a single love draws to beardless Phoebus.) (55-60)

Radulfus seems to have de-mythologized Sincopus' Flora in order to turn his
Flora, possibly the Virgin Mary in classical disguise, into a divine figure. The
poet is indulging in a kind of *trobar clus*, which only initiates can appreciate
fully, and he manifests a classicizing tendency much like Fulcoius'.

Radulfus ends this lengthy prologue with a series of questions directed at
Sincopus (65-74), and the abrupt emergence of the theme of castration, which
dominates the rest of the poem, is a rather shocking explanation of Sincopus'
role as *custos*. Eleventh-century poets usually apply this theme to Saturn,
though castration is a form of punishment for sexual misconduct, as in Fulcoius'
story about the brother and sister bloodletters. In the fabliaux, castration is a
humorous theme often linked with eroticism, but in Radulfus' story it is
associated with greed. The poet's various suggestions accounting for Sincopus'
loss of manhood have led some critics, quite erroneously, to conjecture that the
story is about Abelard and Héloise.[66]

Sincopus begins his story with a typical complaint of the eleventh century, the
impoverishment of scholars (81-88). Motivated by greed, pride, and envy, he
wishes to enroll himself into the priesthood of the Galli, known for their great
wealth. Thus Radulfus turns from an eleventh-century theme to a classical one,
and like the Attis of Catullus, no sooner does Sincopus cut off his testicles—those
"vagrant things" ("res vaga," 98)—than he is surrounded by throngs of Galli and
soon becomes a favorite of Brochus, the high priest. Sincopus prides himself on
his knowledge of sacrifices to various gods, "but the worship of rich Ops," he
says, "was most pleasing to me" ("Divae cultus Opis sed mihi plus placuit,"
124). As planned, he becomes extremely wealthy, and with his fortune he
accumulates a number of parasites who dine at his home even when he is absent.

At this point Sincopus interrupts his narrative to explain what he did with the
remains of his genitalia:

"Denique confitear quia, quae mea membra peremi,
   In cinerem verti soposuique domi,
Et piperi trito miscens aurum quasi servo.
   Nemo mei sacri conscius huius erat . . ."
("At last let me confess that my member which I destroyed
I turned into ash and put aside in the house,

And mixing it with ground pepper, I preserved it like gold.
None of my holy ones was aware of this . . .") (139-42)

Like the miser of *Aulularia*, Sincopus jealously guards his remains within his house, though the love of pure gold has been perverted into a fetishism about genitalia. The pepper container is a comic symbol found in both fabliaux and later *nugae*. In *La vescie a prestre*, an analogue to Chaucer's *Sommoner's Tale*, a wealthy priest is badgered by Jacobins into giving them something of his inheritance:[67]

"Et ke nus n'i amene tenche,"
dient al prestre li .V. Frere,
"dites quel choze c'est, biaz pere."
"Voluntiers voir, c'est me vesie.
Se la voiiés bien netoiie,
mieus ke de corduan varra
et plus longement vos dura:
se poreis ens metre vo poivre."
("That no objections may arise,"
the five friars told the dying priest,
"good father, name the thing at least."
"Most gladly. It's my bladder, men,
and if you'll clean it up you'll then
discover it is better than
the longest-wearing cordovan;
you can use it for a pepper box.")

The priest's bequest connotes that the parasites will receive human waste—that is, the antithesis of wealth—instead of spices, which are symbolic of wealth. In the *Versus de mola piperis*, a trifle located in a thirteenth-century manuscript, a pepper mill is representative of a woman's genitals:[68]

Militis uxorem clamidis mercede subegit
    Clericus, et piperis clam tulit inde molam;
Mane redit, referensque molam praesente marito
    Dixit, "Mantellum redde, reporto molam."
"Redde," maritus ait; respondit foemina, "reddam;
    Amplius ad nostram non molet ille molam."
(A clerk seduced a nobleman's wife for the price of his cloak
And secretly carried away her pepper mill.
The next day he returned, bringing back the
pepper mill, and in the husband's presence
He said, "Give me back my cloak; I've brought back your pepper
mill."

"Give it to him," the husband said; the wife answered, "I will give it
to him,
But he will not grind again in our pepper mill.")

In this story it is the mill and not its contents that is the basis of the wife's pun;
however, pepper, like snowflakes, probably has sexual connotations, as it does
in Radulfus' poem. The symbolic meaning in these later stories may differ
somewhat from Radulfus', yet the symbolic vehicle, a pepper container, provides
a similar opportunity for comedy because of its concrete, mundane, and sexual
or scatological function.

The climax of Sincopus' story occurs when the hero, with bombastic rhetoric,
explains how his followers used his "holy ashes" as ground pepper (149-70).
The scene of the servant boy running to the neighbors for pepper while the
guests discover the hidden treasure has a realistic quality as in the fabliaux, and
it resembles the scene in *Unibos* when the protagonist sends his boy to the
provost for a measuring device. Unlike Fulcoius, whose rhetoric sometimes gets
out of hand, Radulfus has evident control of his language: his meaning is clear,
and Sincopus' melodramatic exclamations intentionally reveal his pomposity.

Sincopus' exaggerated reactions within his own fiction are responsible for his
eventual disgrace. When he returns home and learns of the sacrilege, his
strength leaves him and he falls as if dead, yet he manages to deliver a lengthy
speech criticizing the gods for abandoning him. Absorbed in his own language,
heedless of his servants' ears, the castrate gives full flight to rhetorical bombast:

"Cur genitale meum clepsit vobis latro sacrum,
    Gluttivit nebulo cur genitale meum?
Heu, fortuna, tuae quam sunt vires violentae!
    Opprimis, heu casus, quam subito miseros!
Heu, heu, quam dubium regit orbis climata fatum!"
("Why did a robber steal my genitals, sacred to you [gods]?
Why did a rascal gulp down my genitals?
Alas, fortune, how your strength is violent!
Alas, chance, how quickly you oppress the wretched!
Alas, alas, how doubtful fate rules the regions of the world!") (211-
15)

The servants, who are stunned ("attoniti") when they overhear their lord, crack
jokes in the forecourt:

"'Rebar ego stolidus sic senuisse piper;
Pro muria nostris infertur mentula mensis,
    Carnes intinxi carnibus in domini.'"

("'I'd consider myself stupid if I though pepper thus became aged.
For seasoning his member is brought to our tables.
I dipped my meat in the meat of my lord.'") (228-30)

Once the leaders of the Galli realize that they too have "swallowed the ashes fatal to me" (248), they want to punish Sincopus, who escapes and comes to Philirus, Flora's husband, and becomes the lady's *custos*.

This curious story ends, not with the poet speaking, as may be expected, but with an *envoi* spoken by Sincopus himself:

"En, Zephirine, tibi serie tenus omnia pandi,
    Qualiter et quare dux habear dominae.
Tu ne nostra velis archana recludere cunctis,
    Falsaque ne veris, obsecro, miscueris.
Est horum testis notus iam carmine Pseustis,
    Si percuncteris, proferet ille tibi."
("Look here, Zephirinus, I have revealed to you, in order, everything,
How and wherefore I am considered the guide of the lady.
May you not wish to disclose my secrets to all,
And I beg you, may you not mix false with true.
This matter is made known in the song of Pseustis;
If you will ask him, he will tell you about it.") (267-72)

Zephirinus may be the *senhal* or the pseudonym of Sincopus' messanger—that is, the poet recounting this story—while Pseustis, whose name means "deceitful witness," seems to be the *senhal* of a rival poet who offers an alternate account of Sincopus' story. Bar conjectures that the final couplet "permet de supposer que notre 'épître' constituait une réponse, présentée comme une rectification, à une autre pièce sur le même sujet. S'agit-t-il d'une gageure plaisante entre Raoul et un de ses amis?" (58).   In any case, the symbolic names—even the protagonist's name is a pun[69]—reinforce the likelihood that the tale is pure fiction, one that is understood only "if you are wise." The assertation that "you should not mix false with true" is the exact opposite of Radulfus' statement in another epistle that "true things seem to be mixed with false ones" ("Vera tamen falsis quaedam permixta videntur," 2, 121). Like Fulcoius, Radulfus contrasts "seria" with "ludus" and "frivola"; he distinguishes seriousness and playfulness, tragedy and comedy, but he often is inclined to mix the two genres.[70] Sincopus' plea not to mix false with true contrasts Radulfus' usual mixture of serious and playful and suggests that the fictional speaker's views differ from the poet's.

Radulfus' poem derives its comedy in part from the subject matter, castration. Psychoanalytical critics maintain that the comic impulse of much classical and post-medieval literature emerges from the "reduction of the father to a son" and in such plays as Terence's *Eunuchus* and Shakespeare's *Merchant of Venice* symbolic castration reveals the father's attempt to reassert dominance over the rebellious son or filial representative.[71] In medieval comedy, literal castration is a common subject matter, as in *Du prestre crucefie* and in Radulfus' poem. From a larger perspective, castration is an appropriate comic theme because, as James Feibleman points out, comedy itself "affirms the direction toward the infinite value by insisting upon the absurdly final claims of finite things and events" (95). "Comedy . . . criticizes the finite for not being infinite" (97). Being a "criticism of limitations and an unwillingness to accept them" (94), comedy tends to substitute a part for the whole in its attack upon finite individuals; in other words, Sincopus, defined by the absence of his genitals, is less than an entire man, but is a part of the whole. Radulfus' comedy thus possesses universal qualities, yet it is particularly suitable for a poet whose own production is so limited in time and space. Sincopus' fetishism within the fiction reflects a fetishism on the part of Radulfus and other composers of *nugae*, who exchange prurient trifles as though they were precious relics, not to be seen by the outside world. Such an attitude may explain the singleton manuscripts of works by Baudry and Radulfus, as well as the rarity of popular collections such as the Cambridge Songs.

Among Radulfus' other narratives *epistolae*, none is a true comedy like *Ad Sincopum*, although glimmers of humor do reflect Radulfus' playful temperament. His second epistle, which is the oldest extant version of the Ami and Amile legend, has led critics to odd conclusions about the poem's sources and genre. Francis Bar (77-78) attempts to link this tale with the story of Lantfrid and Cobbo, for in both stories a wife is shared by friends. However, the linguistic commonplaces are only coincidental and the themes of the poems are entirely different: the story of Lantfrid and Cobbo involves the testing of one friend by another, whereas in Rudulfus' epistle, Amicus and Amelius change places because they are similar in appearance. Raby *(SLP* 2:25) considers the poem "a fabliau in praise of friendship . . . fashioned according to the methods of the schools," but the poem utterly lacks the humor of *Ad Sincopum* or, for that matter, of the fabliaux. Radulfus himself asserts that his writing mixes serious and playful (2, 331), yet the poem is a sort of hybrid of epic and romance rather than comedy.

The story falls into two halves: romance and epic motifs characterize the first half, while the magic and brutality of the second half give it the flavor of a fairytale. Like Fulcoius' description of Potiphar's wife, Radulfus' depiction of the princess loved by Amelius is based on Virgil's portrayal of Dido. When Amicus fights in Amelius' place in the duel ordered by the king, Amelius, like Tristan, places a sword between himself and Amicus' wife, who is unaware that she is sleeping with her husband's friend. Amicus, meanwhile, receives Roland's sword from the queen in order to gain victory over Adrastus. In the second half of the story, Amicus, now a leper, is an exile who arrives at his friend's house, Amelius kills his two sons in order to cure his friend, and the dead children are miraculously resurrected. The story thus ends happily, but it lacks the ribald comedy of the fabliaux; its content is alternately militaristic and romantic. The structure of the poem, with its two movements from conflict to resolution, is bipartite like Chrétien's *Cligès* and *Erec et Enide*; like the French poet's narratives, this story is a militaristic romance.

Radulfus' other narrative poems lack comic themes and structure, but the poet's occasional asides are humorous. In his description of his voyage to Caen and Bayeux, for instance, Radulfus jokes wryly when he is offered beer instead of wine:

> Aspernor ciatum dum sencio non fore vinum,
>   Fingo bibisse tamen labraque sicco mea;
> Reddo sciphum puero cui pronus in aure susurro,
>   "Cur propinasti, serve, venena mihi?"
> (I spurn the goblet when I discern it doesn't contain wine;
> I feign drinking yet dry my lips.
> I return the cup to the boy, and leaning over, I whisper in his ear:
> "Why, servant, have you proposed a toast of poison in my honor?") (9, 313-16)

After this joke, the poet swears never to return to Bayeux without his own cup:

> Desero Baiocas, Semeles a prole relictas,
>   Non repetiturus hoc nisi potus iter.
> (I leave Bayeux, abandoned by Semele's son;
> This voyage shall not be repeated unless I have my own brew.) (9, 327-28)

Both this poem and the seventh epistle, describing the exploits of Bohemund, are historical narratives lacking sustained humor. Except for occasional asides, including allusions to popular fables,[72] Radulfus' comic output is limited to one great poem, the ribald *Ad Sincopum*.

The *nugae* include several narrative genres in their infancy, and the poets, few of whom master their craft, have an unhappy tendency of mixing high style with low subject matter. The results are disastrous for comic effect from a twentieth-century and even a thirteenth-century perspective. The generic diversity of the trifles reflects the distinct voices and concerns of individual poets, for unlike the anonymous *ridicula*, forming a homogenous genre, the *nugae* of Egbert, Hildebert, Fulcoius, and others reveal widely differing attitudes about style, humor, and morality. That most *nugae* are attributed to named identities may indicate a greater self-consciousness on the part of the poets, an awareness that their products are unique works of art, a sense that literature has a certain autonomy. This changed attitude is also evident in the greater number of first-person narratives in the early twelfth century, both in Latin and in the vernacular.[73] The evolution in style toward a more controlled grasp of rhetoric is hence accompanied by a growing consciousness about individual poetic craft.

But the craft is crude and the poets' humor is buried beneath it. We may justly criticize some poets for overemphasizing rhetoric at the reader's expense: Egbert pitilessly reduces popular narratives to mere points in time; Fulcoius elevates his style to incomprehensibility. Successful craftsmen, such as Hildebert and Radulfus, do not share the humor of the writers of fabliaux or even of *comediae elegiacae*, and their rhetoric still dominates their storytelling. Hildebert's terse epigrams possess a style and pointedness surpassing Egbert's *exempla*, yet they lack the snap that is requisite for effective jokes and they are missing the amusing obscenity of late medieval *novellini* and Renaissance *facezie*. Radulfus' *Ad Sincopum* is comic only to a scholar capable of appreciating bombast and symbolism, while the tone of the poem, narrated by a pathetic castrate, often borders on tragic. Yet these composers of trifles apparently found their works entertaining. Except for Fulcoius, who is continually extracting philosophical value from secular stories, most of these poets revel in the tale itself, without moralizing or apologizing. The *nugae*, then, are documents of a most peculiar sense of humor at the dawn of the High Middle Ages. They are the pioneering efforts of somewhat isolated scholars struggling to find a medium for a secular impulse.

NOTES

1. Fulcoius uses the word "frivola" to describe the story of the snowchild: "quae vix haec frivola vitas,/Quodque semel discis vix aut nunquam resipiscis" ("such trifles you scarcely avoid,/and hardly ever do you recover what you once learned," 229; epistle 8, lines 60-61).

2. *Poetria Nova* 40-41; lines 693-701 (Margaret Nims' translation, which I use throughout).

3. See Beyer, *Schwank* 68: "die ältesten der uns bekannten Schulschwänke."

4. See Beyer, *Schwank* 70; Horace, *Ars Poetica*, line 139. Cf. Egbert, *Fecunda ratis* (169; part 1, lines 1097-1100) and Geoffrey of Vinsauf, *Poetria Nova* (32): "Hurry up, one and all; now the mountain's in labor, but its offspring will only be a mouse."

5. Cf. *Disciplina Clericalis, Prologus*: "Propterea ergo libellum compegi, partim ex proverbiis philosophorum et suis castigacionibus, partim ex proverbiis et castigacionibus arabis et fabulis et versibus, partim ex animalium et volucrum similitudinibus . . . Huic libello nomen iniungens, et est nomen ex re: id est Clericalis disciplina; reddit enim clericum disciplinatum" ("For that reason, then, have I put together this book, partly from the sayings of wise men and their advice, partly from Arab proverbs, counsels, fables, and poems, and partly from bird and animal similes. . . . This book, to which I have given a title, *Disciplina*

Clericalis, a name that well describes the contents, for it renders the educated man well versed in knowledge"—Hermes' translation, 104).

6. See Egbert 191.

7. Voigt (Egbert 191) gives other variations of the proverb: "Il y avait quatre pelés et un tondu. Il n'y avait que trois tondus et un pelé. Il estit treus pelés et on tondou. Au réserve pour cha d'trois quate plés épi ein tondu."

8. Juvenal 6. 276: "tu tibi tunc, uruca, places fletumque labellis." The word *uruca* means "worm," but in two manuscripts the word used is *curruca* ("cuckold").

9. Satire 2. 3. 153-57 (Fairclough's translation in the Loeb Classical Library edition).

10. *Disciplina Clericalis* 29-30; *exemplum* 19. The same story is found in the *Gesta Romanorum* 436-38; *Caput* 106. Petrus' *exemplum* is the basis of *De clericis et rustico*.

11. 6. 275-78 (Ramsey's translation in the Loeb Classical Library edition). I have altered "uruca" ("poor worm") to "curruca" ("cuckold").

12. See Hervieux 2:553. Both Hervieux (2:513 f.) and Paris ("Les fabulistes latines" 37-51) place *Romulus* in the eleventh century. However, Warnke (Marie de France, *Fabeln* xlviii-lx) believes that *Romulus* was composed after Marie de France.

13. See Wright, *Latin Stories* 20; Cohen, *La "comédie" latine* 1:225-46 (*Lydia*); *Decameron*, Seventh Day, Ninth Tale.

14. See Wright, *Latin Stories* 78-79. The January and May story appears in a Middle English translation of Petrus Alfonsi, but not in the Latin *Disciplina Clericalis* (see Petrus Alfonsi, Hulme ed.). The story also occurs in *Lydia* and in the *Decameron*, Seventh Day, Ninth Tale.

15. See Hervieux 2:614-15. Cf. Marie de France, *Fables* 242; fable 96, lines 41-50 (Spiegel's translation):

Li vilein les ad escrïé,
Dit que ne sunt pas bien alé.
Encuntre l'ewe la deüssent quere—
La la purrunt trover a tere,
La la querunt, si ferunt bien.
Tant ert encuntre tute rien,
Que al val l'ewe n'est pas alee,
Od reddur n'est mie turnee—
En sa mort ne feist ele mie
Ceo que ne vot fere en sa vie.
(The peasant called his men; said he
They were not where they ought to be.
Upstream they ought to look for her—
They'd find her on the bottom there.
So there they looked, with great success.
For she'd so much contrariness

That down the stream she would not go,
But went against the water's flow—
Behaving in her death, this wife,
Exactly as she'd wished in life.)

16. See Wright, *Latin Stories* 13-14; 10. The story also appears in Jacques de Vitry's *Exempla* 94; 227; Poggio's *Facezie* 182-83; 60; and La Fontaine's *Fables* 110; book 3, fable 16. See Thompson 283 (T.255.2: "The obstinate wife sought upstream").

17. This widespread story, emerging in the form of a fabliau, *Du pré tondu* (Montaiglon and Raynaud 4:154-57), is a companion piece to the story of the obstinate wife who drowns in *Romulus* (Hervieux 2:614) and in Marie's *Fables* (238-40; 95). See Jacques de Vitry, *Exempla* (92; 222) and Wright, *Latin Stories* (12-13; 8 and 9) for other renditions.

18. *Satyricon* 118-20. See Hervieux 2:72; 2:217; 2:258-59 for analoguous fables; *De celle qui se fist foutre sur la fosse de son mari* (Montaiglon and Raynaud 3:118-22).

19. *Epigrammaton* 1:48-49; book 1, poem 33 (Walter Ker's translation in Loeb Classical Library edition).

20. *Sabaoth*, "the heavenly hosts," is used in the phrase "Dominus Sabaoth" or "Deus Sabaoth" ("the Lord of Hosts" or " God of hosts"); *Osanna dies* means "Palm Sunday," and *Hosanna*, literally meaning "save, we pray" in Hebrew, is frequently used during ecclesiastical services as a cry.

21. See Skeat 152 ("Draw"). The hypothetical Indo-European *Dheragh* becomes *tragen* in German and *trahere* in Latin. Curiously, the modern Dutch *Drogreden* means "fallacious, fallacy, sophism," and *Drogbeeld* means "illusion." Cf. the Old French *drugier* ("se jouer de, tromper, prévariquer") and *druge* ("jeu, risée, moquerie").

22. A story with similar thematics does appear in Phaedrus 3. 19 ("Aesopus respondet garrulo"): "Once when Aesop was the only servant his master had, he was ordered to prepare dinner earlier than usual. So he went around to several houses in search of fire, and at last found a place to light his lamp. Then, since he had made too long a circuit on the way out, he took a shorter way back, and so returned straight through the Forum. There some chatterbox in the crowd said to him: 'Aesop, what are you doing with a lamp at midday?' 'I'm looking for a *man*,' said he, and hurried away home.

"If that bore managed to get this answer into his head he must have seen that in the judgment of old Aesop he did not pass as a man—a fellow who saw fit to banter another inopportunely when he was busy" (B.E. Perry's translation in the Loeb Classical Library edition).

23. See *Chronicon Novaliciense*, *Monumenta novaliciensia vetustiora* 2:153-56; *Moniage Guillaume* 60-127; lines 406-1823.

24. See Magoun and Smyser 38-40.

25. *Monumenta Novaliciensia* 153. Walter is commanded by the abbot to give up his *cuculla*, mentioned by Egbert also.

26. See Egbert 203.

27. See Bloch 122-33 for Leo's fable.

28. *Die Cambridger Lieder* 100-101. Fulbert, in a poem about himself,says he had "easy teachers" as a boy, but he gives no indication that he indulged in secular letters: "Nam puero faciles providit adesse magistros,/Et juvenem perduxit adhoc, ut episcopus esses" (141: col. 347, poem 16).

29. See *Ruodlieb* 89-101, fragment 7, 26—fragment 8, 129. I use Zeydel's translation throughout.

30. See Ménard 529 f. ("portraits de la laideur"). Cf. the portrait of the ugly servants Spurius in William of Blois' *Alda* (68-71; lines 169-92) and Geta in Vitalis of Blois' *comedia* by that name (Elliott 40-41). Also compare the portrait of Moriuht by Warnerius of Rouen (p. 206-7 below).

31. For Herimannus, see Raby, *History of Christian Latin Poetry* 225-28 and Dronke, *Medieval Latin* 227, n. 1.

32. See Hauréau, *Notice sur les mélanges poétiques* 418.   Several of Hildebert's comic narratives are still published as Martial's attributed poems in the Loeb edition 2:522 (*De Milone*); 2:524 (*Ad Milonem*); 2:530 (*In Turgidum*).

33. Hildebert, *Carmina Minora* 38; poem 47. In spirit this poem is very close to the anonymous, gnomic epigram *Potus Milo sapis*, contained in the same manuscript (Oxford Rawley G.109) holding *Ad Milonem* and *De virgine seni nupta*. The puns on "sapis" are difficult to render into English:

Potus Milo sapis. Non potus deligis idem
    Si bibis ut sapias; desipis ut sapias.
Nec tibi si sicco facundia vixerit ore,
    Necne pota nimis musa diserta tuaque.
Quot sapis ex bacco quot non sapis aure sique ore;
    Hoc unus sapio quod nichil ipse sapis.
(Milo, you sip from the flask. You do not choose this flask
If you sip to be wise; you become insipid in order to gain wisdom.
You don't care if eloquence lives in a dry mouth,
Nor is your muse, having drunk too much, quiet.
As much as you sip of Bacchus, so much are you insipid of ear and mouth;
I alone perceive what you perceive as nothing.)

34. Cf. Martial 2. 49; 8. 12; 2. 7.

35. *Carmina Minora* 16; 24. This poem is very similar to an anonymous, unpublished narrative located in BN lat. 8433, f. 118r:

Dum vir dormit adest mechus, clam Lidia surgit
    Inque thoro famulam collocat illa suam.
Uxorem mechus viciat famulamque maritus
    Sub specie [spem MS] uxoris utraque fit gravida.
Infantem domino dat servula, nupta marito;
    Suscipiens nuptae reicit ille suum.

(While her husband is sleeping, Lydia's lover shows up. She rises secretly,
And she places her maid in [her husband's] bed.
The adulterer vitiates the wife and the husband the maid
In the guise of the wife, and each becomes pregnant.
The servant girl gives a child to the lord, the wife to her husband;
Receiving the one from his wife, he rejects his own son.)

36. See Marcabru 135 (poem 29, lines 19-24), 147 (poem 31, lines 46-54).

37. See Trimpi 331, 336.

38. *Poetria Nova* 245; lines 1567-76 (Nims' translation).

39. This poem is contained on the same folio as *De marito ab uxore turpiter interempto* (Cotton Vit A XII, f. 131r), and it is located in an Oxford manuscript (Oxon. Laud. 86, f. 94r) containing Hildebert's *Milo* poems. The concluding moral application is found only in a Zurich manuscript, published by Werner 13.

40. Located in the *Collection Etienne Baluze* no. 120, f. 332r, and published by Hauréau, *Notice sur les mélanges poétiques* 424. I have altered "viro" to "vero." The poem is based on an Aesopian fable: see Hervieux 2:20-21 (*Anus diligens iuvenum, item puella*); cf. Jacques de Vitry 84; *exemplum* 201.

41. Located in the *Collection Etienne Baluze* no. 120, f. 328v, and published by Hauréau, *Notices sur les mélanges poétiques* 422-23.

42. *Notice sur les mélanges poétiques* 423. Hauréau remarks that "fundite" is a "mot certainement altéré." I have ignored the troublesome word in my translation.

43. Numerous other semi-comic narrative epigrams are located in manuscripts housing works by Hildebert and Marbod, and many of these stories are unpublished. A peculiar narrative epigram, with a plot resembling *Alda* and *De la saineresse*, is located along with Hildebert's *Milo* poems (Oxford Rawley G.109, f. 97, written c. 1200):

Virginis insano Iulianus captus amore
   Femina fit cultu dissimulatque virum
Et sic indutus mulierbriter intrat ad illam.
   Res patet. Abscondit [absadit MS] membra, pudenda patet.
Femina virque procus nec vir nec femina necne,
   Dum volunt credit femina fit neutrum.

(Julian, possessed by a mad passion for a maiden,
Disguises himself as a woman and hides his member,
And thus clothed as a woman, he goes to her.
The deed is made known. He hides his member, but the pudendum is revealed.
The suitor who is woman and man is neither man nor woman,
While they want to take him as a woman, he becomes neuter.)

Also see *Fur erat in furno* (published by Hauréau, *Notices et extraits* 1:236); *Sepe lupus quidam per pascua lata vagantes* (published by Beaugendre as Marbod's, Migne et al., *Patrologiae cursus completus* 171: col. 1628); *Foedere nupta viri nolebat sene potiri* (published by Haureau, *Notice sur les mélanges poétiques* 419).

44. The manuscript also houses Hildebert's *Quid sit vita pudica* (f. 44r) and *De quodam servo* (f. 44v). (*Res mea* is located on f. 75v.)

45. Montaiglon and Raynaud 5:208-10. The theme of drunken women who fall asleep also occurs in *Des. III. dames de Paris* (see Harrison 398-417).

46. *Richars li biaus* 7-17; lines 247-600.

47. Hildebert, "Carmina Miscellanea" 171: col. 1411-12 (not authentic).

48. Hildebert, "Carmina Miscellanea" 171: col. 1400-2 (not authentic).

49. See Werner 55-58.

50. See Baudry 341; poem 238, line 121: "Sed volui Grecas ideo praetendere nugas"; 345; poem 239, lines 34-35.

51. Compare Baudry 156; poem 161, line 197 ("Musa jocosa fuit moresque fuere pudici") and Ovid, *Tristia* 2. 253-54 ("Vita verecunda est, musa jocosa mea"). Also see Baudry 14; poem 36, lines 29-34.

52. William IX 6; *Song* 4, lines 5-6: "Qu'enans fo trobatz en durmen/Sobre chevau." Cf. Fulcoius 250; *Epistola* 15, line 12 ("Quod nichil est,/aliquid quod, rustica fabula, cantas").

53. See Marbod, "Liebesbriefgedichte" 296 and Dronke, *Medieval Latin* 214 f.

54. See Gautier 235 (*Rithmus jocularis*); Peter the Painter 65 (*De choro dominarum*).

55. Epistle 17 is directed to Gervais, Archbishop of Reims (1055-67), Epistle 14 to Richer, Archbishop of Sens (1069-92). Fulcoius' first epistle mentions the actions of Henry IV, king of Germany, in 1080 and 1081. Epistle 2 was written sometime after 1077 or 1080, and Epistle 6 was written after Hildebrand became Pope in 1073 and before Manasses was deposed in 1080. Epistle 7 was penned between 1069/70 and 1073; 11 is directed to William the Conquerer (dead in 1087). Fulcoius apparently flourished in the 1070s and 1080s.

56. See Plutarch, *Romulus* 11. 2: "kalousi de ton bathron touton hoi kai ton olympon onomati moundon" ("They gave to this pit the name 'mundus,' the same as at Olympus").

57. The phrase "permansisse peronem" (62) is troublesome. *Permaneo* means "to hold out, endure;" *pero* is "a kind of boot made of raw hide," but may also mean "saccus coriaceus; sac de cuir" (Maigne d'Arnis col. 1675). Is the robber awaiting his stash bag?

58. Petrus Alfonsi 34-35; *exemplum* 24. This story is found in Wright's *Latin Stories* (24-25; 23) and in the *Gesta Romanorum* 490-91; *Caput* 136.

59. See William IX, *Song* 5 (*Farai un vers pos mi sonelh*); Boccaccio, *Decameron*, Fourth Day, Second Story.

60. See Egbert, *Fecunda ratis* 187; pt. 1, lines 1414-18 (*De quinque lineis amoris*) with Voigt's lengthy footnote listing analogues to the notion that there are five stages of love. Also see Friedman 167-77.

61. See Young 1:6-7: "It was commonly supposed, indeed, that in ancient times a comedy was recited by a single reader, while actors merely accompanied the reading with silent gesticulation.   Still more pervasive were the notions attached to the terms *tragoedia* and *comoedia*, both popularly and in the formal definitions of the erudite.   These two words cease to denote either scenic representation or the exclusive use of dialogue.   Tragedy and comedy were regarded, rather, as forms of narrative, in which dialogue was hardly required . . . Thus the epics of Lucan and Statius and the elegies of Ovid were regarded as 'tragedies', the eclogues of Virgil, as 'comedies', and the satires of Horace, Persius and Juvenal, as either one or the other, according to their varying content and to the point of view of the interpreter."

62. In *De la saineresse* (Eichmann and DuVal 2:106-11), a bloodletter disguised as a female seduces an unfaithful wife. Cf. Marie de France, *Fables* 130; fable 42 (*Del mire, del riche humme, e de sa fille*).

63. Boutémy, "Autour de Godefroid de Reims" 233. It is fairly certain that the poet was born c. 1065, but he disappears from history in 1114, so the date of his death is uncertain. See Bar 3-4.

64. See Bar 153-54 for linguistic borrowings from Ovid. For Dipsas, see *Amores* 1.8; for Bagoas, see *Amores* 2. 2. Eugène Evesque, the editor of *Pamphilus* in Cohen, *La "comédie" latine* (2:169-223), observes "l'intervention de la vieillle, type réaliste, qui avec la Richeut (peu après 1159) et l'Auberée des Fabliaux sera plus ou moins la mère de toutes les entremetteuses modernes de nos littératures occidentales." But it is likely that Radulfus' *Ad Sincopum* is anterior to the *Pamphilus* and that his *anus* is the first known instance of the *vieille* in the High Middle Ages (Fulcoius' Ida not being an old lady but a servant).

65. The lady's complexion of red and white is part of the formal *descriptio* occurring in both elegiac comedy and vernacular romance.   See *Poetria Nova*, lines 571-76; Matthew of Vendôme, *Ars versificatoria*, lines 19-20 (in Faral, "Les arts poétiques" 129); *Milo*, line 22 (in Cohen, *La "comédie" latine* 1:169: "Niveo disputat ore rubor"); *Alda*, line 128 (in Cohen 1:135: "Alba caro nivibus similisque rosis color esset"); *Facetus*, line 219 (Elliott 42: "Candidus et rutilans simul est color ipse genarum").

66. See Bar 153.

67. Harrison 214 (Harrison's translation).

68. Edited and translated by Benson and Andersson 280-81.

69. Sincopus is probably a pun on the noun *sinciput* ("half a head")—i.e., Sincopus is only half a man. *Sincopa* is also a rhetorical term (see Werner 127; line 46).

70. Cf. Radulfus 2, 331 ("permisces seria ludum"); 9, 72 ("Seria dicere quis frivola seu voluit").

71. See Jekels' article in Lauter 43.

72. See 3, 173-76; 3, 353-54; 7, 427-28.

73. The narratives of William IX of Aquitaine and Petrus Alfonsi, as well as the elegiac comedies *Pamphilus* and *De nuncio sagaci*, are all in the first person.

Chapter 3

Satyrae

The eleventh century is the age of venality satire, and nearly every important writer of the time contributed something to the widespread attacks upon the evils of money. In Italy, Peter Damian and Humbert are two major curialists who attack simony, and in Peter's poems, the major characters of later venality satire—bishops and priests, judges and bought witnesses—already appear. In Germany, Egbert composes money passages that smell of the lamp: in one of them the conflict between Pecunia and Sophia anticipates Langland's later conflict between Meed and Reason. Sextus Amarcius' *Sermones* provide glimpses into corruption in real life. In France, Adalbert of Laon's *Carmen ad Robertum* in the early eleventh century is a unique achievement, and by the end of the century a literary milieu emerges with scholars such as Hildebert and Marbod closely influencing one another. One poem, *De nummo, seu satyra adversus avaritiam*, once attributed to Hildebert, exercises an enormous influence on later venality satire. Among the multitude of anonymous works based on this theme, the parodic *Tractatus Garsiae* and the *Evangelium secundum Marcas Argenti* are the most famous. John Yunck has considered much of this literature in *The Lineage of Lady Meed*, yet the production is so vast that Yunck does not mention, much less discuss, several important satirists of ecclesiastical corruption.

With few exceptions, the venality satire of the eleventh century falls outside the confines of comic narrative, for most of these satires lack narrative development and those that do sustain narrative structure are often so bitter in tone that they are tragic rather than comic satires. Egbert's *Quomodo pecunia pepulit sophiam de turre cum vecte* (*Fecunda ratis* 198; pt. 1, 1599-1611), for instance, is a profoundly pessimistic view of money's power; his *De Romanis metuentibus lupum* (*Fecunda ratis* 181; pt. 1, 1288-93), typically Egbertian in its obscurity, is a brief narrative whose money theme is not entirely clear. Only the *Tractatus Garsiae* maintains significant comic narration. This prose tract satirizes the visit of Bernard, Archbishop of Toledo, to Urban II in 1099. Both the archbishop, called Grimoardus by the poet, and the Pope himself are extreme gluttons, and in order to receive an audience with the Pope, the visiting prelate must offer relics of Albinus, representing silver, and Rufinus, representing gold, to the doorkeeper. The Pope and his cardinals engage in a drinking bout when the archbishop arrives, and Gregory of Pavia reads at length from the *Anti-Cato*. After Urban delivers a sermon, he speaks with Garsias, whose double entendres provide the high point of the tract's wit:[1]

> Papa: "Frater Garsia, ego cognosco oves meas."
> Garsias: "Vere cognoscis!" et [iterum] secum: "Nichil enim relinquis in marsupiis earum."
> Papa: "Quid dixisti, [Garsia]?"
> Garsias: "[Domine,] ego dicebam, quod Rodanus fert in mare Ararim."
> Papa: "Frater Garsia, et cognoscunt me meae."
> Garsias: "Cognoscunt, inquam," et secum: "Latronem magnum et emunctorem boni talenti."
> Papa: "[Garsia,] quid dixisti? Non enim intelligo."
> Garsias: "Ego dicebam, quod Zetus in Calais fuerunt filii Boreae."
> (Pope: "Brother Garsias, I know my sheep!"
> Garsias: "Truly you know them!" and to himself: "For you leave nothing in their purses!"
> Pope: "What did you say?"
> Garsias: "I was saying that the Rhone empties the Saône into the sea."
> Pope: "Brother Garsias, and mine know me."
> Garsias: "I agree, they know you." And to himself: "For a great robber and a swindler of high talent."
> Pope: "What did you say? I didn't understand."
> Garsias: "I was saying that Zeus and Calais were the sons of Boreas.")

More drinking leads to the conclusion, when all present fall into a stupor. This "brilliantly executed piece of work" receives the highest praise from scholars. Yunck's comments are illuminating (76):

> Aside from the element of parody, the unknown author says by way of the relics of these fiscal saints much the same thing which was to be said by the meed-satirists of the centuries to follow, whether the allegorical vehicle was *Regina Pecunia*, *Dan Danier*, Sir Penny, Lady Meed, or some other regal figure. Some of Garsias' successors may have spoken more profoundly. None spoke more wittily, or with greater verve and audacity. The technique of heavy irony, spilling over into open abuse, became a favorite of the later satirists.

The themes of eleventh-century satire are not limited to simony and greed. Men, women, and institutions are attacked on other grounds as well. Like the venality satires, these works generally lack narrative development, with two notable exceptions: Warnerius of Rouen's untitled satire against the poet Moriuht, written during the first decades of the century, and Peter the Painter's *De matronis*, composed in the late eleventh or early twelfth century. Like the *Tractatus Garsiae*, these satires are exceptional for their sustained narration and humorous content, though the craft of Warnerius and Peter is inferior. Warnerius' satire, a precious document of early literary activity in Normandy, is written in very poor Latin, and the poet often forgets his purpose and allows his narration to get out of hand. Peter's *De matronis*, laden with clichés of the misogynistic tradition, is simplistic yet culturally fascinating, as it presents a husband who worships his wife "like a goddess," and one is tempted to see a critique of the troubadours' quasi-religious veneration of their ladies. These works contain two fundamental impulses of medieval satire: the attack upon an individual man, a theme inspired primarily by the great satirists of Antiquity, and the attack upon deceitful woman, a theme belonging to the Christian Middle Ages. Further, these poems, like all satires, reveal much about contemporary life, shedding light on historical and cultural events closely associated with literary evolution.

Despite its corrupt state and bad Latin, Warnerius of Rouen's *Satire against Moriuht* is a remarkable document. It provides rare evidence of literary activity in early eleventh-century Normandy a generation before Lanfranc and the school of Bec, and the sustained narration of this lengthy comic tale makes it a unique achievement of its time. This satire also has historical value, as it vividly depicts piracy, slave trading, and necromancy, as practiced in northern Europe. The poet's trenchant humor, his unabashed vulgarity, and his obscure language lead the reader to the open seas, where Danish pirates rape and exile a wandering Irish scholar, and to the court of Rouen, where rival poets viciously attack each other over trifling mistakes.

The two satires of Warnerius may lack high artistic achievement, but they are important documents, indicating that a school of Rouen may have existed at this early time. Both of his poems were written between the death of Richard I (996) and that of Richard II (1026), and they are located in a manuscript holding the pseudo-Plautine comedy *Aulularia* or *Querolus*, probably composed in the early fifth century, and two misogynistic poems, the satires against Jezabel and Semiramis.[2] Most of these poems are "dramatic" literary productions: the *Querolus* is a comic play, a rare link between Roman New Comedy and twelfth-century *comedia elegiaca*. Warnerius' second satire is a "flyting," a contention in dialogue between the poet and a runaway monk from Mont-Saint-Michel; the two misogynistic poems also have dialogue or debate formats. "It is possible," says Dronke, "that these works were assembled in one collection because of certain affinities of form, tone, or theme" (*Poetic Individuality* 77). Magic and sexual perversion are themes occurring in all of these works, and most of them maintain a dramatic structure. The satires against Jezabel and Semiramis are so similar in style and sentiment to Warnerius' satires that scholars view them as products of the school of Rouen as well.

Warnerius' crudity, especially in his satire against Moriuht, leads one critic to rank his work among the most indecent epigrams of Martial, and certainly the frame of this poem, a sober apostrophe to Robert, Archbishop of Rouen (989-1037), and to his mother, Duchess Gonnor, contrasts sharply with the poem's content, in much the same manner as Martials' prefatory epigrams to Domitian contrast with his obscene epigrams.[3] Robert the Pious (996-1031) is covered with praise (5-9), a fact that leads Musset to speculate that the Normans had good relations with France when the poem was being written. In an obscure passage (11-14), Warnerius refers to the deaths of two sons of Richard, first Duke of Normandy and father of Archbishop Robert, but the identities of these lost offspring are impossible to determine. It is likely that the widowed duchess appearing in the narrative (237-66, 327-28) is Gonnor, who served as regent after the death of Richard I. The concluding two lines of the poem complete the frame, as Warnerius turns from Moriuht's vomit to the health of his patron and duchess.

Warnerius' poem consists of three lengthy episodes followed by a prolonged attack upon Moriuht's poetic pretensions. The first two episodes are strictly parallel in structure: twice Moriuht is captured by Danish pirates, and twice he is sold into slavery, once to a nunnery for three cents (92), once to a Saxon widow for a false coin (168). In the final episode, Moriuht learns that his wife and daughter are indentured servants just outside Rouen, and he ransoms both of them, his wife for a half cent (314), his daughter for a quarter cent and a loaf of bread (329-30). After ridiculing the wandering Irishman's physical appearance and sexual appetites, Warnerius spends over a hundred lines (339-452) taking the man to task for composing a pentameter with faulty quantity; ironically, many lines of Warnerius' attack have incorrect quantity.[4] Warnerius' narrative is rambling, almost picaresque, and he is wont to digress at any moment.

Not only does this substantial narrative have a number of metrical errors, but the grammar is frequently incorrect. Twice Warnerius subordinates the wrong clause in a complex sentence (15-16, 369-70); often an incorrect case form is used, but correcting the grammar would destroy the prosody (395, 406, 490). The use of participles and the ablative is imprecise, and there are countless other oddities about the text.[5] Much of the poem remains incomprehensible even when obvious errors in grammar are resolved. Savage death that spares summer cicadas (18-20), the thief who has given the Irish their names (35-36), the conversation that Moriuht has with his wife's owner (305-14), and Mount "Penton," which has gained another rib (343-44), are a few of the poem's more elusive passages.[6] Warnerius is also fond of using unusual words, such as *rabula* (79, 223, 389, 439), *fleumate* (163), *gausape* (192, 310, 447), and *gabeliia* (295).

Warnerius' rhetoric is generally overdone and ineffective. He constantly apostrophizes Moriuht, thereby fluctuating madly between third and second person viewpoints; he constantly changes verb tense, to the point of distracting the reader's attention. His frequent interjections reveal a mock modesty, and his use of *praeteritio* becomes a sort of tic toward the end of the poem. But the *descriptio* of ugliness (221-36), Rabelaisian in flavor, is the earliest amplified instance of the topos in the late Middle Ages, predating less crude descriptions in the *Ruodlieb* and in the elegiac comedies *Geta* and *Alda*.[7]

Though this poem has obvious deficiencies in its composition and prosody, scholars have taken it for "l'un des premiers et des plus singuliers monuments de la renaissance littéraire en Normandie au début du XIe siècle" (Warnerius, "Satire" 197). Dudo of Saint-Quentin, Warnerius' contemporary, mentions a "Northmannica gymnasia" where, French critics believe, grammar and music were taught.[8] But Moriuht's familiarity with grammar, rhetoric, and logic—that is, the trivium—as well as with geometry, one of the components of the quadrivium, is described in a line (51) borrowed directly from Juvenal (3. 76) and is therefore pure fiction. Much of Warnerius' attack on his rival centers on technical literary skills: the Irishman's first speech to the duchess (241-48) is rhetorically inadequate, according to Warnerius, and his great error is using a long syllable in the place of a short one when he writes about Bishop Hugo (d. 989): "Foribus en clausis moratur pontifex Hugo" ("Lo! When the gates have been closed, Bishop Hugo delays," 341). Topical references suggest that Moriuht may be a real personage, a rival *scholasticus*, and Warnerius' depiction of this Irishman rambling about the Norman court, belching forth verses (337), perhaps indicates "la préexistence à Rouen d'une école littéraire originale, fort accueillant aux influences venues d'outre-Manche" (Warnerius, "Le satiriste" 249).

The language of this poem is imbued with phrases and whole lines from the classical writers, especially Virgil, Horace, and Juvenal.[9] Twice Warnerius alludes to the most popular of pagan myths, the love and Venus and Mars, and in the second allusion it is Moriuht who sings of the sweet thefts of Mars (41-42, 321-22). Warnerius' comparison of Glicerium to Dido, after Moriuht has discovered her, is both comic and obscene (282-88). Warnerius' use of the name Glicerium for Moriuht's wife has moved Dronke and Omont to suggest that the poet had read Terence, who uses the name in *The Woman of Andros*, though Musset notes that "ce nom est banal. Gautier de Chatillon l'utilisera plus tard."[10] Moriuht's enigmatic conversation with Glicerium's owner, Baucis (303-14), introduces another name used by classical writers Ovid and Persius.[11] Both Glicerium and Baucis are women appearing in the elegiac comedy *Baucis et Traso*, which is closely related to *Richeut*, the oldest extant Old French fabliau: in the *comedia*, Glicerium is a prostitute, Baucis her go-between or *anus*. It is possible that already in Warnerius' time the two names were used, by learned writers, for prostitutes. Warnerius' references to other classical figures, such as Ilia (115-28), Ascalaphus (286), and Herotes (431), suggest a self-conscious flaunting of his learning, and his reading of Horace's *Ars Poetica* is faulty: he misunderstands a passage at the end of Horace's work, confusing Thales, who fell into a pit, with Empedocles, who fell into burning Aetna (339-40).

Such a text, comments Leblond, is unworthy of notice, except that it testifies to a resurrection of letters:

> L'auteur . . . s'évertue dans un langage, dans une matière dont il vient d'apprendre le rudiment et l'on voit comment il oeuvre le chemin à d'autres.   Car enfin il apporte beaucoup d'éléments qui seront utilisables: une prosodie à peu près correcte, des notions de musique, de mythologie, d'histoire antique, une incitation à se reporter aux grandes sources, pour les thèmes et pour les expressions. (180)

The historical value of the poem is questionable, for it is impossible to distinguish fact from exaggeration, truth from fiction. The Viking capture and rape of Moriuht may easily have occurred in late tenth-century northern Europe, and Moriuht's sale to a nunnery in Corbridge is also possible, as Corbridge was then an important town in northern England with a substantial *monasterium*.[12] But Moriuht, his wife, and his daughter are sold for ridiculously small sums, doubtlessly exaggerated by Warnerius, and the graphic description of Glicerium's enslavement (276-79) is indebted to Juvenal.[13]

Moriuht's paganism and witchcraft seem more fictional than real, though some of his behavior may reflect contemporary practices.   When he escapes the inhabitants of Corbridge in a coracle, the small boat without oars generally reserved for Irish saints, he "sacrifices to the winds" and "calls loudly upon the pagan gods from the entrails of a young woodpecker" (146-48); ironically, passing Danes hear his loud prayers and recapture him.   In a second ritual Moriuht examines the entrails of a human corpse, in which he perceives his wife's *gausape*, or beard (190-202); Beelzebub then informs him of Glicerium's whereabouts.   Finally, Warnerius' recommendation that Moriuht purify himself by dunking his head in a river three times (465-72) seems to draw on a classical topos, though Warnerius may be referring to medieval sorcery as well.

While the literary merits of this satire are not great, it nonetheless belongs to the early history of comic narrative, presenting a low form of comedy with its emphasis on scatology, physical deformity, and sexual perversion. Warnerius' obsession with excrement and urine is part of his vicious attempt to lower Moriuht to the status of an animal, to a "mule wallowing in dung" (297). He makes the link explicit when he sees the hero rolling in hay and dung with Glicerium:

> Nudus cum nuda recubans cur, stulte, capella
>   Ut pecus ad pecudem retro tenes faciem?
> Esne memor quod te nudum nudamque capellam
>   In feno vidi mane jacere fimi?

(When you lie naked with your naked she-goat, why, stupid, do you copulate from behind like a beast on a beast? Do you remember when I saw you both naked, lying in the hay and dung one morning?) (455-58)

Warnerius also denigrates the value of Moriuht's poetry, "worthy of being printed in shit" (338), by linking it with excremental functions:

Grammaticus, rethor, geometra, pictor, aliptes,
   Omnia sit vobis, est caper ipse mihi.
Nam sibi nota magis propriae vesica capelle,
   Quam dialectica vis, quae geometrica sit.
(Grammarian, rhetorician, geometer, painter, wrestler—let him be everything to you—he's still a goat to me. For the bladder of his she-goat is better known to him than dialectical power or geometry.) (51-54)

Warnerius constantly reminds his reader that Moriuht is not a poet, but a bear, a dog, a horse, a wolf, and a worm, in addition to being a *caper* and a *hyrcus*.

Another source of humor is Moriuht's physical imperfection: his baldness. In a scene providing "relief rabelaisien" (Leblond 183), the pirates urinate on the hero's bald pate (70), and when he is caught with a nun in flagrante delicto, the people "strike his bald head with lashes" (138). Twice his baldness is the object of ridicule by characters within the narrative: when he is sold to the nuns, "they mock his great hairless head" ("Derident magnum depile calvitium," 96); when Moriuht leaves Duchess Gonnor's palace,

Hoc monstrum circum juvenes puerique canebant:
   "Calvule, quere cappam, calvule, quere capram."
(Circling this monster, youths and boys were singing: "Little baldy, seek your cap, little baldy, seek you she-goat.") (267-68)

Like the bald man in Egbert's *De uno calvo*, Moriuht does not seek a cap necessary to guard against the cold. But whereas Egbert locates irony in the bald man's rejoicing over finding a comb instead of a cap, Warnerius' humor resides in the pun of "cappa" and "capra."[14]

Warnerius also finds humor in involuntary nudity and sexual depravity. "Genitalia cuncta patebant" (227) is a central theme permitting Warnerius to ridicule the Irish use of kilts (41-44) and Moriuht's barbaric dress:

Ante suum penem gestabat rabula pellem,
   Ante nates caprae tegmina retro nigra,
Calceus et dexter consutus pelle asinina
   Et levus pariter nudus ad usque nates,

Et magis ut dicam, genitalia cuncta patebant,
   Podicis et nigri inguinis atque pili. . .
(This braggart wore a skin over his penis and the black hide of a goat
over his buttocks. His right shoe was a sewn-up ass's skin, and his left
leg was naked up to his rump. Indeed, I may say that his genitals were
entirely exposed, as well as the black piles of his anus and groin . . .)
(223-28)

The poet provides more "relief rabelaisien" in his description of the hero's anus,
in which male and female cats could winter, or a stork or hoopoe build nests
(229-34). Some of Warnerius' sexual humor, such as his description of the
pirates' rape of Moriuht (65-80) or his obscene comment about the price Moriuht
pays for his freedom from the Saxon widow ("Tu liber vulvae pro coitu rigide,"
188), is so vulgar as to shock even the modern reader. Other scenes illustrating
sexual depravity are perhaps less offensive but are nonetheless ribald, as when
Moriuht entertains the nuns of Corbridge (109-14) and when he becomes a
sodomite in Saxony:

Nam multos pueros, monachas, viduasque subegit
   Atque maritatas, esne, poeta, nefas?
Matres nobilium dum percipiunt puerorum
   Corruptas soboles jam fore sic proprias,
Libertate data, mox gente fugatus ab illa. . .
(But he who has plowed many boys, nuns, widows, and wives—is he
not wicked, O poet? When mothers of noble boys perceive that their
daughters will soon be defiled, they grant Moriuht his liberty, and he
is soon driven out by that people . . .) (173-77)

One almost hears Fulcoius' "Spuria stirps, pater est incertus, adultera mater"
when the tyrant who disguises himself as Saturn is caught or the question
terminating *Res mea*: "Quis pocius reus est?"

Warnerius' *Satire against Moriuht* is a unique achievement on several counts:
as an early satire, it is unusual in its emphasis on narrative; as a comedy, it is
remarkable for its great length and its ribald humor; as a work of literature, it
is distinctive because of its historical value. Warnerius' tendency to exaggerate
and his copious borrowings from classical writers reveal the extent to which his
work is fictional, yet one gets the impression that he draws Moriuht from real
life, as this wandering Irish scholar leaps from the manuscript as a rounded real-
life character.

Warnerius' second satire is not a narrative but a debate, and hence it
resembles the satires against Jezabel and Semiramis. As in the *Satire against
Moriuht*, Warnerius addresses Archbishop Robert in the poem's frame. The poet
criticizes Franbaldus for quitting the monastery of Mont-Saint-Michel and its
Benedictine rule so that he could come to Saint-Ouen in Rouen. A debate

between the grammarian Warnerius and the musician Franbaldus ensues, each venemously accusing the other of ignorance. Warnerius' pedantry is less extreme in this satire; nonetheless, he reproaches his enemy for confusing the pronunciation of the prepositions *a* and *ad* and the cases that they govern. This short satire, comments Musset, "est à la fois beaucoup plus obscure et beaucoup moins riche en indications précises; c'est sans doute pourquoi elle a découragé les éditeurs" (254).

The two satires against Jezabel and Semiramis are so similar in diction, tone, and theme to Warnerius' satires that, if they are not by Warnerius himself, they must belong to the same "school" to which he belongs. In the first of these misogynistic poems, each line consists of a question by the poet and a response by the shameless courtesan. The interesting contrast of *contemptus mundi* and *carpe diem* does not alleviate the tedium of the piece's structure. The coarseness of Jezabel's replies resembles Warnerius' crudity in the *Satire against Moriuht*. Although the poet calls Jezabel an *anus*, she is not a go-between but an active, albeit old, seeker of lust. Baucis, who is Glicerium's owner in the *Satire against Moriuht*, is here an old woman: "The greedy man loses his riches," says the poet. "Wrinkled Baucis her molars," replies the harlot ("Perdit avarus opes—Baucis rugosa molares," 139). The text is very corrupt and the poet's pedantry does not help matters: "il se plaît au jeu des énigmes, à tel point que son texte est bien souvent incompréhensible . . . Nous avons fait des observations analogues sur Garnier; son pédantisme, l'obstination à attaquer une personne, le goût scatologique, l'intérêt pour la magie. Quant à la langue, elle a les mêmes caractères dans chacune de ces oeuvres" (Leblond 185).

The satire against Semiramis begins as a comic satire but ends as a romance whose tone is at odds with "un couplet gaillard sur le droit à la jouissance amoureuse" (Leblond 187). The poem is a debate with a prologue, similar in structure to the *comediae elegiacae*, and since it has action, it is closer to drama than to narrative. Like Pasiphae, Semiramis, wife of Ninus, loves a bull. In the prologue the poet manifests a "truculant joviality" (Leblond 186) when he comments on the union:[15]

> Si regina bovem durum quesivit in ervo,
> Cur non regalem portavit vacca coronam?
> Fiat vacca Nini, fiat regina iuvenci.
> (If a queen sought out a rude bull among the vetch,
> Why did a heifer not wear the royal crown?
> Let a heifer be Ninus' bride, if the queen becomes a bull's!) (8-10)

In the debate between the shade of Semiramis and an augur, her brother, the poet reveals his interest in the mechanics of witchcraft. The augur, who wishes to see his sister's bodily shape, not just hear her voice, gradually learns that Semiramis, like Europa, was seduced by Jove, disguised as a bull. This fact excuses her from guilt:

> Divino scortatori proscriptio non est;
> Inculpabiliter talis mihi risit adulter!
> (There is no judgment against a divine seducer;
> Such an adulterer smiled at me without blame!) (173-74)

Unlike the stiff question-answer routine of the satire against Jezabel, this poem is well organized and fluid in its transitions. Yet both poems about women share so many peculiarities in style and syntax that one may tentatively conclude they issue from the same pen.

The three satires against Franbaldus, Jezabel, and Semiramis apparently belong to the "flyting" genre, as does the pre-eleventh-century dialogue between Terence and his "Delusor." According to Karl Young, of the three dramatic traditions that fall outside the Church's dramatic history—classical, mime, and folk—the debate tradition has most in common with "the dwindled legacy from the literary drama of pagan antiquity" (1:1). During the Middle Ages, classical drama had fallen into abeyance. Hrotsvitha of Gandersheim, whose works are contained in a single manuscript, is a rare imitator of Terence, and she herself indicates that her plays were meant to be read, not performed.[16] But the "Carolingian dialogue-poems can be seen as dramatic. All of them, presumably, were read aloud in company, not just in private . . . When they were thus read the different parts were allotted to different readers" (Dronke, *Poetic Individuality* 85). Scholars theorize that even the *Ecbasis captivi* is "a kind of play, or school-declamation aided by mime," and Dronke points out that the fragmentary romance titled *Gesta Apollonii*, composed during the tenth or early eleventh century, may have been thus performed (*Poetic Individuality* 85). Unlike the *Gesta*, however, in which Strabo and Saxo narrate events and quote speakers indiscriminately, without regard for consistency of speaker and character, the three Norman satires, like *Terentius et Delusor*, are thoroughly dramatic in their indications of who speaks what. Further, they lack narrative intrusions of the "he said," "she said" type found in many *comediae elegiacae*.

Apparently the dialogue tradition is quite independent of ecclesiastical drama, though Dronke notes that the late eleventh-century *Sponsus*, like *Semiramis*, begins with a verse prologue (*Poetic Individuality* 85). Even conservative critics concede that "school poems were prepared with a view to recitation rather than singing" (Allen 236), and Baudry of Bourgueil states several times that his *epistolae* were recited.[17] But it is highly unlikely that the satires in dialogue form—or, for that matter, the *nugae* in epistolary form—were performed with the aid of mimes. They were no doubt written and recited by the poets themselves. Baudry's testimony implies that all of the learned Latin literature, the *epistolae* as well as the satires, may well have been recited to an audience. The dialogues and *comediae elegiacae* may have differed only in the number of persons reciting the text. This tradition is distinct from church drama and is related to the rhythmic poetic tradition, for several scholarly Latin writers, including

Herimannus Contractus, Hildebert, and Peter the Painter, incorporate rhythmic poetry into their metrical verse.

The school of Rouen, which existed between 1000 and 1030, had an extremely limited influence: Warnerius was completely forgotten by later writers, and Dudo's style was so obscure that William of Jumièges has to rewrite his history in the 1070s (Warnerius, "Le satiriste" 258). Warnerius' *Satire against Moriuht* is, therefore, an isolated achievement lacking a direct influence on subsequent literary movements. The situation is much different for late eleventh-century writers, many of whom influence each other and thus build a literary milieu providing the basis of the Twelfth Century Renaissance. A popular theme illustrating the close interactions among poets is the age-old attack upon the dangers of wicked women, for nearly every late eleventh-century writer has at least one poem on the subject. The linguistic and thematic commonplaces in these satires suggest that the poets read each other's works.

A typical poem begins with a series of clichés and then moves on to famous *exempla* of evil women. Woman is a fragile thing (*res fragilis*) but, like a dragon, an eating flame (*flamma vorax*). She is a sweet evil (*dulce malum*) who vomits forth cups of venom disguised as honey. She is, of course, the source of all evils (*cunctorum caput malorum*), for it was Eve who precipitated the Fall, and therefore she is the death of souls (*mors animarum*). The poets then mention famous men of the Bible and Antiquity who were deceived by women, the most popular victims being Salomon and David. Hildebert and Peter mention Joseph, the subject of Fulcoius' ninth epistle, and Hippolytus, who appears in Peter's *De illa quae impudenter filium suum adamavit*.[18] Marbod mentions Jezabel, who, along with several other deceitful women, is known to the people in tragedies ("Liber Decem Capitulorum" 3, col. 1699). Beyond minor digressions—Marbod, for instance, briefly describes the trials of Ulysses ("Liber Decem Capitulorum" 3, col. 1699)—these satirists do not develop full-length narratives, the important exception being Peter the Painter.

The only certain biographical facts about Petrus Pictor are that he comes from Flanders and that his *Laus Flandriae* was composed in 1110 or 1111.[19] In his poems, Peter employs commonplaces also used by Marbod and Hildebert; being a contemporary of these famous writers, Peter probably wrote his works around the turn of the century. Of the eighteen poems edited by Acker, nearly half are concerned with religious subjects. One, like Gautier's *Rithmus jocularis*, is a romantic vision of dancing ladies; another is a venality satire; yet another laments the impoverishment of scholars. The narrative satire *De illa quae impudenter filium suum adamavit*, preceded by the misogynistic diatribe titled *De muliere mala*, is definitely a work by Peter, but *De matronis*, existing in a single manuscript side by side with *De muliere mala*, is of doubtful attribution. Boutémy notes that *De matronis* is a metrical poem of leonine hexameters beginning with a rhythmic prologue, just like Peter's *De egestate et fame et siti gule* and his *De excidio Romani* ("Quelques oeuvres inédites" 64). Peter's characteristic tendency to preface metrical poems with rhythmic prologues—a trait that Boutémy considers most banal—induces his editor to include *De matronis* in his corpus (Peter the Painter, *Carmina* xviii).

Perhaps the greatest interest of Peter's *De matronis* lies in the notion of *falsa religio* that he introduces in the prologue, for Peter is writing this story at the very time when the earliest troubadours are worshiping their ladies in a quasi-feudal, quasi-religious fashion.   But by "falsa religio" Peter means "false religiosity"—that is, hypocrisy—for the false wife, who performs "foul acts in secret," merely pretends to be devout (4-11). By praising the chastest of women, Penelope, Anna, and Susanna, she manages to hide her adultery, and her foolish husband, who praises her to the poet, worships her "like a saint":

> Vix ego, vix vere risum potui cohibere
> Post hunc sermonem, dum falsam religionen
> Eius miratur miser utque deam veneratur.
> Nam quod amatorum sit amatrix innumerorum
> Iamdudum novi, quod sit meretrix bene novi.
> (Really, I could scarcely contain my laughter
> After this speech, as the fool admires his wife's false show of religion
> And worships her like a saint.
> For I have long known that she is mistress of innumerable lovers;
> I have known very well that she is a slut.) (16-20)

The central theme of "falsa religio" differs markedly from the troubadour ethos: it is the husband, not the lover, who honors his unfaithful wife "ut dea," "like a saint."

The poet presents three instances of the wife's infidelity, each meant to illustrate the theme of *falsa religio*. In the first episode, the wife pretends to visit a sick friend, a ploy that permits the poet to develop, in ironic fashion, the classical metaphor of love as a disease:

> Sic consolaris languentem, sic medicaris,
> Sic morbum iuvenis dulci lenimine lenis.
> (Thus you console the sick one, thus you doctor him,
> Thus you alleviate the youth's illness with sweet medication.) (40-41)

While certain topoi in Peter's poem also occur in the troubadour tradition, others are the property of Latin poetry. The frequent apostrophes to the adulteress, who wavers between generic Woman and an individualized deceiver, reveal an epigrammatic mode, and the ironic play on "touching" in the wife's second lie to her husband gains its meaning from the four or five stages of love, a theory exploited above all by Latin love poets of the eleventh and subsequent centuries:

"Febre gravi plenam miseri tetigi modo venam,
Sed me tangente fugit febris inde repente . . ."
("I only felt the wretch's pulse, checked his high fever,
And when I touched him, his fever quickly subsided.") (45-46)

The second episode also begins with the wife's lie, which, at first glance, seems to parody an *alba*:

"Nunc est surgendum," dicit, "lacrimisque luendum
Quicquid nocturnus suasit furor atque diurnus.
Surgendum David de nocte propheta probavit,
Vt mens tunc pura Domino libet pia thura.
Hoc Domino gratum tempus, reor, estque beatum,
Templa Dei munda iam cum prece sunt adeunda,
Quare devote factura precamina pro te,
Vir meus, illa peto: curam de rebus habeto!
Tu res carnales, ego tractem spirituales."
("Now is the time to rise," she says, "and to expiate with tears
Whatever the passions of day and night have driven us to do.
David the prophet favored rising at night
So that with a pure and holy mind we could make an offering of incense to the Lord.
I believe this time is most pleasing to the Lord and is blessed by Him;
One should now go to God's holy churches to pray.
So, my husband, while I am ready to pray devotedly for you,
I ask you to take good care of our possessions.
You take care of worldly things; let me handle the spiritual ones.") (57-65)

The wife's use of the gerundive "surgendum" does not differ greatly from the imperative of a contemporary Latin *alba* (Dronke, *Medieval Lyric* 173):

Cantant omnes volucres,
    iam lucescit dies.
Amica cara, surge sine me
    per portas exire!
(All the birds are singing,
already day is dawning.
Rise, dear love, to go out
through the doors without me!)

But there is no doubt that she is really taking her cue from the Psalms (119. 62): "media nocte surgebam ad confitendum tibi super iudicia iustificationis tuae."

Far from being a perversion of an *alba*, a parody of Latin and vernacular love poetry, the wife's lie simply reveals a sound knowledge of the Bible.

The common metaphors of Peter's poem may also remind us of contemporary love poetry, but more than likely Peter is following a well-trod misogynistic tradition.   For example, in the scene of seduction culminating the second episode, a ribald pun equates the sexual act with the religious one:

> Sic flexis orat genibus, sic crimina plorat,
> Sic matutina iacet hora facta supina,
> Sordibus implicitum sic expiat illa maritum.
> (Thus she prays on bent knees, thus she laments sins,
> Thus she lies supine till the break of dawn,
> Thus she atones for the sins of her husband, who is entangled in baseness.) (72-74)

This religio-erotic metaphor differs greatly from the metaphors of troubadour poetry. Another metaphor, which Peter uses three times, is the Ovidian cliché equating woman with serpent (21, 55, 112); the fact that the troubadour Marcabru extends this metaphor through one of his poems (44) is evidence of his Latin learning.

It is only coincidental that the metaphors and thematics of Peter's narrative are reminiscent of troubadour poetry, for close consideration shows that Peter's style and concerns are thoroughly entrenched in the Latin misogynistic tradition. The wife's final deception (103-11), in which she explains to her husband that he will attain heaven through her devotion, is inspired by Virgil and the Bible, and the nature of her deception ("Os aliud fatur, mala mens aliud meditatur," 116) reveals a concern with exterior and interior, truth and fiction, that Fulcoius shares in his story of the snowchild.

This poem may be criticized on several grounds: it is laden with clichés, the diction is somewhat redundant, and the narrative progression is constantly retarded by platitudinous moral outrage. But its developed narrative makes it an unusual, even an outstanding satire, for few satires of the eleventh and early twelfth centuries achieve such development. Unlike Warnerius' *Satire against Moriuht*, which seems to have some basis in contemporary reality, Peter's *De matronis* does not necessarily reflect the mores of his society: Peter is probably not parodying courtly love practices, and the adulteress, unlike Moriuht, is more of a generic type than a rounded individual. Further, the nature of the poem's humor is difficult to assess: the narrator clearly is amused, in sardonic fashion, at the husband's praise of his wife, but his moral outrage at the wife's behavior, similar to the reaction of the narrator of *Res mea*, is sincere and undercuts the comic impulse.   As with Warnerius' ludicrous attack upon Moriuht for misconstruing a line of poetry, the modern reader has a different response to a situation that the medieval writer finds serious, even tragic: we have an impulse to laugh at Warnerius, who proves himself incapable of writing correct hexameters while he attacks Moriuht, and thus we perceive a kind of dramatic irony at the writer's expense; similarly, we find a black irony in the eventual outcome of the wife's treachery—that is, the duped husband's damnation—though Peter himself is not the least amused at this tragic end.   Indeed, our initial reaction to the tale differs from that of the poet, a clerk who knows the stereotypical woman better than real women, who is appalled more than amused at his tragicomedy.

Peter's *De illa que impudenter filium suum adamavit* has so many parallels with *De matronis* that both poems must be his works.[20]   Hauréau has described this narrative as one of the earliest of "ces fables romanesques, appelées, au moyen âge, comédies" (*Notices et extraits* 5:227).   But unlike *De matronis*, this work is distinctly tragic in tone.   It is a variation of the Hippolytus story, as Peter himself indicates ("Prodidit Ypolitum contra ius Phedra cupitum," 14, 77), and it begins with a lengthy prologue titled *De muliere mala*, which contains many commonplaces of misogynistic poems by Marbod, Hildebert, Roger of Caen, and even Marcabru.   Unlike Phaedra, the villain of this story is the mother (*genitrix*), not the stepmother, of her victim.   The son, instead of being mangled by horses, is tossed into a river after being judged, like Joseph, as culpable in attacking his mother.   The story does not end there, as Raby assumes (*SLP* 2:27), but continues with the woman's poisoning of her husband, her second marriage, and her seduction of a *custos*.   Details of the poem recall those of Fulcoius' romantic tale of Potiphar's wife: both women, for instance, accuse the young men of tearing at their clothing.   Like the anonymous *De patricide*, a variation of the Oedipus story, this narrative properly belongs to the realm of tragedy, though satire is also at work in the piece.[21]

Lacking the artistry of the *ridicula* and *nugae*, the satires by Warnerius and Peter nonetheless maintain an impressive narrative structure, and much of the potential humor of these stories—the overt sexuality, the religious parody—resembles the humor of later comic genres.   The episodic plots of both satires are more complex than the repetitious structure of *Unibos*, and they excel compared to the venality satires with their weak narrative development.   The prolonged attack upon a traveling scholar who seduces nuns is precisely the situation at the center of *Richeut*, the oldest extant fabliau.   The purpose of Moriuht's later travels is identical to the protagonist's mission in the *comedia Pamphilus, Gliscerium et Birria*, in which a master and his servant set out to find a woman whose name, incidentally, is Gliscerium.   Indeed, the low comedy of Warnerius' satire—the scatology, the deformities, the sexual perversion—does not surpass the crudity of the fabliaux: in *Le fevre de Creil*, for instance, the description of Gautier's gigantic penis is much more graphic than Warnerius' depiction of genitalia (Pearcy 170).   But the sodomy in the *Satire against Moriuht* is a theme occurring rarely in later comic narratives: the potential sodomy in *Du sot chevalier* remains potential; homosexuality is never actualized in the fabliaux.

Aspects of Peter's satire, despite his moralistic tone, also resemble elements of later comic narratives: the overt religious parody of the adulterous woman engaging in sex as though she were praying is comparable to the climactic scene in *De l'evesque qui benei lo con*, and the behavior of the widow, who "makes herself like new" ("seque novam reparabit," 136), is similar to the actions of the character in *La veuve*:[22]

> Li dame n'a mais de mort cure,
> ains se retifete et escure.

But the potential humor of Peter's and Warnerius' satires is often never exploited for its full value, and in this sense they both differ from the composers of "pure" comic narratives.

The narratives by Warnerius and Peter, being satires, differ from "pure" comic genres—*ridicula*, *nugae*, fabliaux, and *comediae elegiacae*—in fundamental ways. While it is true that the moralistic-philosophical tone of some *nugae*—and some *comediae*, for that matter—detracts from the comic impulse, rarely does the tone shift to the vituperousness of Warnerius or the tragic vision of Peter. This, of course, is the nature of satire: it can fluctuate between comic and tragic moods. While Peter's poem may lack original language and characterization, his narrative is amusing and unique. Warnerius' satire, seeming to be part *comedia*, part fabliau, presents a vivid, rounded character who leaps out of this obscurely written poem a millennium later. Unlike the *ridicula* and *nugae*, which are the ancestors of the later fabliaux and *comediae elegiacae*, the satires belong to a more stable genre, one that does not so much evolve as unfold itself in the final centuries of the Middle Ages.

NOTES

1. Yunck's translation (75).

2. Musset (Warnerius, "Le satiriste" 243-45) suggests 1006 as a possible date for the composition of Warnerius' *Satire against Moriuht*. For Warnerius' second satire, see Musset 259-66; for *Semiramis*, see Dronke, *Poetic Individuality* 66-71; for *Jezabel*, see Leblond 283-87.

3. Cf. Martial's opening epigrams of Book IX.

4. The following lines have incorrect quantity: 99 ("mulierum" is spelled the classical way but pronounced the medieval way); 268 (I have emended the line, but there is still a problem with the final foot); 355; 359; 416; 444.

5. Other oddities about the text include: a peculiar use of the interjection "a" (94); presence of the singular "dactile" (350) instead of the plural, which is necessary for the passage to make sense; the mention that "a short iamb expels both the spondee and the dactyl" (353) when there is no iamb in the criticized

line 341; use of "jurare" in the negative (459)—perhaps the word should be emended to "jurgare" (i.e., "you cannot argue about that").

6. The "fallen soul" ("lapse") of line 19 cannot be death (the vocative is masculine, not feminine), but perhaps refers to Satan. In lines 35-36 Warnerius is apparently punning on the Greek *skotios*, "dark, secret" ("Scotti") and *skotia*, "darkness" ("Scotia")—which explains why they "have taken on these names" ("nominibus sumptis"); the thief again seems to be Satan, manifesting himself as darkness. The literal meaning of line 306 makes no sense ("Her brother seeks to love [her?] throughout his people"); perhaps "frater" should be emended to "fratrem": "She [the "semper putida serva" of line 305] seeks to love her brother . . ." While the "Mons Penton" of line 343 is unidentifiable, the line is certainly an allusion to Persius 1. 92-95, where the friend offers various examples of the absurdities of modern poetic diction, including "costam longo subduximus Appennino" ("we stole a rib from the lengthy Apennines!"). Another enigmatic line is 294 (perhaps "unda" refers to baptism).

7. Cf. *Ruodlieb*, fragment 7, 98-105; William of Blois 171-92; *Geta* 35-350, in Elliott 27-40. Also cf. Martial 9. 47.

8. See Warnerius, "Le Satiriste" 245-46.

9. Warnerius lifts entire lines from Juvenal (line 51 comes from Juvenal 3. 76), Virgil (line 285 is taken from *Aeneid* 4. 76), and Horace (lines 391 and 393 quote *Ars Poetica* 379-80).

10. See Dronke, *Poetic Individuality* 81; Warnerius, "Satire" 196; Warnerius, "Le Satiriste" 246, n. 29.

11. In Ovid (*Metamorphosis* 8. 640 f.) Baucis is a peasant woman; in Persius (4. 21-22) she is an old woman hawking herbs to a fellow slave.

12. The eighth century church belonging to the monastery, St. Andrew's, still survives. See Warnerius, "Le satiriste" 251.

13. Cf. Juvenal 6. 491: "nuda umero Psecas infelix nudisque mamillis."

14. Warnerius is particularly fond of puns: cf. Moriuht-*mors* (49); *ramum*, meaning "branch" or "rod" (112, 113, 134, 165); *gausape*, meaning "woollen cloth, beard [i.e., pubic hair], slut" (192, 310, 447).

15. Text and translation are from Dronke, *Poetic Individuality* 66-71.

16. See Franceschini 295-312. Young comments: "Her product differs from [Terence's] most essentially in the extent of the comic content. Only *Dulcitius* evokes laughter" (1:5).

17. 161, 15-16; 171, 13-14; 178, 9-12; etc.

18. See Hildebert, *Carmina Minora* 50; 26; Peter the Painter, *Carmina* 14; 57-58, 77.

19. See Peter the Painter, *Carmina* xxxv-xxxvii.

20. In both poems, a character contrasts "res carnales" and "res spirituales" (14, 137-38; 16, 65); in both the wife wears makeup after her husband's death (14, 260-65; 16, 143-48). In one the second husband does not love but hates his wife (14, 283); in the other the first husband would hate his wife if he knew the

truth (16, 99). Both poems employ the cliché of the serpent (14, 300; 16, 55, 112-15). Acker notes other commonplaces.

21. See Hauréau, "Notice sur un manuscrit de la Reine Christine" 341-46.

22. See Montaiglon and Raynaud 3:178-85 (*De l'evesque*) and 2:197-214 (*La veuve*). Also compare *De la dame qui fit .III. tors entor le moustier* (Montaiglon and Raynaud 3:192-98) with the wife's behavior in Peter's satire (16, 79 f.).

Conclusion

The *ridicula* and the *nugae* are unique narrative achievements composed at the dawn of the High Middle Ages. The extant rhythms and sequences preceding the *ridicula* and the rare school exercises of Theodulf and other Carolingians indicate the origins of these comic genres and reveal how narrative structure gains sophistication during the transitional centuries separating the Carolingian Revival and Twelfth Century Renaissance. Even though both genres have debts to the past, they represent something new, a kind of primitive short story or novella located at the threshold of a great literary flowering. During the High Middle Ages and early Renaissance, a myriad of comic narrative genres emerge: elegiac comedy, fabliau, *Schwank*, and novella are the best known. These narratives belong to two distinct literary traditions: popular and learned.

The eight extant *ridicula* are indeed the ancestors of the fabliaux and resemble the Old French stories in almost every formal literary aspect. Some similarities—such as the technical form of the genres or their shared plots—could be coincidental, but other similarities are so essential to the nature of these stories and they are so numerous that we may inductively reason that we are reading related genres. But we must keep in mind that we are not dealing with identical genres, and in fact the differences reveal much about the evolution of comic literature during the High Middle Ages and a change in attitude about comedy—and a change in sense of humor—during this seminal period in literary history. The *ridicula* and the fabliaux belong to a popular tradition of comic literature that generally values matter over form, good storytelling over rhetoric. This tradition is distinct from the learned comedy of the *nugae* and the elegiac comedies.

What critics have said about the fabliaux can easily be said about the *ridicula* as well. For example, Bédier's distinction of the "fabliaux simplistes" and the more complex fabliaux can be applied to the *ridicula*: seven of these stories are extremely short and simplistic, consisting of a single incident or of a reduplication of an incident, and they are hardly different from Bédier's "fabliaux simplistes." *Unibos*, in contrast, is a complex tale resembling such fabliaux as *Du bouchier d'Abeville* and *Des trois boçus*. Paul Thiener's observation that, in the fabliaux, "the essence of the plot is motion" (131) pertains also to *Unibos*. This story is repetitive, but this kind of excessive repetition is common in the fabliaux, such as *Des trois boçus*, in which a fool repeatedly disposes of dead hunchbacks.

Not only are the plot structures of *ridicula* and fabliaux similar, but both genres have introductory and concluding frames providing aesthetic distance from the interior fictions (Lacy 111). Unlike the moral conclusions of the fables, the conclusions of *ridicula* and fabliaux are often amoral in stance, as the storyteller sides with the trickster who is clever enough to outtrick someone else.

The plot structure and frames suggest generic kinship, but the similar verse structures of the *ridicula* and fabliaux do not necessarily indicate a relationship between the genres, because many other genres also employ the same type of versification. The octosyllabic couplet that makes up three of the *ridicula* is identical to the verse form of the Old French fabliaux, yet the French octosyllabic couplet is also used in a variety of other genres, such as romance and beast-epic. So it would be a mistake to conclude that similar verse form *proves* a direct relation between the genres.

Also, plots shared by the *ridicula* and the fabliaux do not always provide generic kinship, as the widespread story of the snowchild demonstrates. This story occurs as a *ridiculum*, a fabliau, an *exemplum*, a rhetorical "trifle," an elegiac "comedy," a German *Schwank*, an Italian novella, and a French fairytale. Some of these comic genres belong to a popular current; others belong to a scholarly tradition rooted in a classical past.

But occasionally shared plots do suggest a direct relationship between genres. The conflation of two stories into one, for instance, shows how related genres can merge into a new one. Such is the case of the Grimm fairytale *Das Bürle*, which conflates an episode of *Unibos* with an Old French fabliau, *Le povre clerc*. The *ridiculum* and the fabliau became fused and eventually emerged as a later fairytale.

At times, analogues are so close that common sense tells us the writer of a later work must have had an earlier text before him when he wrote his story, but this kind of direct influence does not always mean that the genres are closely related. For instance, the story of the priest and the wolf (*Sacerdos et Lupus*) is a *ridiculum* that the writer of the *Roman de Renart* must have had before him when he composed his beast-epic, but what is important in comparing *Sacerdos et Lupus* and the corresponding scene in *Renart* is the difference: the French writer turns the *ridiculum* into a beast-fable, not only by making the animal think and talk, but also by omitting the humanistic theme that praises human ingenuity (*ingenium*) and cleverness (*ars*). The *ridicula* are not animal fables; they emphasize human actions, human strengths, and human weaknesses. When animals do show up, they remain dumb beasts.

Technical form and common plots do not in and of themselves prove generic links. But other resemblances between the *ridicula* and fabliau do suggest that the genres are intimately related: similar plot structures; simple diction that, along with simple form, is conducive to low comedy; similar characterization; similar settings; and similar comic themes. All of these shared traits combined lead inductively to the conclusion that the Latin *ridiculum* is the predecessor of the Old French fabliau.

The simple diction of the *ridicula* and fabliaux, like the simple verse form, reveals that both genres belong to the realm of "low" comedy. The *ridicula* generally differ from the contemporary comic "trifles" just as the fabliaux differ generally from the twelfth-century elegiac comedies. *Ridicula* and fabliaux are popular and colloquial, even employing the same clichés;[1] *nugae* and elegiac comedies are scholarly and rhetorical, belonging to a literary tradition of "high" comedy.

Paul Thiener, speaking of the fabliaux, says that "characters must be conventionalized and setting functionalized." The same holds true for the *ridicula*. The characters in the *ridicula* and the fabliaux include merchants, suitors, peasants, adulterous wives, and various kinds of clerics. Unibos is a stock comic character, the peasant with only a single animal like the main character of *Brunain ou La vache au prestre*; his antagonists are unbelievably stupid, like the main character of *Du sot chevalier*. Because most of the *ridicula* are so short, setting is almost non-existent. But in *Unibos*, the settings at the marketplace, in the cottage, and at the town's crossroads are the typical functional settings found in the fabliaux.

Finally, the *ridicula* and fabliaux employ similar themes. All of the *ridicula* depict deception, and often the trickster is outtricked. Four of them have erotic themes, but the eroticism is tame in comparison to the open sexuality of the fabliaux. Other *ridicula* satirize human presumption, overconfidence, and stupidity, and the *ridicula* in general represent an advancement over earlier genres in their emphasis on humanistic themes, such as the celebration of human ingenuity (*ingenium*) and cleverness (*ars*)—themes that are common in the fabliaux (*Des deux bordeors*; *Le lai d'Aristote*). The story of little John shows how a *ridiculum* writer uses an earlier genre—the sixth-century *Vitae patrum*—and makes the theme more humanistic.

While we may conclude that *ridicula* and fabliaux are related genres, we must also understand their differences, which reveal that literary genres, reflecting human consciousness, evolve over time. The *ridicula* are primitive and childlike in their humor, which is labored and obvious, and their climaxes lack punch. Both the *ridicula* and fabliaux share the childlike tendency to delight in physical brutality, but the fabliaux are more scurrilous and sacrilegious in subject matter, their comic inversions sharper and wittier. Audiences' expectations about what is comic change over time—they expect more sophisticated inversions, greater leaps in logic, more shocking sexuality, more biting satire—but the nature of "low" comedy, with its emphasis on brutality and bodily function, is a constant feature, changing only in degree.

The transition from Latin to Old French comic narrative reveals a change in attitude about the comic and a change in attitude about the value of comic literature. While some of the *ridicula* end with "amoral" comments about the genius of man or the cleverness of a trickster, others, like *Unibos*, end apologetically, with the writer distancing himself from his fiction. Fabliau writers are less apologetic and much more open-minded about their ribald fiction. Not only that: they are better writers, perhaps because their attitudes about their fiction are more positive. These new attitudes about comic fiction reflect a changed sense of humor, a changed consciousness, as literature and society emerge from the Dark Ages.

Even though the *ridicula* and fabliaux are closely related genres, one must recognize their important differences in language and outlook, differences that are associated with the emergence of the vernacular as a primary mode of literary expression and also with great cultural changes that explain the shift from early medieval to late medieval society. In contrast, the evolution of learned comic literature from early epigrams to longer *epistola* and eventually to the elegiac comedies is gradual and continuous, both because of the nature of stable tradition and because of the shared language.

The strongest link between *nugae* and later Latin narrative is the methodology of abbreviation and amplification. Just as Hildebert, in *De Milone mercatore*, probably abbreviates the theme of Matthew of Vendôme's *Milo*, Geoffrey of Vinsauf condenses the snowchild theme in his *Poetria Nova*. While the tendency to abbreviate appealed particularly to eleventh-century writers, the technique of amplification undergoes an evolution. The early extended narratives, the *epistolae* and metrical declamations, seem preparatory for the best comic narratives in Latin of the High Middle Ages. Late eleventh-century writers, we have seen, use the techniques of amplification mentioned by Geoffrey, and the *descriptiones* of beauty and ugliness anticipate more formal portraits of later centuries.

Writers of *nugae* and *comediae* even employ the same metaphors and clichés as they construct their rhetorical pieces: for instance, Radulfus' comment to Sincopus, "Mollis enim durum gutta cavat lapidem" ("For the gentle drop hollows the hard stone," 6, 18) occurs almost verbatim in the *Facetus*: "Et durum lapidem gutta cadendo cavat" ("The drop of water hollows out the hard rock by its fall," 200). Similarly, the cliché of the honied tongue and poisoned mind appears in Fulcoius' *Epistola* VIII as well as in *Baucis et Traso* and *De nuncio sagaci*;[2] the metaphor of the sterile field and fertile wife, found in both Hildebert's *De Milone* and Matthew's *Milo*, also occurs in *Alda* and *Baucis et Traso*.[3]

The predominant themes of the elegiac comedies—seduction, deception, craftiness (*ars*)—are those of the earlier *nugae*. Sexual encounters, usually adultery and sometimes rape, often form the central themes of the comedies, and servants and old ladies act as go-betweens and bauds. The tone of these erotic adventures may vary considerably: *De tribus puellis*, for example, in which a poet judges the beauty of three maidens and then seduces the fairest, is romantic like Gautier's *Rithmus jocularis* and Peter the Painter's *Exacta cena*. In *Alda*, on the other hand, the ugly servant Spurius provides comic relief, and in the seduction scene the "marché de viz" theme reduces romanticism. In only three of these poems is deception of a non-sexual nature; obviously these writers were obsessed with the sexual act, whether in the form of titillating eroticism or crude rape, and stock topoi and metaphors run throughout the comedies. Not only are some of the scenes in the *nugae* and *comediae* nearly identical, but both genres share learned Latin themes, such as the *gradus amori*.[4] A dominant theme in several of these works, including the very early ones like the *Facetus* and *Pamphilus*, is *ars*, craftiness, with its accompanying themes of *fraus* and *ingenium*, themes that are common enough in the *ridicula* and *nugae*. *Nugae* and *comediae* also reveal legal concerns, like the metrical declamations, in the judgments that terminate several of them.[5] Finally, many of the didactic or philosophical themes found in the *nugae*—such as Fulcoius' and Radulfus' concerns with interiority and exteriority, truth and falseness—also occur in the elegiac comedies, although the writers do differ in their attitudes about the usefulness of literature.[6]

Certain themes and motifs of the *comediae elegiacae* are also shared with vernacular fabliaux and romances, for many of the Latin works tend toward ribald comedy, while others approach romantic seriousness. But Faral, noting commonplaces shared by *comediae* and fabliaux, goes too far when he concludes: "Le fabliau du XIIIe siècle, en tant que genre littéraire, est issu du conte latin du XIIe siècle, et par conséquent, en dernière analyse, remonte, par cet intermédiaire, à l'antique comédie latine" ("Le fabliaux latin" 384). Nykrog, in contrast, notes three important differences between *comediae* and fabliaux: the rhetorical style of the *comediae*, the character of the wily slave or servant, and the classical names of the *comediae*'s characters are unique to elegiac comedies. Nykrog further points out the possibility that early fabliaux, such as *Richeut*, may well have influenced elegiac comedy, such as *Baucis et Traso* (1-1i).

Hunt investigates a quite different group of shared themes and motifs with impressive success: the commonplaces found in four elegiac comedies and Chrétien de Troyes' romances. Hunt theorizes that the *comediae* "formed the literary bridge between the study of the *auctores*, especially Ovid, and the creation of 'romances' for oral recitation":

> They may well have been included in Chrestien's youthful Ovidian reading and, like many medieval writers, he may have regarded them as genuine works of the Sulmonensian . . . Chrestien's *comandemanz Ovide* (*Cligès* 1-2), i.e., *praecepta Ovidii*, could refer to almost any Ovidian or pseudo-Ovidian work on an amatory theme. (142)

His conclusion that "the *comediae* represent *oeuvres de transition* between the *imitatio auctorum*, or school exercise, and courtly narrative presented to a patron" (155) may be a little pat, but at least Hunt is aware of the real origins of elegiac comedies—which are not, as Faral contends, "l'antique comédie latine," but school exercises, *nugae*.

As early attempts at composing high comedy, the *nugae* lack the immediately discernible comedy of the *ridicula*. Although some of the *nugae*, preoccupied with the crudity of the latrine or influenced by simple themes of the fairytale, differ from lower forms of comedy only in their style, the general impulse of these poems is toward refinement of expression, beginning with the pedantic attempts of Egbert and culminating in lucid epigrams and extended narratives having occasional comic success and serious intellectual preoccupations. The arcane style and vocabulary of this poetry suggest a need to impress a coterie of appreciators, and allusions and unintelligible passages may contain keys held by that audience. Unlike the *ridicula*, which are all anonymous, the *nugae* and *comediae elegiacae* are usually attributed to well-known members of the Church. We may conclude that these scholarly productions reveal a more self-conscious attitude of the poets, who are often troubled by their prurient excursions into the secular and who make their individual mark on a given body of work.

The placement of the *ridicula* and *nugae* at opposite ends of the comic spectrum is a critical viewpoint that should not be oversimplified. The *ridicula* in sequence form, for instance, elevate the common tale with their stylistic excellence and are comparable to the formal structures of William IX's narratives and the Old French *Richeut*.[7] Yet most *ridicula* are composed in prosaic rhythmic lines that allow an emphasis on matter instead of manner, like the Old French octosyllabic couplet. The *nugae* and the *comediae elegiacae*, though sharing certain themes with the lower forms of comedy, belong to another tradition, one emulating classical models and generally valuing manner over matter.

From a larger perspective, the *ridicula* and *nugae* mark the beginning of two comic traditions that persist into the Renaissance, when comic drama emerges as a truly representational, objective form. While the *ridicula* and even the fabliaux may have been linked with some type of live performance, their progeny, the novelle and *Schwänke*, probably were not. In contrast, the *nugae* and *comediae elegiacae* were probably recited to audiences, but these "performances" were non-dramatic from a classical or modern viewpoint. Like narrative, the comic drama of the High Middle Ages may be divided into low and high forms. The Old French farces, like the comic scenes in church drama, no doubt owe much to the non-dramatic fabliau tradition, as does the later *commedia dell'arte*.[8] These "low" forms differ from academic Renaissance drama in much the same way that *ridicula* differ from *nugae*, or fabliaux from *comediae elegiacae*, for low comedy, unlike high comedy, generally ignores the classical tradition. At least one Renaissance playwright, Aeneas Silvius Piccolomini, who later became

Pope Pius II, has an apologetic attitude regarding his early comedy *Chrysis* that hardly differs from the eleventh-century churchmen's retractions of their trifles.[9] In contrast, the greatest Renaissance playwright, Shakespeare, was capable of combining both traditions in his plays, which are influenced by the popular tradition as well as by the classical heritage.

NOTES

1. Consider, for instance, the figure of speech "you're drunk!" meaning "you're a fool!" in *Unibos* (stanza 55), *Jouglet* ("Robert," fet ele, "estes vous yvres?" 302, in Eichmann and DuVal 1:130); *Du Chevalier qui fit les cons parler* ("ne soiez ivres," Harrison 226), and *Des tresces* ("Ne me tenroiz pas si por ivre," 298, in Montaiglon and Raynaud 4:77).

2. The Ovidian cliché of poison ("venenum") lurking beneath honey is applied to the *anus* Dipsas (*Amores* 1. 8. 104: "impia sub dulci melle venena latent") and also occurs in Petrus Pictor's *De illa que impudenter filium suum adamavit* ("Sub specie mellis distillat pocula fellis," 323), Marbod's *De meretrice* ("O genus hominum! mellita venena caveto," "Liber Decem Capitulorum" col. 1699), *Baucis et Traso* ("Lingua mihi dulcis, tibi plena venenis!," 127, in Cohen 2:74), and *De nuncio sagaci* ("Mel portas ore, set fel latitat tibi corde," 154). Cf. Fulcoius 8, 34; 8, 50.

3. Cf. William of Blois 206 ("sterili semina perdit humo"); *Baucis et Traso* 153-54 in Cohen 2:76 ("Non herbis, ut tu, segetes subvertere novi,/Uberiora tibi carmine rura dare"); also cf. *Pamphilus* 77-79, 560-61, for the merchandising metaphor used by Hildebert in *De Milone*.

4. In both *Milo* and *Pamphilus*, for instance, lovers are interrupted, as the narrator is in Gautier's *Aeole, rex fortis*: when Milo catches his wife with the king, "rumpuntur basia" (129, in Cohen 1:172); when Pamphilus hears a knock at the door, he speculates, "Vir fuit aut ventus" (652). Cf. *Aeole, rex fortis*: "Dum sumus in latebris, ferit ictibus ostia crebris." For the occurrence of the *gradus amoris* in elegiac comedy, see *De nuncio sagaci* 52, *Pamphilus* 235, and *Baucis et Traso* 197, in Cohen 2:77.

5. *Pamphilus*, *Milo*, and *Alda* all have legalistic conclusions, much like Hildebert's *De quodam servo*, *Res mea*, and other *nugae*.

6. See *Baucis et Traso* 197, in Cohen 2:77 ("veris falsissima miscet"); *Milo* 253, in Cohen 1:177 ("Non falero falsum"). Compare Geta's philosophizing that "Geta is nothing" (280, in Elliott 38) with Fulcoius' poem about "nothing" (*Epistola* XV).

7. The technical form of Williams' *Farai un vers pos mi sonelh* (*Song* V) is very similar to the *rythmi caudata continentes* of *Richeut*. See Faral, "Le Conte de *Richeut*" 263-64.

8. See Nicoll 169-75, 179-87.

9. "Anneas Silvius, parvenu aux plus hautes dignités ecclésiastiques, a regretté profondément les oeuvres profanes qu'il avait écrites avant son entrée dans les ordres, et il aurait voulu à ce moment faire disparaître toutes les traces de son activité littéraire d'inspiration paienne" (Piccolomini, *Chrysis* 5-6).

Appendix

Texts and Translations
of the Poems
(Excluding the Short *Nugae*)

RIDICULA

Modus Florum

1. Mendosam quam cantilenam ago,
    puerulis commendatam dabo,
    quo modulos per mendaces risum
    auditoribus ingentem ferant.
2a. Liberalis et decora
    cuidam regi erat nata,
    quam sub lege huius modi
    procis obponit querendam:
2b. Si quis mentiendi gnarus
    usque ad eo instet fallendo,
    dum cesaris ore fallax
    predicitur, is ducat filiam.
3a. Quo audito Suevus
    nil moratus infit:
    "Raptis armis ego
    dum venatum solus irem,
    lepusculus inter feras
    telo tactus occumbebat.
    Mox effusis intestinis
    caput avulsum cum cute cedo.
3b. "Cumque cesum manu
    levaretur caput,
    lesa aure effunduntur
    mellis modii centeni,
    sotiaque auris tacta
    totidem pisarum fudit.
    Quibus intra pellem strictis,
    lepus ipse dum secatur,
    crepidine summa caude
    kartam regiam latentem cepi,
4. "Que servum te firmat esse meum."
    "Mentitur," clamat rex, "karta et tu!"
    Sic rege deluso Suevus falsa
    gener regius est arte factus.

Modus Florum

1.   I compose a "lying song" that I recommend for little boys [to sing]. Through lying little measures they will bear great laughter to listeners.

2a.   A courtly and comely daughter was born to a king. For her hand, the king, according to the custom of the time, made the following pledge to [potential] suitors:

2b.   If anyone expert in lying could pursue deception to such a point that he got the king to call him a liar, that man would marry the daughter.

3a.   Upon hearing of this, a Swabian spoke up immediately: "When I was hunting alone, with my weapons in hand, I struck down a young hare, along with other wild animals, with my spear. After its intestines poured forth, I cut off its head, tore it away with the skin.

3b.   "When I raised the cut-off head with my hand, a hundred measures of honey poured from the wounded ear and just as many peas poured out of the fellow ear. When these were stripped and the hare was cut up, within its skin, at the very base of the tail, I found a royal charter

4.   "Which proclaims that you are my servant!" "Liars!" exclaims the king, "both the charter and you!" Thus when the king was tricked, the Swabian became a royal son-in-law because of his deceptive cunning.

Modus Liebinc

1a. Advertite,
    omnes populi,
    ridiculum
    et audite, quomodo
    Suevum mulier
    et ipse illam
    defraudaret.

2a. Vix remige
    triste secat mare,
    ecce subito
    orta tempestate
    furit pelagus,
    certant flamina,
    tolluntur fluctus,
    post multaque exulem
    vagum littore
    longinquo nothus
    exponebat.

3a. Duobus
    volutis annis
    exul dictus
    revertitur.
    Occurrit
    infida coniux
    secum trahens
    puerulum.
    Datis osculis
    maritus illi
    "De quo," inquit, "puerum
    istum habeas,
    dic, aut extrema
    patieris."

4a. Anni post hec quinque
    transierunt aut plus
    et mercator vagus
    instauravit remos:
    ratim quassam reficit,
    vela alligat
    et nivis natum
    duxit secum.

1b. Constantie
    civis Suevulus
    trans equora
    gazam portans navibus
    domi coniugem
    lascivam nimis
    relinquebat.

2b. Nec interim
    domi vacat coniux;
    mimi aderant,
    iuvenes secuntur,
    quos et inmemor
    viri exulis
    excepit gaudens
    atque nocte proxima
    pregnans filium
    iniustum fudit
    iusto die.

3b. At illa
    maritum timens
    dolos versat
    in omnia.
    "Mi," tandem,
    "mi coniux," inquit,
    "una vice
    in Alpibus
    nive sitiens
    extinxi sitim.
    Inde ergo gravida
    istum puerum
    damnoso foetu
    heu gignebam."

4b. Transfretato mari
    producebat natum
    et pro arrabone
    mercatori tradens
    centum libras accipit
    atque vendito
    infante dives
    revertitur.

Modus Liebinc

1a. Pay attention, everybody, and listen to a funny story about how a wife cheated a Swabian and he cheated her.

1b. A little Swabian, a citizen of Constance, carrying his goods in ships across the sea, left his wanton wife at home.

2a. Scarcely did he cleave the harsh sea with his oars than lo! suddenly, a tempest arises, the deep rages, the winds contend, and the waves are borne up. After much turmoil the northwind lands the wandering exile on a far-off shore.

2b. Meanwhile, his wife is not idle at home; mimes attend her, and forgetful of her wandering husband, she joyously receives youths who follow [them]. On the following night she conceives a son, and she bears the illegitimate child on the appointed day.

3a. When two years have passed, the wanderer returns. The unfaithful wife runs toward him, dragging the little boy with her. After they exchange kisses, the husband says to her, "By whom did you bear this child? Tell me, or you will suffer the worst."

3b. Fearing her husband, she thinks of a lie wherever she can: "Once, in the Alps, I thirsted for snow and quenched my thirst [by eating snow]. That's how I become heavy and bore this boy in a cursed pregnancy, alas!"

4a. Five years or more pass by, and the wandering merchant repairs his oars. He remakes his broken boat, ties his sails, and takes the snowchild with him.

4b. When he crossed the sea, he advertised his son [for sale], and he gave him to a merchant for earnest money. He received a hundred pounds and, after selling the child, returned home.

Modus Liebinc

5a. Ingressusque domum
ad uxorem ait:
"Consolare, coniux,
consolare, cara:
natum tuum perdidi,
quem non ipsa tu
me magis quidem
dilexisti.

6. Sic perfidam
Suevus coniugem
deluserat;
sic fraus fraudem vicerat:
nam quem genuit
nix, recte hunc sol
liquefecit.

5b. "Tempestate orta
nos ventosus furor
in vadosas sirtes
nimis fessos egit,
et nos omnes graviter
torret sol, at il-
le nivis natus
liquescebat."

De Lantfrido et Cobbone (Sequence)

1a. Omnis sonus cantilene   trifariam fit.
Nam aut fidium concentu sonus constat
pulsu plectri manusve,
ut sunt discrepantie vocum variis
chordarum generibus;

1b. Aut tibiarum canorus   redditur flatus,
fistularum ut sunt discrimina, queque
folle ventris orisque
tumidi flatu perstrepentia pulchre
mentem mulcisonant;

2a. Aut multimodis gutture canoro idem sonus redditur
plurimarum faucium, hominum volucrum animantiumque,
sicque in pulsu guttureque agitur.

2b. His modis canamus carorum sotiorumque actus,
quorum [in] honorem pretitulatur prohemium hocce pulchre
Lantfridi Cobbonisque pernobili stemmate.

3. Quamvis amicitiarum
genera plura legantur,
non sunt adeo preclara
ut istorum sodalium,
qui communes extiterunt
in tantum, ut neuter horum
suapte quid possideret

Modus Liebinc

5a.   After entering his house, he says to his wife: "Console yourself, my wife. Console yourself, my dear. I have lost your son, whom not even you loved more than I.

5b.   "A storm arose and a raving wind drove us, exhausted, into sandbanks full of shoals, where the sun burned all of us fiercely, melting him who was born of the snow."

6.   Thus the Swabian deceived his unfaithful wife. Thus fraud had conquered fraud. And him whom snow engendered, rightly the sun melted.

Lantfrid and Cobbo (Sequence)

1a.   The sound of song is threefold: either it is rhythmic, consisting in the harmony of a cithern, in the beating of a stick or of the hands, so there are dissimilarities in the various accents and in the types of strings;

1b.   Or sound is rendered by wind instruments, the melodious blowing of flutes and other instruments, each distinguished by the use of cheeks, lungs, and mouths, and from full breath beautiful music sounds sweet to the mind;

2a.   Or harmony is created in various ways by the melodious sound of many throats, of men, of birds, and of animals, and thus sound is produced by the hands and by the lungs.

2b.   By these means we should sing about the deeds of our loved ones and of our companions in whose honor is inscribed this pretty prologue: Lantfrid and Cobbo, both of noble stock.

3.   Although one may read about many kinds of friendship, there has never been a more remarkable one than that of these two companions, who experience so much together that neither of them possessed anything as his own,

[nec] gazarum nec servorum
nec alicuius suppellectilis;
alter horum quicquid vellet,
ab altero ratum foret;
more ambo coequales,
in nullo umquam dissides,
quasi duo unus essent,
in omnibus similes.

4.   Porro prior orsus Cobbo
dixit fratri sotio:
"Diu mihi hic regale
incumbit servitium,
quod fratres affinesque
visendo non adeam,
immemor meorum.
Ideo ultra mare revertar,
unde huc adveni;
illorum affectui
veniendo ad illos
ibi satisfaciam."

5.   "Tedet me," Lantfridus inquit,
"vite proprie tam dire,
ut absque te solus hic degam.
Nam arripiens coniugem
tecum pergam exul, tecum,
ut tu diu factus mecum
vicem rependens amori."
Sicque pergentes litora maris
applicarunt pariter.
Tum infit Cobbo sodali:
"Hortor, frater, maneas:
redeam visendo [te]
en vita comite;
unum memoriale
frater fratri facias:

6.   "Uxorem, quam tibi solam
vendicasti propriam,
mihi dedas, ut licenter
fruar eius amplexu."
Nihil hesitando manum
manui eius tribuens hilare:
"Fruere ut libet, frater, ea,
ne dicatur, quod semotim
nisus sim quid possidere."

neither riches nor servants nor household goods of any kind; if one of them should desire anything, it would be guessed at by the other; in this way they were both equal, in nothing ever separate, as if two were one, in all things alike.
4.   Then once Cobbo, the first to speak, says to his brotherly companion, "For a long time this royal service has been a burden on me, for I am not free to visit my brothers and my relatives, and I am forgetful of my own; for that reason I must return beyond the sea whence I came here; by returning to them I shall there gratify their affections."
5.   "My own life," replies Lantfrid, "will be too difficult for me if I have to live alone without you. So taking my wife, with you I shall live as an exile, with you, as you have done with me for a long time, and I will thus repay you for your love." They then proceed to the shores of the sea, equally attached to one another, and Cobbo says to his friend, "I beseech you, brother, stay behind. I will return to visit you—come now, we are friends for life!—[but] you should offer me something to remember you by as a brother to a brother.
6.   "Your wife, whom alone you have repeatedly praised as your own, you should give to me, so that frequently I may enjoy her embraces." Without hesitation Lantfrid gave his hand to the other's hand cheerfully. "Enjoy her as you will, brother, so it may not be said that, separated from you, I relied upon a possession."

Classe tunc apparata
ducit secum in equor.
7.   Stans Lantfridus super litus
cantibus chordarum ait:
"Cobbo frater, fidem tene,
hactenus ut feceras,
nam indecens est affectum
sequendo voti honorem perdere;
dedecus frater fratri ne fiat."
Sicque diu canendo
post illum intuitus,
longius eum non cernens
fregit rupe timpanum.
8.   At Cobbo collisum
fratrem non ferens
mox vertendo mulcet:
"En habes, perdulcis amor,
quod dedisti, intactum
ante amoris experimentum.
Iam non est, quod experiatur ultra;
ceptum iter relinquam."

De Lantfrido et Cobbone (Rhythmic version)

1.   Cum insignium virorum   gesta dictis fulgeant,
dulcibus ecce iam decet   ut modolis clareant,
quatinus illorum facta   fidem nobis augeant.
2.   Sepe namque, que videtur   ociosa cancio,
pura nobis imputatur   fidei devocio,
ceu scolastici ludentes   canimus in timpano.
3.   Quodam tempore fuerunt   duo viri nobiles,
sicut fabule testantur   et scurrarum complices,
unus Cobbo vocabatur   Lantfridus et consodes.
4.   Unus patria de una   natus est nobiliter,
alter ex altera natus   omine flebiliter;
in una domo penetrantes   serviebant pariter.
5.   Primus enim unus horum   dixit, Cobbo nomine:
"Amplius nolo morare,   Lantfride carissime,
sed alterius parebo   dictis, frater obtime.
6.   "Trans maria navigabo: procreant pericula
mei servi et propinqui   in terra domestica;
forsitan illorum sanguis   erit mihi gloria."

When the fleet of ships appeared, Cobbo led her with him to the sea.

7.   Lantfrid, standing upon the shore, sings a song with his cithern: "Brother Cobbo, be faithful, as you have been so far, for the love that merely follows desire is shameful and leads to dishonor; a brother should not disgrace a brother." And thus long singing, Lantfrid watches Cobbo leave, and when he could no longer see him, he breaks his timbrel on a rock.

8.   But Cobbo, afraid that his brother would dash himself to pieces, calms him by soon returning. "Come," he says, "take back what you gave me, for sweet love, untouched, before the deed of love. Now there is nothing to be further proven; I shall abandon my planned voyage."

Lantfrid and Cobbo (Rhythmic Version)

1.   Since the deeds of distinguished men glitter in words, it is fitting, here and now, that they resound in sweet melodies because their actions increase our faith.

2.   For often, we finally judge what seems a useless song as the holy zeal of our faith when we scholars, playing, sing it to a timbrel's beat.

3.   Once upon a time there were two noblemen whom popular stories, told by minstrels, have made well known: one was named Cobbo and the other, his comrade, Lantfrid.

4.   One was born a noble in a certain country; the other was born in unfavorable conditions in another country. Having entered the same court, they served equally well.

5.   Once Cobbo was first to say, "I may no longer stay, dearest Lantfrid, for I must submit to another's commands, best brother.

6.   "I must sail across the sea. My servants and neighbors are stirring up troubles in my native land. Perhaps their blood will be my glory."

7. Primus Cobbo ad Lantfridum   dixit inter epulas:
    "Multas valde tesaurorum   posui divicias,
    quas tibi fieri volo: mihi dono capias."
8. Lantfridus ei respondit: "Meum est hoc facere.
    Tu trans mare me venisti   visitando querere;
    ego tibi multa bona   debeo [rependere]."
9. "Dic mihi, quomodo tu vis   fieri placabilis?"
    . . . .

    "Uxor ad amandum tua   mihi est amabilis."
10. Cuius uxor Segesvita   fulgebat in talamis,
    splendor solis utque lune   rutilat in radiis,
    ac pre cunctis speciosa   videbatur feminis.
11. Cobbo tantum perscrutare   volens amicitiam

    . . . .

    . . . .
12. . . . .

    "nam et ego tesaurorum   posui divicias,
    quas tibi fieri volo: mihi dono capias."
13. Lantfridus enim per manum   uxorem accipiens
    tradidit Cobboni, fidem   illius prospiciens,
    usque ad naves, cum illa   pergeret, egrediens.
14. Cumque in citarizando   accepisset nenias,
    cantico cordarum dixit: "Cobbo, fidem teneas!"
    atque repetebat usque: "Cobbo, fidem teneas!"
15. In occursum quidem suum   cum venissent invicem,
    Lantfrido cum iuramento   suam reddit coniugem:
    "Sine crimine ac firmus   permansi in stabilem."

Heriger

1. Heriger, urbis   Maguntiacensis
    antistes, quendam   vidit prophetam,
    qui ad infernum   se dixit raptum.
2. Inde cum multas   referret causas,
    subiunxit totum   esse infernum
    accinctum densis   undique silvis.
3. Heriger illi   ridens respondit:
    "Meum subulcum   illuc ad pastum
    nolo cum macris   mittere porcis."
4. Vir ait falsus: "Fui translatus
    in templum celi   Christumque vidi
    letum sedentem   et comedentem.

7.   Then Cobbo said to Lantfrid when they were at table: "I have put aside a great deal of my wealth; I want it to become yours. Take what I give you."
8.   Lantfrid replies: "It is *my* duty to do this. You have crossed the sea to live with me. I ought to repay you for the many favors I have received from you.
9.   "Tell me, how would you most like to be pleased?"
. . . .
"You would behave like a true friend if you gave me your wife to enjoy."
10.   Lantfrid's wife, Segesvita, glittered in her room. The brilliance of sun and moon reddens in her rays, and she seemed more splendid than all other women.
11.   Cobbo, wanting to test Lantfrid's friendship
. . . .
. . . .
12.   . . . .
13.   Then Lantfrid, seizing his wife by the hand, delivered her to Cobbo, and paying close attention to his friend's faithfulness, he accompanied them to the ship as his wife was leaving.
14.   Then he sang mournful songs on a harp. As he played he sang, "Cobbo, be faithful!" and often repeated "Cobbo, be faithful!"
15.   Finally when the two friends came back together again, Cobbo returned the woman to Lantfrid and swears: "I have remained true to you, faultless and steadfast."

Heriger

1.   Heriger, Bishop of Mainz, once met a certain boaster who said he was transported to hell.
2.   While this man was describing the many features of hell, he mentioned that all of it was girded by an extremely thick forest.
3.   Laughing, Heriger replied to him, "I'd better not send my swineherd there to feed his lean swine."
4.   The liar continued: "I was also carried to the throne of heaven, and I beheld Christ, joyfully sitting and eating.

5. "Iohannes baptista   erat pincerna
atque preclari   pocula vini
porrexit cunctis   vocatis sanctis."

6. Heriger ait: "Prudenter egit
Christus, Iohannem   ponens pincernam,
quoniam vinum   non bibit umquam."

7. . . . .

8. "Mendax probaris,   cum Petrum dicis
illic magistrum   esse cocorum,
est quia summi   ianitor celi.

9. "Honore quali   te deus celi
habuit ibi?   Ubi sedisti
Volo, ut narres,   quid manducasses."

10. Respondit homo: "Angulo uno;
partem pulmonis   furabar cocis.
Hoc manducavi   atque recessi."

11. Heriger illum   iussit ad palum
loris ligari   scopisque cedi,
sermone duro   hunc arguendo:

12. "Si te ad suum   invitet pastum
Christus, ut secum   capias cibum,
cave ne furtum facias!"

De Iohanne abbate

1. In gestis patrum veterum   quoddam legi ridiculum,
exemplo tamen habile,   quod vobis dico rithmice.

2. Iohannes abba parvulus   statura, non virtutibus,
ita maiori socio,   quicum erat in heremo,

3. "Volo," dicebat, "vivere   secure sicut angelus,
nec veste nec cibo frui,   qui laboretur manibus."

4. Respondit maior: "Moneo,   ne sis incepti properus,
frater, quod tibi postmodum   sit non cepisse sacius."

5. At minor: "Qui non dimicat,   non cadit neque superat!"
ait et nudus heremum   interiorem penetrat.

6. Septem dies gramineo   vix ibi durat pabulo;
octava fames imperat   ut ad sodalem redeat.

7. Qui sero clausa ianua   tutus sedet in cellula,
cum minor voce debili   "Frater," appellat, "aperi!

8. "Iohannes opis indigus   notis assistit foribus;
ne spernat tua pietas,   quem redigit necessitas."

9. Respondit ille deintus: "Iohannes factus angelus
miratur celi cardines,   ultra non curat homines."

5.   "John the Baptist was the cupbearer and offered cups of excellent wine to all the saints who were summoned together."

6.   Heriger replied, "Christ behaved wisely by making John the cupbearer, since the Baptist never drinks wine."

7.   . . . .

8.   "You have proven yourself a liar when you said that Peter is the head cook there, for he is the doorkeeper of those highest gates.

9.   "With what honor did the Lord of heaven entertain you there? Where did you sit? Tell me, what did you eat?"

10.   The man responded, "[I sat] in a corner; I stole a piece of lung from the cook. I ate that, and then I returned [to earth]."

11.   Heriger ordered him to be tied to the stake with rope and to be beaten with broom, all the time reproving him with harsh words:

12.   "The next time Christ invites you to dinner to share his food with you, make sure that you do not steal!"

Brother John

1.   In the tales of our forefathers I read a funny story, yet useful as a moral tale, which I recount to you rhythmically.

2.   Brother John, short in stature but not in virtues, said to his superior, with whom he lived in the monastery,

3.   "I want to live like an angel, free from cares, enjoying neither clothing nor food, the products of manual labor."

4.   The superior replied, "I warn you, brother, do not be o'erhasty beginning something that had sooner not been undertaken."

5.   But the lesser brother retorted, "Nothing lost, nothing gained!" and naked, he enters the inner recesses of the monastery.

6.   He hardly lasts seven days there subsisting on a diet of herbs; on the eighth day hunger overcomes him, so he returns to his cellmate.

7.   His cellmate, meanwhile, sits comfortably in the little cell after closing the door late at night, and John, with a weak voice, calls, "Brother, please open!

8.   "John, needing your help, stands outside the well-known door; may your pity not scorn him whom necessity drives back."

9.   "John has become an angel," the monk inside replied. "He gazes at heaven's gates, no longer thinking about men."

10. Iohannes foris excubat   malamque noctem tolerat
    et preter voluntariam   hanc agit penitentiam.
11. Facto mane recipitur   satisque verbis uritur,
    sed intentus ad crustula   fert patienter omnia.
12. Refocillatus Domino   grates agit ac socio,
    dehinc rastellum brachiis   temptat movere languidis.
13. Castigatus angustia   de levitate nimia,
    cum angelus non potuit,   vir bonus esse didicit.

Sacerdos et Lupus

1. Quibus ludus est animo   et iocularis cantio,
    hoc advertant ridiculum;   est verum, non ficticium.
2. Sacerdos iam ruricola   aetate sub decrepita
    vivebat amans pecudis,   hic enim mos est rusticis.
3. Ad cuius tale studium   omne patebat commodum,
    nisi foret tam proxima   luporum altrix silvula.
4. Hi minuentes numerum   per eius summam generum
    dant impares ex paribus   et pares ex imparibus.
5. Qui dolens sui fieri   detrimentum peculii,
    quia diffidit viribus,   vindictam querit artibus.
6. Fossam cavat non modicam,   intus ponens agniculam,
    et ne pateret hostibus,   superne tegit frondibus.
7. Humano datum commodo   nil maius est ingenio!
    Lupus, dum nocte circuit,   spe prede captus incidit.
8. Accurrit mane presbiter,   gaudet vicisse taliter;
    intus protento baculo   lupi minatur oculo.
9. "Iam," inquit, "fera pessima,   tibi rependam debita.
    Aut hic frangetur baculus,   aut hic crepabit oculus."
10. Hoc dicto simul impulit,   verbo sed factum defuit,
    nam lupus servans oculum   morsu retentat baculum.
11. At ille miser vetulus,   dum sese trahit firmius,
    ripa cedente corruit   et lupo comes extitit.
12. Hinc stat lupus, hinc presbiter   timent, sed dispariliter,
    nam, ut fidenter arbitror,   lupus stabat securior.
13. Sacerdos secum mussitat   septemque psalmos ruminat,
    sed revolvit frequentius   "Miserere mei, Deus!"
14. "Hoc," inquid, "infortunii   dant mihi vota populi,
    quorum neglexi animas,   quorum comedi decimas."
15. Pro defunctorum merito   cantat "Placebo Domino,"
    et pro votis viventium   totum cantat psalterium.
16. Post completum psalterium   commune prestat commodum
    sacerdotis timiditas   atque lupi calliditas.

10. So John must sleep outdoors and endure the harsh night; most unwillingly he undergoes this penance.

11. In the morning he is let in and is criticized by words enough, but intent upon little crumbs, he patiently endures everything.

12. Revived, he gives thanks to the Lord—and to his comrade; immediately he endeavors to move a hoe with his weakened limbs.

13. Checked by necessity, reproved for caprice, John decides, since he could not become an angel, to be a good man.

The Priest and the Wolf

1.   Those who would like to hear a jest and a funny song should listen to this "ridiculum"—it's true, not fiction.

2.   Once there was a country priest who, at a ripe old age, loved his flock [of sheep] and lived a simple life.

3.   Everything would have suited him fine were it not for a small forest, the nurse of wolves, that was nearby.

4.   By their great number these wolves diminished the number of his flock, making odd numbers even and then even numbers odd.

5.   Afraid that he would lose his entire flock, he seeks vengeance by his cunning, for he had no confidence in his strength.

6.   He digs a large pit and places a little lamb within; he covers it with leaves so his enemies would not discover it.

7.   Nothing greater is given to man than his genius! A wolf, wandering at night in hope of prey, fell into the pit, a captive.

8.   In the morning the priest runs to the hole and rejoices that he has thus conquered his enemy.

9.   "Now," he says, "worst of all beasts, I shall repay you what I owe you. Either this stick will break or your eye will rattle."

10. After saying this, he strikes, but the deed fails the word, for the wolf, preserving his eye, holds the stick in his teeth.

11. The old wretch, drawing himself up firmly, falls into the hole when the bank breaks, and he becomes the wolf's companion.

12. Here stands the wolf, there the priest. Each is afraid, but unequally, for I am quite sure that the wolf was the more secure.

13. The priest mutters and ruminates on the seven psalms, and he repeats most frequently, "Pity me, O Lord!"

14. "The prayers of the unfortunate people," he says, "whose souls I have neglected, whose tithes I have eaten, cause this predicament."

15. For the benefit of the dead he sings, "I will be pleasing unto the Lord," and for the prayers of the living he sings the entire psalter.

16. After he completes the psalter, the priest's fear and the wolf's cleverness are presented with a common opportunity.

17. Nam cum acclinis presbiter   perfiniret "Pater noster"
    atque clamaret Domino   "Sed libera nos a malo,"
18. Hic dorso eius insilit   et saltu liber effugit,
    et cuius arte captus est,   illo pro scala usus est.
19. Ast ille letus nimium   cantat "Laudate Dominum"
    ac promittit pro populo   se oraturum amodo.
20. Hinc a vicinis queritur   et inventus extrahitur,
    sed nunquam post devotius   oravit nec fidelius.

Alfrad

1. Est unus locus   Homburh dictus,
   in quo pascebat   asinam Alfrad,
   viribus fortem   atque fidelem.
2. Que dum in amplum   exiret campum,
   vidit currentem   lupum voracem,
   caput abscondit,   caudam ostendit.
3. Lupus accurrit,   caudam momordit;
   asina bina   levavit crura
   fecitque longum   cum lupo bellum.
4. Cum defecisse   vires sensisset,
   protulit grandem   plangendo vocem
   vocansque suam   moritur domnam.
5. Audiens grandem   asine vocem
   Alfrad cucurrit: "Sorores," dixit,
   "cito venite,   me adiuvate!
6. "Asinam caram   misi ad erbam;
   illius magnum   audio planctum;
   spero, cum sevo   ut pugnet lupo."
7. Clamor sororum   venit in claustrum,
   turbe virorum   ac mulierum
   assunt, cruentum   ut captent lupum.
8. Adela namque,   soror Alfrade,
   Rikilam querit,   Agatham invenit,
   ibant, ut fortem   sternerent hostem.
9. At ille ruptis   asine costis
   sanguinis undam   carnemque totam
   simul voravit,   silvam intravit.
10. Illud videntes   cuncte sorores
    crines scindebant,   pectus tundebant,
    flentes insontem   asine mortem.

17. For while the priest, bent over, was finishing the "Pater noster" and exclaiming to God, "And deliver us from evil,"

18. The wolf leaps on his back and, with a jump, escapes free. Thus he used the old man, by whose cunning he was captured, as a ladder.

19. The priest, most joyful, sings "Praise to the Lord" and promises to pray for the people from now on.

20. His neighbors look for him and, once they find him, draw him out [of the pit]. But never again did he pray with more devotion and faith.

Alfrad

1.   There is a place called Homburg where [a num named] Alfrad pastured a she-ass that was strong in body and faithful.

2.   When the ass sallied forth in the full field, she saw a gluttonous wolf running toward her. She hid her head and showed her tail.

3.   The wolf ran toward her and bit off her tail; the ass lifted both legs and battled long with the wolf.

4.   When she felt her strength weakening, she let out a great shout, wailing and calling her lady as she is dying.

5.   Hearing the loud shout of the ass, Alfrad runs forth. "Sisters," she says, "come quickly! Help me!

6.   "I sent my dear ass to the field, and now I hear her loud lamentation. I hope she is beating the fierce wolf."

7.   The shouting of the sisters reaches the cloister. A crowd of men and woman gather to capture the bloodthirsty wolf.

8.   Adela, Alfrad's sister, looks for Rikila and finds Agatha. They went forth to lay low the strong host.

9.   But the wolf, when the ass's sides burst, devoured a river of blood and flesh and entered a forest.

10. Seeing that, all the sisters tore their hair and beat their breasts, bewailing the death of the innocent ass.

11. Denique parvum   portabat pullum;
    illum plorabat   maxime Alfrad,
    sperans exinde   prolem crevisse.
12. Adela mitis,   Fritherun dulcis
    venerunt ambe,   ut Alverade
    cor confirmarent   atque sanarent:
13. "Delinque mestas,   soror, querelas!
    Lupus amarum   non curat fletum;
    Dominus aliam   dabit tibi asinam."

Unibos

1. Rebus conspectis seculi   non satiantur oculi;
    Aures sunt in hominibus   amicae novitatibus.
2. Ad mensam magni principis   est rumor Uniusbovis;
    Praesentatur ut fabula   per verba iocularia.
3. Fiunt cibis convivia,   sed verbis exercitia;
    In personarum drammate   uno cantemus de bove!
4. Natis natus ridiculis   est rusticus de rusticis;
    Natura fecit hominem,   sed fortuna mirabilem.
5. Gravis fati commercio   boves emit pauper homo;
    Sub exemplis agricolae   terram laborat scindere.
6. Eventus per horribiles   nunquam ducit duos boves;
    Nec simul pungit stimulo   nec uno ponit sub iugo.
7. Frustra fortunam vincere   sua certat pauperie;
    Duro fatorum stamine   boves perdit assidue.
8. Sequax unius fit bovis   excoriatis relinquis.
    A vicinis deluditur;   Unusbos miser dicitur.
9. Tristis sors mugientium   bovem rapit novissimum;
    Iam res minor fit elegi   egestate vocabuli.
10. Exinanito nomine,   evacuato bostare,
    Tergus disponit vendere   denudato cadavere.
11. Corpus linquit quadruvio   sumpto bovis amphibalo;
    Super iumenti sellulam   ponit vitae fiduciam.
12. Ad forum postliminii   bovis fert vestem mortui;
    Non tardat se per semitas   dum festinat ad nundinas.
13. Sed ut intrat emporium,   facit venale corium,
    Quod putat magni precii   sicut decorem pallii.
14. Participes commercii   capacitatem corii
    Pedum mensurant terminis   sutorum testimoniis.

12,1 vestem] pestem MS

11. Finally they bore the small animal away. Alfrad wept for her the most, for she hoped to have a distinguished progeny from her.

12. Gentle Adela and sweet Fritherun both came to comfort Alfrad and to cheer her.

13. "Stop your sad complaining, sister! The wolf doesn't care about your bitter tears, and the Lord will give you another ass."

Unibos

1. Men's eyes are never filled enough by the remarkable sights of this world. Their ears are ever eager to hear new tales.

2. As a play with witty words, the story of Unibos is presented at the table of a great prince.

3. There are guests at the feast, a bandying of words. Accompanied by performing actors, let us sing of Unibos!

4. Son of ridiculous sons, he is a peasant from peasants. Nature made the man, but fortune produced wonders.

5. This poor man has bought oxen—they are cruel fate's lot—and imitating farmers, he tries to split the earth.

6. But the worst luck prohibits him from leading two oxen. He never strikes two at once; he never puts two under the same yoke.

7. Vainly he struggles to conquer his destined poverty; he continuously loses oxen, thanks to the coarse thread of the Fates.

8. Now he follows one ox—the others have been skinned. His neighbors, mocking him, call him wretched "One-ox."

9. Bitter destiny deprives him of his last lowing ox. Now things stand worse than his nickname would indicate.

10. With his good name gone and his stalls emptied, he plans to sell the hide once the corpse has been stripped.

11. He leaves the carcass on the crossroad, takes the ox's hide, and places it, his last hope for survival, upon his mule's saddle.

12. He brings the skin of his dead ox to a market beyond the border. Narrow paths do not slow him down as he hurries to the fair.

13. As soon as he enters the marketplace, he offers the skin for sale, thinking it most valuable, like a fine cloak.

14. With shoemakers looking on, merchants measure the breadth of the skin to the tips of the hooves.

15. Unibovem nullus iuvat;   solus pellem magnificat.
    Pro nummis octo tunicam   bovis largitur sordidam.
16. Post expletum commercium   ascendit iumentum suum,
    Distento ventre turgidus   retrorsum vertendo gradum.
17. Omen habens argenteum   intrat lucum frondiferum;
    Qui dum ventris purgat lacum,   nummatum trahit meritum.
18. Anum dum certat tergere,   herbam festinat rumpere,
    Sed herbam vellens repperit,   quod gens avara diligit.
19. De nummis tres sextarios   mox offendit absconditos
    Quos in flaccenti sacculo   ponit mox facto turgido.
20. Super iumentum concitus   totis imponit viribus
    Casu repertas vir opes;   ad paternas redit lares.
21. Reversus saccum disligat;   infantem stultus advocat,
    Quem mittit pro sextario   praepositi iustissimo.
22. Quaerit puer sextarium,   praepositus officium;
    Pandit puer negotium   nimis simplex argenteum.
23. Largitur vas praepositus   infanti donans ocius;
    Unibovem pauperrimum   stupet factum ditissimum.
24. Post tergum vadit pueri   ferentis lancem tritici;
    Massam videt argenteam   fumosam dum lustrat domam.
25. Nummorum visis montibus   dicit complosis manibus:
    "Huius egeni gaudium   est furtum, non commercium.
26. "Non est in musac cesarum   nec corbanan pontificum
    Argenti tantum pretium,   quantum tegit tugurium."
27. Irritatus praeposito   respondet valde livido:
    "Non est hoc furtum noctium,   sed corii commercium.
28. "Post huius regni terminum   sollempne fit emporium;
    Dum data bovis tunica   argenti ridet copia.
29. "Non est mercatum simile   sicut de bovis tergore.
    Exemplum de me paupere   si vis tenere, suscipe!"
30. Post haec ministri publico   conveniunt in trivio,
    Villae maior, praepositus,   templi sacerdos inclitus.
31. Oeconomus attonitus   suis refert comitibus
    Famam novi commercii,   unius questum corii.
32. Tunc gavisus praepositus,   fartus tantis rumoribus,
    Profunda dat suspiria,   cum pompa dicens talia:
33. "Vobis dicam miraculum,   revelabo prodigium,
    Aperiam consilium   celandum saluberrimum.
34. "Si vultis esse divites,   si fortunati, comites,
    Quae sum facturus, facite,   sequenda nunc perpendite!
35. "A nostris tabernaculis   omnis fortuna sterilis
    Descedet per commercium,   commerciorum maximum.

15. None of the offers satisfies Unibos—he alone values the skin highly. Yet for eight cents he sells the shabby hide of his ox.

16. After this deal, Unibos fills his belly, climbs his mule, and heads back home.

17. Chance smiles on him as he enters a thick wood: while relieving himself, he discovers a treasure of coins.

18. In fact, as he seeks to wipe himself, tearing handfuls of grass, under a tuft he finds what greedy people love.

19. He uncovers three bags of silver coins hidden in the grass and soon his saddlebag bulges with them.

20. Using all his strength, he places his newfound wealth on top of the mule and returns to his father's hearth.

21. Back home, the fool unloads his bag and calls for his son, whom he sends to the provost for an accurate measuring device.

22. The boy goes for the measurer. The provost asks about its purpose, and the simpleton reveals the story about the silver.

23. The provost takes out the instrument and gives it to the swift boy. He is amazed that the destitute Unibos is now extremely wealthy.

24. The provost, hurrying behind the boy, who carries the wheat balance, finally perceives a silver mass brightening the smoky cottage.

25. Upon seeing the mountains of coins, the provost, clapping his hands together, exclaims, "This poor man's joy comes from theft, not business.

26. "Neither the emperor's vault nor the pope's coffer conceals as much silver as this cottage."

27. Angry, Unibos replies to the envious provost: "This does not come from stealing in the dark of night, but from the sale of my ox-skin.

28. "Beyond this realm's border is a weekly market. When a seller offers an ox-hide, merchants offer him plenty of silver.

29. "There is no business like selling ox-skins. If you wish to follow my example—a poor man's—then do so."

30. After this the officials—the town mayor, the provost, and the distinguished priest of the church—convene in a public square.

31. The stunned provost, who is treasurer of the church, informs his companions about the news of the recent sale and the enormous profit gained from a single hide.

32. Filled with joyful tidings and sighing deeply, the provost pompously hails his colleagues:

33. "I'll tell you about a miracle and reveal a marvel. Indeed, I'll give you a most useful bit of advice, but you must keep it secret.

34. "If you want to become wealthy and blessed, my friends, follow my advice and do what I shall do.

35. "All evil fortune will depart our houses through a great business deal—the greatest of all deals.

36. "Est mercandi felicitas   quam transmisit divinitas,
    De vitulorum coriis,   de vitularum spoliis.
37. "Hic noster pauper Unibos   habet multos denarios
    Quos non mensurat numero   sed ferrato sextario.
38. "Est fortunatus subito   unius pellis precio,
    Quam vendidit in proximo   eventu felicissimo.
39. "Non est opus sub imbribus   nobis arare amplius
    Si probatis una die   locupletem de paupere.
40. "Sed quod narro commercium   occultum sit per triduum!
    Si trapezetae saperent,   argentum nunquam tunderent.
41. "Est facta demonstratio   commercii de commodo;
    Fiat deliberatio   quid nobis sit in animo!"
42. Ad haec suspirans presbiter   prior respondet impiger,
    Plenus novae letitiae   plus quam possit ostendere.
43. "Si mutaretur in bovem   uxor quam duxi nobilem,
    Pro tanti lucri spe bona   mox careret pellicula."
44. Mox maior villae tertius,   habendi cui non est modus,
    Quae concepit ex fabula,   eructavit prodigia:
45. "Per istum iuro baculum,   per corpus hoc, per spiritum,
    Si ruminant diluculo   mei boves in stabulo . . ."
46. Dextras furtivo foedere   vicissim certant tangere
    Ut clam boves excerebrent,   interfectos excorient.
47. Firmati per stultitiam   procedunt ad insaniam;
    Mactant boves crudeliter   excoriantes acriter.
48. Suspendunt carnes trabibus;   pelles taxant in curribus.
    Quiete noctis tempore   petunt mercatum transfugae.
49. Plaustra pelles vehentia   locant sub arrogantia
    In mercati confinio   inani pleni somnio.
50. Respectum per silentia   vibrant per fori stadia;
    Interpretari sub prece   sperant a multitudine.
51. Vulgus transit, vulgus redit,   nullus sub cura consulit;
    Non est qui quaerat cupide   commercium de tergore.
52. Post intervalla temporum   maior tenendo stimulum
    Clamat in rauco gutture: "Quis vult has pelles emere?"
53. Assunt sutores sordidi,   quibus sunt septem solidi,
    Quibus placet coemptio   uno signato corio.
54. Dicit sutor: "Quantum dabo   hoc pro bovino corio?"
    Respondet maior subito: "Tres libras da continuo!"

39,1 nobis arare] arare nobis MS
43,1 in bovem] unibovem MS
43,2 bona] boni MS

36.   "The Lord brings us the opportunity of selling the skins of our calves and our cows.

37.   "Our poor Unibos has so many silver pieces, he can't measure them without a wheat measurer.

38.   "He is suddenly enriched by selling a single hide, which by happy chance he sold nearby.

39.   "If you agree to become rich instead of poor in a single day, we need no longer plow in the rain.

40.   "But let's keep this business secret for three days, for if the minters should find out, they would never strike silver coins.

41.   "I have described this business opportunity to you. Now let us decide what we shall do."

42.   At this the priest, sighing deeply, eagerly responds first; he is full of a newfound joy—more than he can ever show.

43.   "If the woman I have married could be turned into a fine ox, she would soon lack her little hide in my hope for so much gain."

44.   Then the mayor of the village, whose possessions are immeasurable, having heard the provost's tale, belched forth oaths:

45.   "I swear by this staff, by this body, by this soul, my oxen won't be chewing cud in the stable at dawn."

46.   They eagerly shake hands to seal their secret compact: to behead their oxen and skin the dead animals.

47.   Confirmed in their stupidity, they rush to madness; they savagely slay their oxen and zealously strip them of their hides.

48.   They hang the flesh on beams and stack the skins in their carts. In the deep of night, they go to market like traitors seeking an enemy camp.

49.   Haughty and full of foolish dreams, they place the carts full of skins at the edge of the marketplace.

50.   They glance rapidly and silently around the confines of the marketplace; they expect to do business with an entreating multitude.

51.   People come, people go, and not one shows any interest in the hides; no one eagerly inquires about the skins.

52.   After some time the mayor, brandishing his staff, cries in a hoarse voice, "Who wants to buy these skins?"

53.   Lowly shoemakers who have seven cents approach. They are interested in buying only a single intact hide.

54.   One of them asks, "How much do I have to pay for this ox-hide?" The mayor replies quickly, "Three pounds at once!"

55. Sutor inquit: "Es ebrius!"   Maior ait: "Sim fatuus.
    De tribus libris minimum   non dimittam denarium."
56. Tunc infit sutor setifer: "Dicis ioculariter."
    Econtra maior somnifer: "Tres libras!" clamat firmiter.
57. Vulgaris ammiratio   sonoro mox fit in foro;
    Est vulgus in spectaculis   relictis mercimoniis.
58. Ira commotus presbiter   maiori dicit duriter:
    "Insulse, nescis vendere   quod praesentas hic publice.
59. "Hac hasta discerno meum   trium librorum corium.
    Solve, sutor, marsuppium!   Audisti fixum numerum."
60. Quam mensuram commercii   profert sensus presbiteri.
    Sutor subinfert: "Stultior   non est in terra venditor.
61. "De qua sint hi provincia,   dicant tres in praesentia,
    Qui putant boum tergora   divitiarum maxima!
62. "Decem nummorum corium   ad magnum levant precium.
    Nudis plantis incedite   huius coloni patriae!"
63. Alternat ex obprobriis   utraque pars sub iurgiis;
    Sutorum congregatio   irato crescit animo.
64. Ducuntur a lictoribus,   praesentantur iudicibus,
    Traduntur exactoribus,   corripiuntur legibus.
65. Reddunt per vadimonium   conventionem tergorum
    Quam posuerunt in foro   Unibovis consilio.
66. Persolvunt legis debita,   revertuntur ad propria,
    Exhaustis in marsuppiis,   ociosis in curriculis.
67. Denudati pecunia,   armati tres mestitia
    Conantur interficere   Unibovem meridie.
68. Infra caeli tentoria   non sunt audita talia,
    Quae perpetravit Unibos,   ut sedaret stultissimos.
69. Versutus mites reddidit   ut tres iratos respicit;
    Insania prudentia   respondent per ludibria.
70. Mori dum tremens aestimat,   occasionem simulat
    Mortem pingens in coniuge   tincta suillo sanguine.
71. Uxor dolosi sub dolo   strata iacet tugurio
    Quasi sit vere mortua,   occisa sponsi dextera.
72. Cadaver foedum sanguine   corpus apparet feminae;
    Crudeles mansuescere   incipiunt pro crimine.
73. Qui venerant occidere   certant percussam plangere,
    Increpantes Unibovem   flendo mactatam coniugem.

55,1 Sim] sum MS
57,2 in spectaculis] inspectaculis MS
59,1 librorum] librarum MS
70,2 tincta] tinctam MS

55. The shoemaker replies, "You must be crazy." "Maybe I am," replies the mayor, "but I will not budge a penny under three pounds."

56. Then the surly shoemaker says, "You're joking," and in reply the mayor, still sleepy, says steadily, "Three pounds."

57. Filled with surprise, the people in the crowded marketplace soon leave their goods aside to attend the show.

58. The priest, moved to anger, says sternly to the mayor: "Fool, you don't know how to drive a bargain with the merchandise you offer these people.

59. "I swear by this staff that my hide is worth three pounds. Open your purse, shoemaker—you have heard the required sum."

60. The priest is endowed with such business know-how that the shoemaker replies, "There is not a stupider salesman on the face of the earth.

61. "Let these three men, who think ox-hides are the greatest riches, tell us here and now what country they are from.

62. "They value ten-cent hides at the highest price. People from that country must walk barefoot!"

63. Each side exchanges reproaches and insults; the group of shoemakers becomes increasingly irritated.

64. Finally, the three fools are led away by bailiffs and presented to judges; they are led before overseers and rebuked according to the laws.

65. As a fine they must give up all of the hides that they put on sale on Unibos' advice.

66. They pay off the legal fines and return home with empty purses and vacant carts.

67. Stripped of money but full of resentment, they decide to kill Unibos at high noon.

68. Never has such a deed as Unibos performed to soothe the stupid threesome been seen under heaven.

69. The sly Unibos is able to render the three angry men gentle when he sees them; craftiness counters madness with a trick.

70. Trembling, thinking he is about to die, he devises a plan: he paints his wife deathly red with swine blood.

71. The crafty man's wife lies apparently dead in the cottage, as if she had been killed by her husband.

72. The woman's body is like a corpse caked with blood; seeing this atrocity, the cruel men forget their anger.

73. Those who came to kill now lament the beaten woman, and as they lament the slaughtered wife, they reproach Unibos.

74. Simul dicunt ferociter: "Heus, insensate compater,
    Qua causa tu durissima   perpetrasti facinora?
75. "Confusionis trux faber   nos seduxisti nequiter;
    Ut mercatum probavimus,   mortem tuam tractavimus.
76. "Magnum damnum, stultissime,   adquisisti de coniuge;
    Non est culpa mediocris   vitam fugasse coniugis."
77. Inquit securus Unibos   magis seducens tres viros:
    "Sanabile flagitium   perpetravi per gladium.
78. "Si mecum pacem facitis,   si cordis iram rumpitis,
    Vivam cito videbitis,   interfectam quam cernitis."
79. "Fiat, fiat!" hilariter   dicunt seducti pariter:
    "Repellimus a pectore   pestes inimicitiae."
80. Dum sic perpendit Unibos   loqui tres adversarios,
    Ad cistam currit ligneam   sumens salignam bucinam.
81. Lustrat cadaver coniugis   sub testibus erroneis;
    Bis lustrat, saepe bucinat,   horam surgendi praedicat.
82. Lustratione tertia   tamquam virtute mistica
    Dum nomen sponsae nominat,   quiescentem resuscitat.
83. Exurgens uxor impetu   astat deformis habitu;
    Iubetur ab Unibove   ut se mundet a sanguine.
84. Confestim lota facie,   induta meliuscule,
    Apparet speciosior,   vultu mundato pulchrior.
85. Seducti per Unibovem   mirantur pulchritudinem
    Resuscitatae feminae,   stupentes illam plaudere.
86. Dicunt suppressis vocibus: "Nunquam tam pulchram vidimus
    Istius formam feminae,   quae surrexit in hac die.
87. "Ante mortem turpis fuit;   de morte pulchra rediit.
    Felix mors, quae pulchrificat,   quae deformes condecorat!
88. "Quam felix sonus bucinae   qua renovantur vetulae!
    Sponsae nostrae decrepitae   pro multo fiunt tempore.
89. "Si nos divina gratia   honoraret hac bucina,
    Occideremus coniuges   pro rugis detestabiles.
90. Precemur hunc Unibovem   ut nobis praestet ad vicem
    Vel ut vendat hanc bucinam   quae turpem tollit maculam!
91. "Tubam certemus emere   ut sponsas interficere
    Uno possimus tempore   ornandas pulchritudine.
92. "Cum resonabit bucina,   fugabitur mors aspera
    Sicut in hac probavimus,   exanimem quam vidimus.
93. "Facturi sumus alteras   de redivivis nuptias.
    Offeramus pecuniam   ut nobis vendat bucinam!"
94. Oblato magno munere   tubam merentur emere;
    Post comparatam bucinam   vertuntur in insaniam.

90,1 Precemur hunc Unibovem] Precemur unibovem MS

74. Together, they shout wildly: "Why, unfeeling man, why did you commit this dastardly crime?

75. "Wicked sower of confusion, you evilly seduced us; however, just as we agreed upon our unfortunate business venture, we have agreed upon your death.

76. "And because of your wife, fool, you shall receive the greatest punishment: murdering one's wife is not a venial sin."

77. Confident, Unibos speaks and tricks the threesome yet more: "This crime, which I committed with a sword, is in fact curable.

78. "If you make peace with me, if you quell the anger in your hearts, you will see this woman, whom you now perceive dead, come back to life."

79. "So be it! So be it!" the three men, equally deceived, exclaim gladly. "We shall remove our sworn hatred from our breasts."

80. After sizing up his three babbling enemies, Unibos runs to a wooden chest and takes out a willow flute.

81. While the fools observe him, he circles his wife's corpse. Twice he circles, and while playing the instrument continuously, he foretells the moment of her resurrection.

82. With the great powers of a magician, on the third pass he revives his wife from her sleep at the exact moment he utters her name.

83. Rising promptly, his wife, horrible in appearance, stands before the threesome; Unibos then orders her to wash off the blood.

84. When her face is washed and she is better clothed, she immediately seems most beautiful, comelier of face and limbs.

85. The fools, tricked by Unibos, marvel at the beauty of the revived woman. Astonished, they nonetheless voice their approval.

86. With hushed voices they say: "We have never seen this woman, who has just now been revived, appear so beautiful.

87. "Before her death she was ugly, but from death she returned fair. Blessed is the death that beautifies and improves the unsightly!

88. "How sweet the sound of the flute that rejuvenates old women! Our own wives have also been decrepit for a long time.

89. "If this flute would bestow some of its miraculous power upon us, we could also kill our wives and their cursed wrinkles.

90. "Let us beg Unibos to lend it to each one of us, or perhaps he might sell us this flute that removes ugly age spots.

91. "Let's try purchasing this flute so we may kill our wives and later have them adorned with beauty.

92. "When we play the flute, cruel death will fly away, just as it did with this woman whom we saw dead.

93. "With rejuvenated wives, we shall celebrate second nuptials. Let us offer Unibos money so he will give us his flute."

94. They manage to buy the horn once they have offered much money, and after their purchase, they turn their minds to madness.

95. Duobus dicit presbiter: "Oro, precor, sollempniter,
Ut primus interficiam   sponsam mihi carissimam.
96. "En, praestetur gratissima   mihi vitalis bucina!
Minorabo per iugulum   presbiterissae senium.
97. "Post me secundus bucinam   assumet saluberrimam
Qui prior suam feminam   occidet sicut vitulam."
98. Petitiones annuunt   sacerdotis quem diligunt
Ut occidat, ut iugulet,   ut occisam resuscitet.
99. It sacerdos cum bucina   armatus ex insania;
Moriturae dat basia   stricta coma feminea.
100. Cultellum monstrat presbiter;   ridendo dicit mulier:
"Quid vultis, care, facere?   Nolite dure facere!"
101. Sacerdos ait loetifer: "Te iugulabo dulciter;
In iuvenili corpore   resurges voce bucinae."
102. Solum "Vae!" clamat femina,   percussa iacet mortua;
Stultus paterfamilias   exclamat: "Deo gratias!"
103. Apponit ori bucinam,   sufflat per arrogantiam;
Dum ter iacentem circuit,   obscenis verbis arguit:
104. "O simulatrix callida,   surge, dolosa simia!
Petulca sicut asina   leva caput de bucina!"
105. Auditis his clamoribus   amens suam praepositus
Festinat interficere   sub spe vitalis bucinae.
106. Ad orbatum presbiterum   venit post homicidium
Ut sibi praestet bucinam   qua suscitet praepositam.
107. Tandem recepta bucina   sacerdotem de femina
Interrogat hac mortua,   si surrexit iuvencula.
108. Interroganti dicitur: "Haec a te non videbitur
Donec limen ecclesiae   tua petet cum coniuge."
109. Sponsaecida praepositus,   privatus mentis sensibus,
Ad domum portat propriam   seductionis bucinam.
110. Nunquam sacerdos altius   mestis tubae mugitibus
Bucinavit profundius   quam fatuus praepositus.
111. Quantum tubae concavitas,   tantum prodest ventositas:
Ut revixit presbitera,   sic surrexit praeposita.
112. Maior villae non est minor   in reatu, si tardior,
Qui sponsae vitam dissipat,   qui bucinat, non suscitat.
113. Tres glebulae, tres mortuae·   praesentantur ecclesiae
Orto tristi diluculo   cum lugubri spectaculo.
114. Sponsorum sub insania   infossantur cadavera;
Tres occultantur coniuges   per threnas lamentabiles.

107,2 hac] ha MS
113,1 glebulae] gebulae MS

95. The priest says to his companions: "I pray, I solemnly beg of you, to let me be the first to kill my dear wife.

96. "Come now, this resuscitating flute should bring me great happiness. First, however, I will end my wife's old age by slitting her throat.

97. "After me, one of you, having first killed his wife like a heifer, will play this rejuvenating flute."

98. The other two, who adore the priest, agree to his request that he kill, murder, and resuscitate the dead woman.

99. Excited by such foolishness, the priest takes off with the flute. He kisses his wife, who soon must die, and he touches her hair lightly.

100. When the priest shows his wife the knife, she says to her smiling husband, "What are you planning, dear? Don't do anything wicked."

101. The murderous priest replies: "I will strangle you gently, and then you will arise in a youthful body when I play this flute."

102. The wife emits a single "alas!" before she falls down dead, and the foolish husband cries out his thanks to God.

103. He places the flute to his lips and plays presumptuously, but after circling the prostrate body of his wife three times, he begins to curse her offensively.

104. "Come on, you sly faker! Get up, you little monkey! Stubborn as a mule, raise your head to the sound of this flute!"

105. At the moment the priest's shouts are heard, the foolish provost is in the act of killing his wife, hoping to revive her with the life-giving flute.

106. And after the murder, he visits the newly widowed priest to receive the flute that he believes will resuscitate his own wife.

107. When he finally gets the flute, he asks the priest about his dead wife—did she arise as a young girl?

108. The priest replies to the provost: "You will not see my wife until she arrives at the church door with your wife."

109. The wife-killing provost, taking leave of his senses, carries the trickster's flute to his own house.

110. Never did a cleric, with sad bellowings of horn, play more clearly, more deeply, than the foolish provost.

111. His playing, however, is as profitable to him as the empty air within the flute. Just as the priest's wife had revived, so arose the provost's.

112. The town's mayor is not the least, although the last, in committing the crime. He takes his wife's life and plays, but she does not arise either.

113. The three dead women, now mere clay, arrive at the church as the sad dawn arises over the mournful procession.

114. After this lunacy, the corpses are buried, lowered into the graves to the tune of mournful dirges.

115. Discedentes a tumulis   in profundis suspiriis
     Tres susurrant adinvicem: "Occidamus Unibovem,
116. "Qui gazas nostras sustulit,   suis verbis nos tradidit,
     Dum dixit iuvenescere   anus mugitu bucinae!
117. "Auctor tanti periculi   a nobis possit conteri;
     Eius invadat verticem   amara mors ignobilem!"
118. Mentis commoti fluctibus   ad arma currunt protinus
     Artificem versutiae   occisuri durissime.
119. Calliditas Unibovis   plena multis ingeniis
     Superavit iactantiam   trium virorum fervidam.
120. Ad suos currit Unibos   quondam pauper denarios.
     Massam de nummis accipit;   armatos hostes decipit.
121. Equam trahit de stabulo,   caudam levat plus solito;
     In naturae foramine   nummos certat inmergere.
122. In medio tugurio   equae firmatur statio;
     Mox iumento candidum   expandit unum linteum.
123. In foribus tugurii   adsunt tres adversarii;
     Dum minantur Unibovem,   causam vident mirabilem.
124. Tres stant in domus limine   volentes interficere
     Unibovem, sed non valent,   de novo facto dum stupent.
125. Observantes officium   Unibovis argenteum,
     Qui costas equae dum fricat,   partum nummorum provocat.
126. Exclamant: "Quid est, Unibos,   quod iumentum denarios
     Aperte tibi parturit,   miram causam nobis parit?"
127. Caute respondet Unibos: "Videtis hos denarios?
     Fundit nummos huius equae   venter pro vili stercore.
128. "Per noctes equa singulas   tales iactat pecunias,
     Obs, regina pecuniae,   ani sedet foramine."
129. Repente visis talibus,   auditis his sermonibus,
     Hostes iram reiciunt,   Unibovi sic inquiunt:
130. "Si de fortuna gaudeas,   vende nobis hoc animal!
     Deponemus tres odium   si comparamus turgidum."
131. Vestitus tegnis Unibos   ad tres hoc dicit socios:
     "Non est hanc dare facile   genitricem pecuniae.
132. "Huius sub pelle bestiae   arca latet laetitiae;
     Non est hec vilis bestia   quae tanta parit munera."
133. "Si de tua substantia   tua laetetur anima,"
     Illi dicunt, "carissime,   ne differas hanc vendere!"
134. Versipellis mox Unibos   ad brutos dicit tres viros:
     "Iumentum vendam nobile,   sed non pro parvo munere.
135. "Vos vidistis, quid peperit;   cognoscitis, quid hic pluit.
     Si nummorum latibulum   vultis, conferte precium!
136. "Sed ut sitis benivoli,   conferte libras quindecim!
     Plures in brevi tempore   libras reddet pro stercore."

115. Leaving the graves, the three lunatics, sighing deeply, whisper to each other, "Let's kill Unibos,

116. "Who took our money and then tricked us when he said that an old woman could be rejuvenated by the lowing of a flute.

117. "We should destroy the author of such mischief—let a cruel death fall upon his peasant head!"

118. Mentally unbalanced, they rush forth and gather arms to kill the master of stratagem.

119. But Unibos' cleverness, brimming ever with new tricks, again overcomes the angry threats of the three men.

120. The once-poor Unibos runs to his coins, grabs a mass of them, and succeeds in tricking the armed host.

121. He draws his mare from the stable, lifts her tail quite high, and plunges the coins into nature's opening.

122. He makes the mare stand in the middle of the cottage and then spreads a white linen cloth over the beast.

123. His three enemies, standing outside the hut and threatening Unibos, witness a marvelous event.

124. Standing on the threshold, they want to kill Unibos, but they are stunned into inaction by the new event.

125. They observe Unibos working over some silver coins: while rubbing the mare's flanks, he seems to produce a quantity of coins.

126. They exclaim, "What is this, Unibos? What is this beast that is clearly producing coins for you and a marvel for us?"

127. Unibos replies cautiously: "See these coins? This mare's belly excretes coins instead of worthless dung.

128. "Every night she pours out such wealth that surely Ops, the queen of abundance, must sit at this opening."

129. Once they see the money and hear the story, the anger of Unibos' enemies immediately abates, and they say to him:

130. "Enjoy your good fortune and sell us this animal! If you do, we three shall end our hatred once we have bought this swollen beast."

131. Unibos, full of tricks, says this to the three friends: "It's not easy just giving away this source of wealth.

132. "There is a wonderful treasure chest hidden in this beast's hide; surely this animal, which bestows such gifts, is not a cheap one."

133. "If you wish to delight further in your great wealth," they threaten, "my dearest Unibos, no longer delay selling the mare to us."

134. The crafty Unibos then says to the senseless three: "I'll sell you my noble beast, but not for a small price.

135. "You see what it has produced, and you know what it has showered. If you want a coin-ladened treasure chest, you must pay the price!

136. "Give me fifteen pounds—may you be so kind. In a short time my beast will repay your pounds in kind instead of excrement."

137. Tres illi libras quindecim   ut persolvunt Unibovi,
     Equam ducunt ligamine   custodientes cupide.

138. Festinus inquit presbiter: "Audite me, sicut decet!
     Iumentum volo ducere   ad stabulum domus meae.

139. "Qui sum primus ecclesia,   sim primus in custodia;
     Diluculo recolligam   quam donavi pecuniam!

140. "Sit prima nox presbiteri,   secunda sit praepositi,
     Maioris nox sit tertia   sub aequitatis trutina!"

141. "Fiat," dicit praepositus;   "Sit," dicit maior tertius.
     "Haec est nostra concordia   sub miti patientia!"

142. Equam procurat presbiter   dans hordeum celeriter.
     Per nocturnas vigilias   equae praebet auriculas.

143. Facto tamen diluculo   sacerdos a praesepio
     Communem trahit bestiam,   ut deponat pecuniam.

144. Illa putans ad aratrum   deduci sibi cognitum
     Sub cauda laxat squibulas,   sicut solet, foedissimas.

145. Dum stercoris quassatio   auditur a presbitero,
     Nummos putat procedere   ex alvo brutae bestiae.

146. Clamat sacerdos: "Pueri,   abscendite, domestici!
     Solus meam recolligam,   quam donavi pecuniam."

147. Cum sacerdos scrutinium   per fimum facit foetidum,
     Unum minutum repperit   quod festinanter accipit.

148. Iumentum cum sex mensium   olim fuisset parvulum,
     Vulnus suscepit stipite   ani tenelli limine.

149. Ibi minutum substitit,   in cicatrice latuit,
     Equa cum nummos reddidit,   quos Unibos subintulit.

150. Illa scrobs alti vulneris   invenienti profuit
     Dum commovit pecuniam   inclinus hordeaceam.

151. Est vulgare proverbium: "Quod non prosit, non est malum";
     Ani lesi molestia   presbitero dat gaudia.

152. Praepositus per studium   sacerdotis petit domum,
     Ructatricem pecuniae   certans mane requirere.

153. "Iumentum praesta, presbiter!   Ex una nocte locuples
     Manebis omni tempore   nummorum multitudine."

154. "Dedam equam, praeposite,"   dicit sacerdos tepide.
     "Intempestive reddere   equam me cogis hodie.

155. "Aurorae gallicinio   exierunt ab utero
     Male cocti denarii,   recentes, hordeacei."

156. Cum magnis potentatibus   equam ducit praepositus;
     Idem tamen quod presbiter   praeter minuta possidet.

157. Iumentum nocte tertia   maior claudit domo sua
     Reperturus diluculo   quod fetebat in angulo.

152,2 certans] certam MS

137. After paying Unibos fifteen pounds, the threesome lead the mare away with a rope, greedily guarding it.

138. The priest speaks eagerly: "Listen to me, you must! I want to be the first to lead the beast to my house-stable.

139. "Since I am the foremost member of the church, I should be the first to keep it. At dawn I shall collect the money I have given Unibos.

140. "Let the first night be mine, the second the provost's, and the third the mayor's, according to the scale of equity."

141. "So be it," says the provost. "Yes," adds the mayor.   "This is our agreement. Let us be patient."

142. The priest cares for the mare, giving it barley. His ears are cupped toward the mare during his nocturnal vigil.

143. When morning comes, the priest leads the shared beast from its stall so it may deposit the money.

144. Thinking she's being led to her familiar plow, she lets go a foul apple, as she is wont, from beneath her tail.

145. When the priest hears the dung's splatter, he believes that coins are coming from the heavy beast's belly.

146. The priest cries, "Houseboys, leave! I alone will gather up the money I have given."

147. When the priest has examined the filthy pile, he discovers a tiny coin, which he quickly picks up.

148. Long ago, when the beast was a six-month-old filly, it wounded its anus on a tree stump.

149. In that scar a small coin hid itself and stood firm while the mare emitted the other coins Unibos had placed there.

150. The deep wound profited the prospector as, bending down, he loosened the barley money.

151. There is a popular proverb: "What is not good is not necessarily bad." The annoying wound gives the priest joy.

152. The provost, meanwhile, joyously seeks the priest's house in the morning, hoping to procure in his turn the belcher of wealth.

153. "Give me the beast, priest. After this one night you should be forever rich with innumerable coins."

154. The priest replies lukewarmly, "I'll give you the mare, provost, but you force me to give the mare up prematurely on this day.

155. "At the break of dawn, only underdone coins, mostly barley, came out of its belly."

156. Nevertheless, with much authority the provost leads the mare away, but he gets the same thing the priest did, with the exception of the small coin.

157. On the third night the mayor likewise stables the beast, and at dawn he also finds a stinking pile in a corner.

158. Comedit hordeaceum   equa communis pabulum,
     Quae stercus foetoriferum   horis concepit noctium.
159. Quid sit facturus Unibos   contra commotos aemulos
     Meditatur in lectulo   frequenti cum suspirio.
160. Conveniunt cum turbine   ferrata tres in acie,
     Post nocturnam caliginem   adeuntes Unibovem.
161. Viri clamant tres pariter: "Exi, sceleste fraudifer!
     Occidende crudeliter   mactaberis carnaliter."
162. Respondet adversariis   qui quaeritur sub stipulis:
     "Praesto sum vester Unibos;   vos meos dico dominos.
163. "Si vultis interficere   quem quaeritis durissime,
     Vobis narrabo quomodo   perire velim subito.
164. "Sunt mortis multa genera,   unum finem dant omnia;
     Ut vobis satisfaciam,   modum mortis mox eligam.
165. "Quae mors fiat amarior   in mundo sive tristior,
     Nunquam probastis, domini,   nec probetis, dulcissimi.
166. "Dicam tamen pacifice   qua ratione perdere
     Me possitis in hac die   aut cras futuro tempore.
167. "Ligate me de funibus   aut de contortis restibus;
     In apotheca mittite   in qua me missum claudite!
168. "A doctis carpentariis   stringatur tonna circulis;
     Tonnam cum meo corpore   ad mare magnum volvite!
169. "Cum tonna me dimergite,   ad abyssum transmittite;
     Hac arte me confundite!   sic peream me iudice."
170. "Fiat tibi," tres inquiunt,   "hoc mentes nostrae cupiunt,
     Ut tali morte pereas,   a nobis ut sic exeas."
171. Nectunt loris Unibovem   in terra detestabilem
     Qui, postquam tonna clauditur,   in ripa maris sistitur.
172. Clausus sic fatur Unibos   magis seducens tres viros:
     "Confiteor hic hodie,   reclusus sum iustissime.
173. "In agone iudicii   sum constitutus ultimi;
     Propter diem novissimum   deponite nunc odium!
174. "Miser manus erigere   in hoc non possum carcere;
     Heu, lumbos vexant brachia   per maledicta vincula.
175. "Pietatis viatico,   apothecae spiraculo
     Mendacium non profero,   caritatem pronuntio.
176. "Bisseni sunt denarii   in fundo mei loculi
     Quos bibite, piissimi,   ad honorem summi dei!"
177. Caritativus presbiter   fatetur temporaliter:
     "Donec bibamus dulciter,   in tonna dormi dulciter!"
178. Tres festinant ad pocula   bibituri precamina;
     Sedent, loquuntur nimium,   bibunt vinum clarissimum.

158. The shared mare had eaten a meal of barley and engendered only bad-smelling dung during the night.

159. Meanwhile, Unibos, sighing frequently in his bed, worries about what he should do with his enraged and envious rivals.

160. These three assemble like a whirlwind, assume proper battle formation, and finally approach Unibos' house once night's darkness has dissipated.

161. All three then call out together: "Come out, you filthy liar! We shall butcher you most cruelly; shortly, we'll cut you to pieces."

162. Hidden under his straw mat, Unibos replies to his enemies: "Here I am, your Unibos, and I call you my lords.

163. "Before you kill me, whom you seek most keenly, let me first tell you how I should prefer to die a quick death.

164. "There are many ways of being killed, but all lead to the same end. So, in order to meet your ends and mine, why not let me choose the manner of my death?

165. "Surely, my lords, you would not approve, nor indeed should you, my dear friends, that I should undergo too bitter or too cruel a parting from this life.

166. "I, however, will reveal to you peaceably how you should destroy me, either today or at a future time.

167. "Tie me up with rope, bind it tightly around me, get a barrel, and shut me up in it.

168. "The barrel should be sealed with bands by skilled coopers; then, with my body inside, throw the barrel into the mighty sea.

169. "Carry me out to the deep sea and sink me and the barrel. In this way you destroy me, and I die according to my wishes."

170. "Let it be as you wish," the three say. "We also desire that you perish such a death and thus depart from this world."

171. They bind Unibos, the most detested man on earth, with cords. Afterward he is enclosed in a barrel and placed on a cliff near the sea.

172. From inside, Unibos, deceiving the three men as usual, says the following: "I confess, here and now, that I have been imprisoned most righteously.

173. "Indeed, I am now ready to meet my last judgment. My lords, on behalf of this new beginning, please end your hatred now.

174. "Miserable that I am, I cannot free my hands in this prison. The cursed cords, alas, torment my arms and legs.

175. "As a result of your charity, of these last rites kindly given, I can no longer lie to you as I speak from this barrel—I must demonstrate my love of you.

176. "There are twelve coins at the bottom of my money box. Buy drinks, my kind fathers, and toast to the Lord Almighty!"

177. The priest, now turned a loving man, speaks in a courteous manner: "While we drink sweet wine, sleep sweetly in this barrel."

178. The three hurry to their cups to make holy toasts. They sit and they talk while they drink a fine wine.

179. It cum porcinis gregibus   sonoris grunnientium,
     Subulcus transit pervius   in pharetratis renibus.
180. Dum porcos audit Unibos   tonnae fricare circulos,
     Exclamat: "Adversarii,   ah, non sunt adhuc ebrii."
181. Horret subulcus de sono   Unibovis incognito;
     Vas quernum tangit baculo   dicens incluso misero:
182. "Pro quo clausus es crimine   in apotheca, perdite?"
     Prompte respondet Unibos: "Honores nolo maximos.
183. "Huius coloni patriae   me compellunt cotidie
     Me volentes efficere   praepositum potentiae.
184. "Ergo nunquam praepositus   ero meis aetatibus,
     Nam sufficit quod habeo;   honores regni renuo."
185. Subulcus inquit cupidus: "Me decet honor maximus;
     Ego pro te praepositus   efficiar ditissimus.
186. "Compulsus sum fataliter   apothecam tuam, miser,
     Hoc fuste meo tangere.   Certa me tonna ponere!"
187. Subulcus pellit circulos,   multum laetatur Unibos.
     Aperitur vas ligneum;   fit fortunae commercium.
188. Eicitur, dissolvitur,   festinanter dimittitur;
     Duris fit liber vinculis   qui iacuit sub circulis.
189. Subulcus intrat concavum   vas aptans corpus proprium
     Quasi sentiret lectulum   de floribus compositum.
190. Trux vas opturat Unibos;   strictim reponit circulos.
     Per locos transit invios   ducens porcos pinguissimos.
191. Reversis potatoribus   tres de potationibus,
     Dum tonnam volvunt in mare,   audet subulcus dicere:
192. "Fiam, fiam praepositus   sub vestris voluntatibus;
     Maris ne iacter fluctibus   a vobis iam edomitus."
193. Plenus vino praepositus   in indignationibus
     Subulco dixit simplici: "Non est haec vox dulcis mihi.
194. "Tonnam certate volvere,   o socii, certissime.
     Fit fluctuum praepositus   hic Unibos nequissimus."
195. In ponto salso mergitur,   apotheca colliditur,
     Subulcus, heu, conteritur,   a cunctis obliviscitur.
196. Fatuitatis divites   tres persolvisse compares
     Existimant novissimas   Unibovis exequias.
197. Post haec in die tertia   sollempni tamen feria
     Visitaturus fatuos   redit magistros Unibos.
198. It per villae quadruvium   tenens in dextra baculum,
     Porcorum multitudinem   deducens ante faciem.
199. Distente prudens bucinat,   subulci more sybilat,
     Rufos cum furvis convocat,   dente laedentes territat.

199,2 furvis] fursis MS

179. Meanwhile a swineherd passes by the barrel with a herd of swine grunting noisily. With arrows in his quiver, he crosses the road toward it.

180. When Unibos hears the pigs rubbing against the barrel's bands, he exclaims, "Oh no! My enemies decided not to get drunk!"

181. The swineherd shudders at the mysterious sound coming from the barrel. He taps the oaken vessel with his stick and says to the imprisoned Unibos:

182. "For what crime, O lost soul, are you enclosed in this barrel?" Unibos replies readily: "I refused the highest honors.

183. "The people of this country urge me daily to become their leading provost.

184. "But never in my life will I become their provost, for what I have suffices me, and I reject the honors of this world."

185. The greedy swineherd answers, "Great honors, however, well befit me. I, taking your place, could become a wealthy provost.

186. "Indeed, fate must have driven me, you wretch, to tap your barrel with my staff. Now help me put myself in the barrel instead of you!"

187. The swineherd dislodges the bands while Unibos greatly rejoices. The wooden barrel is finally opened, and the business of Lady Luck is done.

188. Unibos is pulled out, untied, and quickly released. Now he is free of fetters, free of the bands that once held him.

189. The swineherd enters the hollow barrel in Unibos' place and adjusts his own body as if he were settling upon a little bed of flowers.

190. Unibos seals up the wooden barrel and replaces the bands firmly. Then leading the fat pigs away, he enters a trackless waste.

191. When the three bibblers return from drinking and begin to roll the barrel seaward, the swineherd boldly says:

192. "All right, I'll be your provost. I give in to your wishes. So don't throw me into the sea! I am ruled by your desires!"

193. The provost, full of wine, replies indignantly to the swineherd: "I don't find those words very amusing.

194. "Let's roll this barrel, O comrades, with strong hands. Let this wicked Unibos become provost of the waves."

195. The barrel is thrown in the salty sea. There is it dashed apart, and the swineherd, alas, is destroyed. No one remembers him.

196. All three men, still rich in foolishness, think they have finally paid their due to the dead Unibos.

197. But three days later, at a weekly fair, Unibos returns to visit his foolish masters.

198. He enters the center of the town holding a staff in his right hand and leading a multitude of pigs in front of him.

199. He plays his horn fully and carefully, and whistling like a swineherd, he calls together the red and the dark pigs and prods the alarmed animals with his prong.

200. Qui viderant Unibovem   eius dicebant similem,
     De quo fama volaverat   quod mortuus iam fuerat.
201. Nuntiatur praeposito,   maiori cum presbitero,
     Quod Unibos revixerit   in ponto qui mersus fuit.
202. Tres illi surgunt stupidi   famam credentes somnii,
     Suis quassantes genibus   subsellia poplitibus.
203. Formam vident Unibovis   procini ductricem gregis.
     Ipsum sed esse non putant;   occidisse putaverant.
204. Recognoscunt Unibovem;   vident porcorum divitem.
     Interrogant, quis dederit   tot porcos aut vendiderit.
205. Respondet sub prodigio: "Maris praecipitatio,
     Ad regnum felicissimum   ivi per praecipitium.
206. "Inde nunquam recederem   si non amassem coniugem
     Quam vidistis resurgere   veracis tubae murmure.
207. "Non fuit culpa bucinae,   sed bucinantis pessime,
     Omnes si vestrae feminae   modo sternunt sub pulvere.
208. "Heu, cur in pueritia   me non iactastis ad loca,
     Unde felix regredior,   revertor eruditior?
209. "Me iactastis per odium   ad propitiatorium,
     Ubi porcorum sunt greges   per nullum numerabiles."
210. Sub ammirationibus   prius dicit praepositus:
     "Nos pernarum spes optima   monet temptare maria.
211. "Me quisquis erit stultior,   parebit," dicit stultior.
     Petunt fluctus aequoreos   post quos incedit Unibos.
212. Motus marini personant,   grunnire porcos estimant;
     Requirunt ab Unibove   qua sint porcinae semitae.
213. Sed Unibos periculum   dicens designat pessimum:
     "Ubi litus est altius,   ubi mare profundius,
214. "Illuc festini currite;   sine metu vos mergite!
     Maiores porci sunt aquis   quam sint in terris aridis."
215. Unibovis consiliis   tres dant se praecipitiis;
     Sub capitali frenesi   per saltum stulte mortui.
216. Inimici consilia   non sunt credenda subdola,
     Ostendit ista fabula   per seculorum secula.

200. Those who see him say he looks just like Unibos, whose recent death is now a matter of gossip.

201. The provost, the mayor, and the priest learn that Unibos, whom they had thrown into the sea, has been resurrected.

202. Thinking he is a ghost, they spring up stunned, and their knees and hams shake the benches.

203. They behold the shape of Unibos leading the drove of swine, but they do not think it is Unibos himself—they were sure they had killed him.

204. At last they must recognize that it is he, and seeing his wealth in pork, they ask him who had given him or sold him so many animals.

205. He replies with a miraculous lie: "Tumbling beneath the sea, I traveled to a marvelous realm on the ocean's floor.

206. "I would never have returned here from that place if I did not love my wife, who you saw rise again by the sound of the true flute.

207. "It wasn't the fault of the flute if your wives now snore under dust—it was your bad playing that is to blame.

208. "Ah, why didn't you throw me down there when I was a boy? Still, even now I return a happy, wiser man.

209. "In your hatred you threw me to my atonement, a place where there are so many pigs they cannot be counted."

210. Admiring Unibos, the provost speaks first: "The hope of acquiring such pigs drives me to assail the sea also.

211. "Anyone less perceptive than I should follow me," says the dolt. So they seek the sea's waves while Unibos walks behind.

212. The sea resounds, and the three men think they hear pigs grunting. They ask Unibos where lies the trail of the pigs.

213. And Unibos indicates the place where the danger is greatest: "Where the cliffs are highest, where the sea is deepest,

214. "There you should run quickly, and throw yourselves in without fear. You'll find more pigs in these waters than on dry land."

215. With this advice the three throw themselves off the cliff. In deadly frenzy they die foolishly in the salt sea.

216. As this story reveals, the deceitful counsel of the wicked should never be believed.

NUGAE

Res mea

"[R]es mea, dum noctem nondum vocat aurea luna,
    I prior et socios elige," miles ait.
Paruit illa viro famulis commissa duobus
    Infaustoque prior omine carpit iter.
5 Nil agis, infelix, non haec custodia salva est,
    Quae tibi perpetui causa doloris erit.
Dum licet et nondum pudor est violatus in illa,
    Vxorem nulli crede, marite, tuam.
Ba[c]chus erat quartus qui praecedebat euntes,
10   Previus ille tribus triste docebat iter.
Sensit equus domine dominam titubare cadendo,
    Sensit et infirmo pondere terga premi.
Prosilit et vino pariter sompnoque gravatam
    In media fertur destituisse via.
15 At comites poti non respexere cadentem;
    Plenus uterque mero, cecus uterque fuit.
Illa relicta iacet, rediere duo male sani,
    Excipit hos stabulis militis aula suis.
Tota domus vigilat, dominam pars sobria quaerit,
20   Sobria pars loquitur, potus uterque tacet.
Interea coniunx infelix nocte futura
    In venerem ponit spem sibi, potus erat.
Dum redit, oppressam sompno vinoque sepultam
    Invenit, at minime comperit esse suam.
25 Substitit et famulum precio, precibusque minisque
    In vicium stupri cogit, at ille favet.
Frangitur ecce pudor, pudor integritatis honeste,
    Et servata federa rumpit amans.
Miles abit, tandem dominam famulosque requirit.
30   Invenit hos potos, illa relicta fuit.
Dum dubitat lusumque sua se comperit arte,
    Dedecus inmensum dissimulare parat.
Fama rei seriem patula collegerat aure;
    Dissimulare potest, fama tacere nequit.

11 cadendo] candendo MS
25 precibusque] precibus MS

Res mea

"My dear, while the golden moon does not yet bring night,
Go ahead and choose your companions," says the knight.
Entrusted with two servants by her husband, she gets ready
And proceeds on a journey with unlucky omen.
5   Do not go, unfortunate one; this custody is not safe.
It will cause everlasting sorrow for you.
While it is still possible, while her honor has not yet been violated,
Entrust your wife to no one, husband.
Bacchus preceded the travelers as a fourth;
10   Foremost, he led the unhappy way for the threesome.
The lady's horse feels the lady totter as she falls over;
It feels its back pressed by a light weight.
It leaps, and she, burdened with wine as well as sleep,
Was set down, the story goes, in the middle of the road.
15   But her drunk companions did not look back at her falling;
Both full of wine, both were blind.
She lay [on the road], left behind; the two men, not feeling well, have
       returned.
The knight's household receives them in his quarters.
The entire household keeps watch: the sober part inquires about the lady,
20   The sober part starts talking, but the drunkards remain silent.
Meanwhile the unlucky husband, during the coming night,
Places his hope of salvation in Venus, and there was drinking.
When his wife returns, she is obviously burdened with
Sleep and immersed in wine, and he does not even recognize her as his own
       [wife].
25   He values her as though she were a servant, and with entreaties and threats
A servant forces her to a place of violation while the knight gives him his
       permission.
See how honor is shattered, the honor of honest chastity,
And a lover breaks the established laws!
The knight goes away; then he asks about his lady and the servants.
30   He encounters the two drunkards—[they tell him] she was left behind.
Though he is not certain, he thinks he has been deceived by his own
       cunning;
His immense shame convinces him to keep the affair secret.
But open talk of the event brought crowds of people together in the palace;
He could pretend things were fine, but he couldn't quiet rumor.

35 Quis pocius reus est? Domini mandata peregit
    Servus, at illa stuprum victa sopore tulit.
Ergo sopor dominam, domini violencia servum
    Defendit, solus miles adulter erit.

Fulcoii Belvacensis, *Epistola VIII*

Fulco, plena doli mihi prandia tradere noli:
Nanque cibis potum similem paro, sit tibi notum.
Detrahis absenti, fallax assurgis eunti.
Hac in perfidia quis Acestes, quae fuit Ida
5 Collige, parque pari tibi noveris arte parari:
Mercator quidam quandam sibi comparat Idam
Corpore formosam varia sed mente dolosam,
Custodem rerum quam deputat. Inde dierum
Paucis expletis celer impatiensque quietis
10 Visit nundinas estates atque pruinas.
Qui labor est gratus; plures ad lucra moratus.
Cum vasis vestes cumulat studiosus Acestes,
Nec mercis quicquid monstratur ubique reliquit
Vt sic placaret quam sic vehementer amaret.
15 Haec culpando moras dum menses odit et horas,
Impatiens peperit. Quae det mendatia quaerit
Quid commentetur dum vir lucrando moretur,
Quo mitem faciat sponsum, quo credula fiat.
Et sic indennis crescit puer estque triennis.
20 Gaza, merce graves deducit navita naves.
Occurrendo viro coniunx in robore miro,
Audax figmenti, tendens puerum venienti,
"En," ait, "hunc sine te tribuerunt numina de te.
Sic sic egisti, pater, hunc absens genuisti.   fol. 141v
25 Coniugis oblitum dum quero nocte maritum,
Dum iuvat insanos amplexus reddere, vanos
Quaerere concubitus, vehemens hoc visito litus,
Quem sic arderem tanquam te, sponse, viderem.
Te non audivi, mea vota videre nequivi.
30 Cum magis exarsi, nivis hoc in gutture sparsi.
Pro te consumpsi, vice seminis ignea sumpsi.
Hoc desiderio pregnans, hoc nomine fio.
Hoc, pater, in nato tua, coniunx, ora notato."
Fit sponsus letus sed non in corde quietus:

18 mitem] mittem MS

35 Who is the guiltier? A servant followed the commands
Of his lord while the lady, overcome by sleep, endured violation.
Therefore sleep excuses the lady, the lord's impetuosity
Excuses the servant. Only the knight will be [accused as] the adulterer.

Fulcoius of Beauvais, *Epistle VIII*

Fulco, don't send dishes full of fraud to me,
For you should know that I am preparing a drink similar to your food.
You disparage the absent, but you rise deceitfully when they return.
In such perfidy consider who was Acestes, who was Ida,
5   And you will learn how you are provided a match for you in cunning.
A certain merchant married a woman named Ida,
Whose body was beautiful, but whose fickle mind was deceitful,
And he placed her in charge of his possessions. Then,
When a few days passed, overhasty and impatient with quiet,
10   He visits markets for whole summers and whole winters on end.
His work pleases him, and he awaits a greater profit.
Eager Acestes accumulates garments along with vases;
He does not overlook any gain wherever it appears,
In order to please her whom he loves so ardently.
15   She, complaining of his absence and hating the days and months,
Impatient, gave birth. She wonders what lies she should tell,
What fictions she should invent while her husband is delayed by profits,
So that she might make her husband mild and herself believable.
Meanwhile, a blameless boy grows up and three years pass.
20   The sailor draws his ships, heavy with treasure, with goods, into port.
When her husband runs forth to meet her, the wife, with astonishing vigor,
Bold in her fiction, stretches the boy to the oncomer
And says, "Behold, the gods granted you this boy in your absence.
Yes, father, it is true: you produced this son, you engendered him when you
were away.
25   When I was seeking my husband, forgetful of his wife, at night,
At the time when it is most pleasing to exchange heated embraces, to seek
fruitless coition,
I was burning with passion, and I visited this shore;
I was burning for you as if I saw you, my husband.
I did not hear you, nor could I see my prayers.
30   When my passion blazed even more, I sprinkled snow in my throat.
I took it in place of you; burning, I took it in lieu of your semen.
Because of this desire, through this agency, I became pregnant.
Observe your features, husband (and father), in this son."
The husband appears joyful but is unquiet in his heart.

35 Quippe liquet puerum nive, grandine non fore verum.
    Sponsae cum nato dat munus et oscula grato.
    Nec mora, "Perpendi causas et facta rependi.
    Merces, sponsa, para; Neptuni flagret ut ara
    Fac prius et mundi. Tempus uocat," inquit, "eundi."
40 Preparet heredem iubet haec, res servet et edem.
    "Quem non viderunt, quem fata deusque dederunt
    Notis ostendam divis et vota rependam."
    Est quoniam natus, non amplius incomitatus
    Merces augebit sed et ipsum cuncta docebit.
45 Paruit ergo, parat sponsus quaecunque rogarat.
    Fraudis plena nihil metuit de pignore fraudis.
    Discedunt laeti. "Memor," addidit, "esto niveti;
    Nostros per fluctus serva, karissime, fructus."
    Distracto puero facta pro fraude molesto.
50 It, redit. Ut mestus queritur sed pectore festus:
    "Immemor ipse nivis, visum diris ita divis,
    Admisi sobolis membris incendia solis.
    O soror, o laetum non functum morte nivetum,
    Carne nec exutum fero sed cum carne solutum."
55 Percussit simili percussus vulnere pili.
    Sic fuit ars arti, fuit et fraus obvia fraudi.   fol. 142r
    Sermo quidem gratus vulgi. Sum premeditatus
    Quid velit, inque mera lunae quid nescio spera
    Astruit. Apparet quod inumbrat cum mage claret
60 Vulgi simplicitas. Quae vix haec frivola vitas,
    Quodque semel discis vix aut nunquam resipiscis.
    Dicis latronem sic permansisse peronem
    Dum radios binis, scandendo per ardua, spinis
    Obstruit in luna, quae furtis officit una.
65 Hoc ego non legi sed mecum sepius egi
    Qua foret hoc opera de falsis promere vera
    Si foret in specie quod falso dicitur in re.
    Vnde quod audebo, sic te, perverse, docebo:
    Res est fallaci tibi ficta tuoque sequaci.
70 Fur vult furari nec vult furando notari.
    Vult metuendo crucem spinis obducere lucem.
    Non vult monstrari quisquis male vult operari.

35 Indeed, it does not appear likely that his son could be born from snow, from
   hail.
   He gives gifts and kisses to his wife and the dear child.
   Immediately he says, "I have considered your reasons and pondered upon the
   results.
   Prepare my wares, wife. First make sure the altar of Neptune
   And of the sacred pit is blazing. It's time to go," he says.
40 He orders her to prepare the heir and to look after the property and the
   house.
   "Him whom the fates and god have not seen, whom they granted,
   I will show him to the known divinities and give them thanks."
   Since he has a son, the merchant is no longer unaccompanied,
   But he will expand his business and teach him everything.
45 Thus she obeyed him and she prepares whatever her husband had requested.
   Full of fraud herself, she has no fear concerning the pledge [i.e., child] of
   fraud.
   Joyful they depart. "Be careful," she added, "with the snowchild.
   Protect our offspring in the open seas, dearest."
   He sold the boy who was irksome because of the committed fraud.
50 He leaves; he returns. He laments as if sad, but he is joyful in his heart.
   "Forgetting he was born of snow—as seen good to the dire gods—
   I let the sun shine on my offspring's limbs.
   O sister, all joy is gone because of the snowchild's death.
   I do not bring his bones back, for they were dissolved along with his flesh."
55 Having been cheated, he struck back with a similar blow of the javelin.
   Thus cunning checked cunning, and fraud fraud.
   This is a pleasing popular tale. I have wondered
   What the story means, and I don't know what on earth it shows.
   What is in the dark becomes clear when
60 The simplicity of the common people becomes bright. Such trifles you
   scarcely avoid,
   And hardly every do you recover what you have once learned.
   You say that thus a robber awaited a leather boot
   When, scaling steep places, he obstructed the moon's rays,
   Which alone hindered this theft, with two thorns.
65 This I did not read, but I have often thought to myself
   By what means it may be possible to distinguish true things from false,
   If what is said to be false in fact were also false on appearance.
   I shall teach you, perverse one, as much as I dare:
   This story is invented for your fallacious self and for your follower.
70 The robber wants to rob and does not want to be known for his robbery.
   In fear of the gallows he wants to cover up the moon with thorns.
   Whoever wants to commit evil does not want to be pointed out.

Sed viciis fuscat si quis virtute choruscat,
Et spinis pungit cum verbis verbera iungit.
75 Sed caveat latro quia lux lucebit in atro.
Nec poterunt tenebrae lucem convincere crebrae.
Illa manus pereat, flammas quae portat et undas,
Quae linguam iungit, pariter quae pungit et ungit.

Radulfi Tortarii, *Epistola VI*

Sincope, formosae custodia provida Florae
    Ne Paris argutis fallat, adesto, dolis.
Claude fores, clatros, et vectes obice portis,
    Muni tecta domus iugibus excubiis.
5 Acrisius Danen sublimi clauserat arce,
    Amotis maribus sola ministrat anus;
Ferrea turris erat, nulla de parte patebat,
    Non erat ulli fas appropiare viro;
Danes in gremium furtim dilabitur aurum,
10   Intumuit subito nubilis alvus eo.
Haec ego non retuli te posse putem quia falli,
    Aut praetium passi sumere velle stupri:
At speties fulvi faciles hebetare metalli
    Cum soleat sensus, tu stabilito tuos.
15 Crebro suadelis anus inportuna paratis
    Pota venena cavis evomit auriculis;
Tedia difficilem frangunt aliquando puellam,
    Mollis enim durum gutta cavat lapidem.
Urbem fama tenet, nescis aut supprimis unus
20   Garrit rivales illa duos iuvenes;
Dicitur Artimises unus sed Xanticus alter,
    His ardet flammis Flora decens geminis,
Corpore proceri, forma prestante decori,
    Bis quinos fratres exuperant spetie.
25 Candidior lana capud hircum Xanticus alba,
    Membra tegit tunica multicolore sua;
Depingit caligas simplex color, his et aristas
    Expressas omnis inspitias generis.   f. 121v
Funditur Artimisis planus de vertice crinis
30   Non niger aut flavus, buxeus at pocius;
Vestibus inscriptos flores mirabere seros,
    Narcissum, rosulam, lilia, peoniam;

12 passi] fassi MS

But he darkens with vices if anyone glitters with virtue,
And he pierces with thorns when he joins blows to words.
75 But let the robber beware, since light will light in the darkness.
Nor can thick darkness overcome light.
May that hand perish, which carries flames and water,
Which joins the tongue, which at the same time both punctures and soothes.

Radulfus Tortarius, *Epistle VI*

Sincopus, cautious guard of beautiful Flora,
Beware lest Paris deceive you with cunning frauds.
Close the doors, lattices, and set the bolts on the doors,
Protect the roof of the house with continuous guards!
5   Acrisius had closed up Danae in a high stronghold,
Only an old woman attends her while men are far removed;
The tower was made of iron, it opened on no sides,
It was impossible for any man to make her his own;
Gold falls down stealthily into Danae's belly,
10 The veiled womb suddenly swells with it.
I don't tell you this because I think you can be deceived,
Or are willing to receive the wages of her permitted violation;
But while easy sight of a tawny quarry is wont to weaken
A person's senses, you harden yours.
15 Repeatedly the troublesome old woman vomits forth
With ready persuasions drinkable potions in her hollowed lobes;
Boredom sometimes subdues a difficult girl,
For the gentle drop hollows the hard stone.
Rumor charms the city you don't know it, or you keep it to yourself
20 It babbles about two rival youths;
It is said that Artimises is one and Xanticus the other,
For these the comely Flora burns with her twin fires;
Tall in body, becoming in their excellent figures,
They excel their ten brothers in their beauty.
25 Brighter than the white wool is the shaggy head of Xanticus;
He covers his members with his multicolored tunic;
His boots are of a single color, and in these ways you may perceive
Clearly visible plants of all kinds.
The evenly cut hair of Artemises spreads out from his crown,
30 Not black or flaxen, but rather the color of boxwood;
You will marvel at the late flowers inscribed on his clothes,
Narcissus, little roses, lilies, peonies;

Induitur longas vernanti flamine suras,
   Presentat fruges calceus omnimodas;
35 Semper amiciri referuntur scemate tali.
   Primo detrito scema recurrit idem.
Si calles, poteris qui sint cognoscere signis,
   Dotibus insignes militiaeque duces.
Zelotipus Panemos avertere non valet istos
40   A Florae facilis lenibus obsequiis.
Et quia praeclaram sit sortitus genituram,
   Nequaquam denis fratribus inferior,
Conqueritur Florae quia non potiatur amore,
   Eius iocunda nec fruitur spetie.
45 Felix qui Florae iugi potiatur amore,
   Cuius sic facies nix veluti renitet,
Nec candor tantus perpenditur esse molestus,
   Cocci vernantis cum rubor insit ei.
At non parte viget color idem corporis omni
50   Gratia nec membris omnibus est eadem:
Congruit ergo suo mire speties sua membro,
   Nil in ea fedum nil videas mutilum;
Illius igne peris prudenter qui sapis omnis,
   Me quoque nil miror si capit eius amor.
55 At tua fors sodes non est mea, Sincope, Flora,
   Nam tua pulcra quidem sed mea pulcra magis.
Totius hec orbis, tua civis solius orbis.
   Est tua nota tibi, sed mea nota Iovi.
Iam tua nupta viro sed adhuc constat mea virgo.
60   Inberbis Phebi quam trahit unus amor.
Dic michi, sic valeas, tibi credita sic sit amica,
   Sic plagas tumidae suffugias dominae,
Sic tibi credat herus nec edat sibi viscera zelus,
   Sic numquam fidei deroget ille tuae,   f. 122r
65 Quid tua commisit, verearis ne profiteri,
   Mentula testiculis cur careas geminis?
Forsitan hos ferro Perifras praecidit acuto
   Iamque veternosis ulceribus putridos,
Aut te fasce suo ramex inmensa gravabat,
70   Plebeiae raptus virginis aut pudor est,
Aut est ignoti generis vim passa puella,
   Pauperis aut uxor munere lusa tuo.
Heus age, quid verum responde dixeris horum,
   Cura tibi Florae qualiter acciderit.
75 "Nil," ait, "indignum me" Sincopus "accipe passum,
   Nam me tam turpem nolo putes hominem.

He is clothed by a cloth making his long calves springlike;
His shoe reveals all kind of fruit.
35 They are said to be always clothed in such a fashion.
When the first suit has worn away, the same fashion returns.
If you are wise, you will be able to tell who they are by signs,
Distinguished by their qualities and leaders of warfare.
The jealous Panemos is not able to drive them away
40 From gentle service to facile Flora.
And since he has received an excellent begetting,
Not at all inferior to his ten brothers,
He complains to Flora because he may not obtain her love,
Nor enjoy her playful beauty.
45 Happy is he who may enjoy the perpetual love of Flora,
Whose beauty glitters just like the snow,
Nor is such dazzling white considered to be evil,
Since the redness of the spring oak berry is in her;
But the same color does not flourish in all of her body
50 Nor is the same grace in all of her members:
Accordingly her beauty is wonderfully suited to her limbs,
Nor would you see in her any foul blemish;
All of you who savor it pine away discreetly from its fire;
Do not be surprised that I would also pine if her love captures me.
55 But your Flora, Sincopus, is, if you please, not my lot,
For yours is indeed pretty, but mine is even prettier;
She is an inhabitant of the entire earth, yours the citizen of only a city,
Yours is distinguished for you, but mine is distinguished for Jove;
Now yours is married to a man, but mine still remains a virgin,
60 Whom a single love draws to beardless Phoebus.
Tell me, so far as you have strength, as this mistress is entrusted to you,
As thus you shun the snares of a proud lady,
As thus the lord entrusts her to you and jealousy does not eat up his entrails,
As never does he detract from your honesty,
65 What brought it about, unless you fear to acknowledge it openly,
For what reason do you lack your member and two testicles?
Perhaps Perifras cut them off with sharp metal
And now they are withered with dull sores,
Or perhaps a rupture with its burden grieved you immensely,
70 Or the decency of a common virgin was ravished,
Or the girl of a scarcely known family was prostituted,
Or the wife of a poor man was deluded by your gift;
Alas, speak! Tell me which of them you will admit is the truth,
How the guardianship of Flora befell you.
75 "Listen what I have undergone," says Sincopus, "not at all unworthy,
For I do not want you to think I am such a base man;

Est nobis animus non sic ut rere remissus,
    Qui se tam fedis illaqueet maculis.
Sed quoniam queris mihi cur genitale recidi,
80   Ne speres aliud, pando tibi brevius.
Artis grammaticae tumidus de cognitione,
    Exundans animis nec locuplebs opibus,
Angebar iugi succensus pectoris estu.
    'Quid facis? en nullae sunt tibi diviciae
85 Unde vel exiguum crescat facis emolumentum.
    Si nummos habeas semper honorus eris;
Nullus honos inopi tibi, nullus amicus egenti;
    Aurum si desit littera nulla placet.
Anne vides Gallos Hecates incedere pingues,
90   Serica quos vestit et clamis et tunica?
Auro cum caris honerantur brachia gemmis,
    Suras circumdat purpureum tegimen,
Auratos pedibus soccos ac vertice mitram.
    Turribus assimiles aspicis esse lares,
95 Horrea frumento, cellaria plena Falerno,
    Scrinia multimodis accumulata gazis.
Si fierem similis, quirem mox hec adipisci;
    Obstant his soli, res vaga, testiculi.
Nam disciplinae cum sim gnarus mediocris,
100   Etsi non summus flamen, honestus ero.'
Attritu cotis gladium, sed corde trementi,   f. 122v
    Nam rubigo vetus roserat, exacuo,
Et penetrans caeci secreta silentia tecti,
    Uno dissecui vulnere membra michi.
105 Ingens afflixit dolor hinc confinia cordis,
    Cordis defectus vulnera subsequitur.
Centurias Magnae Matris non haec latuere,
    Gallorum turmis visitor assidue,
Submittunt qui me collegia praemonuere,
110   Quod sua ditarer opido si sequerer;
Nil magis obtabam, concessi, 'sanior,' inquam,
    'Vobis coniungar flamen et efficiar.'
Mox ubi convalui sacris adsisto choreis,
    Consecror et tactus unguine flamineo;
115 Summi pontficis circumdabat infula Brochum
    Unicus affectus quem mihi nexuerat;
Ritus sacrorum didici moresque deorum,

85 facis] fac MS

My mind was not remiss as you believe,
Entangling itself in such foul sins.
But since you ask me why I cut off my genitals,
80 Lest you hope for more, I shall tell you the story briefly.
Swollen with knowledge of the grammatical art,
Overflowing with brains but not wealthy in substance,
I was vexed, irritated with perpetual burning of the breast:
'What are you doing? Look! You have no riches
85 Or means whence to make a small gain grow;
If you have money you will always be honored;
There is no honor for you destitute, no friend for the needy;
If gold is lacking, no letters are pleasing!
Have you not seen the fat Galli of Hecate proceed,
90 Whom silk shirts and tunics clothe?
Their arms are loaded with gold and precious jewels;
Purple coverings enclose their calves,
Gilded slippers on their feet and coifs on their heads;
You see their hearths are similar to towers;
95 Their granaries are filled with corn, their cellars with Falernian,
Caskets heaped up with many kinds of treasures.
If I were like them, I would soon seek to acquire these possessions;
Only these testicles—vagrant things—stand in the way.
For since I am acquainted with their common discipline,
100 Although I am not a priest, I will be honored.'
By rubbing flintstones I sharpen a sword, but with a trembling heart,
For rust had eaten the old instrument away,
And entering the secret silences of the dark house,
With an incision I cut away my members;
105 Hence an enormous pain tormented the confines of my heart;
A weakening of the heart immediately followed the wound.
These things have not been hidden from the order of the Great Mother;
I am visited eagerly by throngs of Galli;
The fraternity, which admonished me before, now raises me,
110 So that I would be very much enriched by their order if I should follow it;
No more did I oppose them; I submitted. 'Healthier,' I said,
'Let me be joined to you and made a priest.'
Soon when I recovered my health, I stood out at the holy dances,
And I am consecrated, touched by the priestly ointment;
115 The fillet of Brochus, the high priest, is placed around my head;
An uncommon love bound him to me;
I learned the sacred rites and the ways of the gods,

Vellet quisque sibi quae rata liba dari:
    Aprum Telluri sed caprum caede Lieo,
120   Iunoni vitulam daque Iovi vitulum,
    Agnam Thetis amat, Venus at sine felle columbam,
      Infernus taurum tergore Pluto nigrum;
    Orgia Saturni scio quae sint orgia Martis,
      Divae cultus Opis sed mihi plus placuit;
125 Admoveor sacris instructus in omnibus aris,
      Brochi pontificis relligione minor;
    Exhibeor talis qui deberem venerari,
      Plebibus acceptus carus et imperio.
    Delectabilium succrescunt plurima rerum,
130   Vulgi mirantis summa per ora feror;
    Dives agris, dives positis in faenore nummis,
      Dives vernaclis, dives eram pecore.
    Sed tibi si multas consultus colligis escas,
      Quos ex his plures non deerunt sacies:
135 Obsideor per continuos hinc hospite soles,
      Aedibus a nostris non redit esuriens;
    Incidit aversis discrimen ob id mihi fatis
      Omni dum nostrum panditur hospitium.   f. 123r
    Denique confitear quia, quae mea membra peremi,
140   In cinerem verti seposuique domi,
    Et piperi trito miscens aurum quasi servo.
      Nemo mei sacri conscius huius erat;
    Me quoque legitime non rebar posse litare,
      Ni mecum gererem dum sacra perficerem.
145 Totum tantillo credebam pulvere salvo,
      Meror erat nullus dampna tulisse prius.
    Ergo felici prolapsu dum rota currit,
      Invida fortunam fata tulere bonam.
    Hora gentandi venere domum michi noti,
150   Nam sic consuerant, tunc ego sed deeram;
    Procundus lautas illis meus apparat escas
      Multarum dominus tempore quo fueram.
    Heu mihi, qui volui mea probra tibi reserari,
      Propalabis enim pluribus illa vagis!
155 Heu sors dura! piper nequaquam habuisse minister
      Hac vice condiret dicitur unde cibos;
    Sumere fas epulas nec erat sic illecebrosas,
      Ni cum rugoso praepositas pipere.
    Sedulus ergo puer vicinos pervolat omnes.

What appropriate cakes to be given to them, each as he desires:
Slaughter a boar for Earth but a goat for Bacchus;
120 Give a female calf to Juno and a male one to Jove;
Thetis loves a lamb, Venus a dove without gallbladder,
Infernal Pluto a bull black of hide;
I know the secret revels of Saturn, the secret revels of Mars,
But the worship of rich Ops was most pleasing to me;
125 I am consulted, versed in all the holy altars,
Second only to the piety of the high priest Brochus;
I am presented as he who ought to be worshiped,
Received dearly by the people and the emperor.
Very many delightful things increased in number;
130 I am celebrated in the mouths of the admiring people;
I was rich in land, rich in moneys laid out at usury,
Rich in slaves, rich in livestock.
But if you, having considered the matter, assemble many foods for yourself,
Because of these foods there will be a great abundance of men not absent
      from your table.
135 Hence I was beset by guests every day;
They did not go away hungry from my home;
Because of this the turning point of my adverse fates came about
While my lodging was open to all.
At last let me confess that my member, which I destroyed,
140 I turned into ash and put aside in the house,
And mixing it with ground pepper, I preserved it like gold.
None of my holy ones was aware of this;
I also did not think that I would receive favorable omens legitimately
If I did not carry them with me when I performed holy offices;
145 So much did I believe in such a little powder being safe,
I bore no grief at injuries that I had endured before.
Thus while the wheel turns with a lucky gliding,
The envious fates bore away my good fortune.
At the hour of breakfast my followers came to my house.
150 For thus they were wont, though I was then away;
My servant prepares elegant plates for them
At that time when I was lord of many plates.
Alas, poor me! who wanted to unlock to you my many shameful acts,
For you will divulge them to many wanderers!
155 Alas, heavy fate! It is said that the waiter had no pepper
With which he could then season the food;
It was not right to consume thus such enticing dishes,
Unless they were offered with shriveled pepper.
Therefore the zealous boy flies to all the neighbors;

160   Tedet convivas quod facit ille moras,
      Qui mussant, 'latet hac forsan quod quaerimus archa,'
      Indice monstrantes interius positam.
      Quo pudor, heu, quo fas, quo iusta licentia fugit!
      Heu stolidi temerant iura statuta patrum!
165 Archellam frangunt sacros cineresque revellunt,
      Quos tritum credunt esse piper fatui;
      Inde popinatos condire cibos properarunt;
      Talibus et laeti se recreant epulis,
      Unde saginati nostro redeunt genitali.
170   Commisisse scelus nescit eques reprobus.
      Post biduum redeo, dolet infortunia nemo,
      Necdum cognoram quae mihi contigerant;
      At disiecta meae custodia praenotat archae
      Detrimenta novae tristia mesticiae;   f. 123v
175 Thecae dum rimas perscrutor, rimor opaca,
      Forte resignaret si michi depositum.
      Cernentes nostri me percunctantur alunni:
      'Num casu piperis sollicitaris, here?
      Inprudens claustris archae conviva revulsis,
180   Altilium pingues condiit inde dapes.'
      Auribus haec hausi posquam, sine mente remansi;
      Viribus elapsis exanimis cecidi.
      Cum fletu largo privatus pignore caro,
      Merens vociferor, 'O Opis, ecquid ago?
185 Dii conferte boni, per quae vos crimina lesi?
      Votane persolvi, dignane liba dedi?
      Libavi vestris inpurus forsitan aris;
      Inspexi fibras ventre satur pecudum.
      Non est legitimo fortassis victima caesa
190   Ordine, Sabaeum thus neque propositum?
      Nescius a superis Stigios secludere divis,
      Haud Stiga secrevi Ditis ab aethre Iovis?
      Nec sacra distinxi statuit quaecumque vetustas
      Manes a larvis abfore pauca ratus?
195 Forsan metiris quae tempora, secla vel annos,
      Frigus et autunnum caumaque verque novum
      Inprobus ascripsi, vates o Phebe, sorori,
      Quosque regit menses Cinthia clara, tibi,
      Ipsius incessus, tempestivos maris estus,
200   Nimbos atque nives, aera perspicuum,
      Corpora quae furtim crescens animata subimplet,

177 percunctantur] percunctatur MS

160 The guests are perturbed by his delays.
They mutter, 'Perhaps what we're looking for is hidden in this chest,'
With fingers indicating that it lie within.
Where does shame, alas, where do justice, lawful freedom flee!
Alas, the idiots profane the established laws of the fathers!
165 They break the little chest and pull out the holy ashes,
Which the fools think is ground pepper;
Then they hasten to spice their gormandized food;
Joyful, they refresh themselves with such dishes,
Whence they return to their homes fattened with my genitals.
170 The false knight does not know the crime he has perpetrated.
After two days I return. No one laments the misfortune,
Nor yet did I know what had happened to me;
But the broken lock of my chest is at last known,
The sad losses of this new cause of mourning;
175 While I examine the cracks of the covering, I explore the shadows,
If perchance any of my deposit should unseal.
Perceiving me, my disciples ask me:
'By chance are you concerned about the pepper, my lord?
Your guest, not caring about the chest, tore the locks off,
180 Whence he seasoned his dinner rich with fat fowl.'
As this information struck my ears, I remained senseless;
With my strength fallen away, I fell as if dead;
With a great cry, deprived of my dear pledge,
Lamenting I call out, 'O Ops, did I do anything wrong?
185 Do you band together, good gods, for the injuries by which I have offended
      you?
Didn't I pay offerings, didn't I give worthy cakes?
Perhaps I made libation at your altars when I was impure;
Sated, I inspected the entrails in the cattle's stomach.
Perhaps the victim was not slaughtered in the lawful
190 Manner, and the Sabaean incense was not offered?
Ignorant of separating the Sitgian gods from those above,
Did I not at all distinguish the Styx of Pluto from the aether of Jove?
Did I not distinguish whatever holy time was at hand,
Having reckoned in detail how the shades were removed from ghosts?
195 Perhaps you measure the times, centuries or years,
The cold and autumn and the heat and new spring
That I reckoned poorly, O seers of Phoebus, sisters,
And you measure the months that clear Cynthia rules for you,
The ebb, the seasonal heaving of the sea,
200 Rainstorms and snows, the clear aether,
The bodies that, growing, are secretly filled with life,

Deficiens eadem non minus extenuans?
Sidus Saturni iocundum forte vocavi,
   Difficilemque Iovis atque gravem Veneris.
205 A me vestra tenax est si mutata potestas,
   O dii, defitiam nec merear veniam;
Non est a nobis si quae veneratio vobis,
   Debuit attribui more repensa suo;
Ergo si decuit qualem me iugiter egi,
210   Si non offendi, si bene vos colui,   f. 124r
Cur genitale meum clepsit vobis latro sacrum,
   Gluttivit nebulo cur genitale meum?
Heu, fortuna, tuae quam sunt vires violentae!
   Opprimis, heu casus, quam subito miseros!
215 Heu, heu, quam dubium regit orbis climata fatum!
   Orbis habet nullum sed mage remigium.'
Talia dementans querula cum voce profarer,
   Aures servorum nec caveo bibulas;
Adstant attoniti mirantes dicta patroni,
220   Seque diu versis vultibus aspitiunt.
O genus ingratum servi, genus ore prophanum,
   Plenum rimarum, fraudibus expositum!
Atria progressi mussant altrinsecus illi,
   'Quae sunt quae dominus verba, papa! loquitur?
225 Forsan condivit sibi quod genitale recidit,
   Igni combussit, miscuit et piperi.
Numquid non cineri mixtum piper esse notasti?
   Rebar ego stolidus sic senuisse piper;
Pro muria nostris infertur mentula mensis,
230   Carnes intinxi carnibus in domini.'
Urbis perlatas haec dispersere plateas,
   Rumor et hic vicos ruraque longa replet.
Foeda sacerdotum replet aures fama spadonum,
   Quorum mox holidis amoveor choreis.
235 Arceor a phanis, vetor appropiare sacellis,
   Sacraque si tangam liba prophana putant,
Obruor et spurtis inflato gutture sputis,
   Inque meum nomen flegmatis imber adest.
Edicto statuunt ne quis me colligat urbe,
240   Et quae contulerant omnia surripiunt,
Nec cessat tetrum subnectere tristia fatum,
   Accumulans dictis deteriora malis;

224 papa] pape MS

Departing but at the same time not diminishing?
Perhaps I invoked the star of Saturn as playful,
And Jupiter as difficult and Venus as serious.
205 If your firm authority has been altered by me,
    O gods, then let me be wanting and not obtain your grace;
    If there is no reverence from me toward you,
    Reverence ought to be given, paid back in the proper way;
    But if the way I continually behaved was fitting,
210 If I did not offend, if I worshiped you well,
    Why did a robber steal my genitals, sacred to you,
    Why did a rascal gulp down my genitals?
    Alas, fortune, how your strength is violent!
    Alas, chance, how quickly you oppress the wretched!
215 Alas, alas, how doubtful fate rules the regions of the world!
    The world is nothing but much rowing.'
    While raving, I uttered these laments aloud;
    I did not care about my servants' ears, ready to hear;
    They stand there stunned, marveling at their patron's words,
220 And, faces turned, they look at each other for a long time.
    O ungrateful race of servants, race profane in mouth,
    Full of chinks, accessible to frauds!
    Gaining the forecourts, they mutter on both sides,
    'What are these words that our lord, alas! speaks?
225 Perhaps he pickled his genitals that he cut off;
    He burned them in fire and mixed them with pepper.
    Do you know whether the pepper was mixed with ash?
    I would consider myself stupid if I thought pepper thus became aged;
    For seasoning his member is brought to our tables;
230 I dipped my meat in the meat of my lord.'
    Through the city's broad streets these tidings spread,
    And this news fills villages and remote farms.
    The eunuch priest's disgraceful fame fills ears;
    Soon I am removed from their rank dances.
235 I am kept at a distance from the temples; I am forbidden to make amends in
      the chapels,
    And if I touch the holy cakes, they think them defiled,
    And I am covered with dirty spittle from swollen throats,
    And in my honor falls a shower of phlegm.
    By edict they established that no one assemble with me in the city,
240 And what they had given everyone snatches away,
    Nor does black fate cease to add pains,
    Heaping up worse things with wicked words;

Pessima quippe volat velotior alite fama,
    Vulgaturque malum promtius a populis.
245 Denique, commissae fuerant qui fraudis iniquae
    In me signiferi nobilibus geniti;   f. 124v
    Nequaquam obprobrium poterant tolerare malignum,
    Qui mihi fatales glutierant cineres.
    Hii biberant omnem furia potante furorem;
250 . Aspirarat eos ut puto Thesiphone.
    Perlustrant igitur lucos, loca devia, saltus,
    Urbes atque agros, ruraque seu frutices,
    Cruribus effractis mihi qui manibusque recisis
    Invento linguam detraherent opicam.
255 Quos ubi persensi me perdere velle, refugi;
    Liqui vero meum cum patria genium,
    Prolixaque via percurri milia multa.
    Ad Floraeque virum pervenio Philirum.
    Vidit ut inberbem me, percunctatur an essem
260   Integer, obduxit pallidus ora pudor.
    'Adsum servitio,' dixi, 'vir maxime, vestro.
    Quis sim vel qualis quaerere nolo velis.'
    'Esto comes Florae,' respondit vir vafer ille;
    'Sic fies nostra dignus amicicia.'
265 Laetus oboedivi verbis iocunda monentis,
    Obsequor et Florae, spernar amando licet.
    En, Zephirine, tibi serie tenus omnia pandi,
    Qualiter et quare dux habear dominae.
    Tu ne nostra velis archana recludere cunctis,
270   Falsaque ne veris, obsecro, miscueris.
    Est horum testis notus iam carmine Pseustis,
    Si percuncteris, proferet ille tibi."

The worst rumor indeed flies quicker than a bird,
And the evil is spread by the people more quickly.
245 At last, because of the unjust fraud that I undertook,
Those who were leaders, born of noble stock, were against me;
Not at all were they able to endure malicious scandal,
Those who had swallowed the ashes fatal to me;
These drank all their rage when their madness was drunk;
250 Thesiphone, I believe, infused them.
Then they purify the groves, unfrequented places, woodlands,
Cities and fields and farms and bushes.
With my legs broken and my hands cut off
They would withdraw my foolish tongue with a device.
255 When I realized they wanted to destroy me, I fled;
Indeed, I left my people along with my country,
And on a long road I have hastened many miles.
I come to Philirus, husband of Flora.
He sees that I'm beardless, inquiries whether I am whole.
260 Wan shame covers my mouth.
'I am here, great man,' I say, 'at your service;
I don't want you to try seeking who or how I am.'
'Be the companion of Flora,' replies that crafty man;
'Thus you will become worthy of my friendship.'
265 Joyful, I obeyed the words promising pleasant outcomes,
And I obey Flora, although I am despised by him who would be loved.
Look here, Zephirinus, I have revealed to you, in order, everything,
How and wherefore I am considered the guide of the lady.
May you not wish to disclose my secrets to all,
270 And I beg you, may you not mix false with true.
This matter is made known in the song of Pseustis;
If you ask him, he will tell you about it."

SATYRAE

Warnerii Rotomagorum, *Satyra contra Moriuht*

Rotberto domino subnixo presulis ostro,   fol. 2r
    Et matri dominae illius eximiae,
Vuarnerius, dubia non spe confisus utrisque,
    Nunc et post obitum vivere per Dominum.
5   Francorum decus est Rotberti vita superstes,
    Regis precipui nobilis atque pii;
Vos columen magnum, turris bene fida bonorum,
    Non casura cito, adtribuente Deo.
Ille regit Francos, armis Marteque superbos;
10   Vos bene Nortmannos, sanguine, cede feros.
Proles Richardi duo sunt retinacula mundi,
    Quattuor, o! utinam, ve tibi mors, taceam,
Quattuor in regno superessent lumina nostro,
    Si duo non ferres, filius et pater est.
15   Sed quia defunctos non prodest plangere nostros,
    Mortis ab exitio carne resurget homo.
Mi pie presul, ave! salve per secula, salve!
    Non nobis decus hoc invideas, fera mors.
His nobis parcas quantum tibi, lapse, cycadas,
20   Dum ruis a sella, igne velut stipula.
Nititur hoc regnum sicut suflamine tectum,
    Quo perstante vigor, quoque ruente dolor.
Parce, Deus, vivis, precor, et miserere sepultis,
    Te miserere decet nosque rogare pater.

25   Sed quoniam jam tempus adest incepta moveri,
    Ecce canam meritum carminis et stimulum.
Servitio vestro cum me Rotomago dedissem,
    Heu! fortunatum vidimus ecce caprum.
Solis in occasum jacet insula, Scottia dicta,
30   Fertilis, a populo non bene culta suo;
Ut dicunt plures, hanc gens si gnara teneret,
    Vinceret Italiam fertilitate sua.
Haec, paradisiacam prospectans undique vitam,
    Heu! nutrit Scottos et fovet inlepidos,

11 Proles Richardi] Proles ri Richardi MS
21 Nititur] Mititur MS
23 sepultis] ceptus MS, *corr. marg.* sepultis

Warnerius of Rouen, *Satire against Moriuht*

Warnerius, trusting confidently in each, bids Archbishop Robert, propped by the noble purple, and his mother, most excellent lady, to live now and forever in the Lord [1-4].

King Robert, that extraordinary, noble, and pious leader, is still well and alive, much to the glory of the French [5-6].

The archbishop and his mother are like a mighty column, like a strong tower for the virtuous that, with God willing, will not soon topple [7-8].

King Robert rules the French, proud in arms and Mars; well do you two rule the Normans, savage in blood and slaughter [9-10].

The sons of Duke Richard are the two halters of the world. There would be four but alas! your deaths! oh, let me remain silent! Four luminaries would remain in our kingdom if you, death, did not bear off two they were son and father. But it doesn't help to lament the dead, for from death's destruction man will rise again in the flesh [11-16].

Hail, my pious bishop! God bless you during your reign, God bless you! Do not, savage death, envy us this glory. Spare as many of this family as you spare summer cicadas for yourself, O fallen soul, when you rush down from your saddle like a stalk on fire. The kingdom relies on this man just as a roof depends on a stay: while he stands, there is strength; if he falls, there is grief [17-22].

Spare the living, Lord, I beg of You, and pity the dead. It is fitting that You pity, Father, and that we beg [23-24].

But since it is now time to begin my undertaking, I will write about the merits of poetry and the goad of song. When I had devoted my talent to your service, Rouen, alas! I beheld [a poet who was] a lucky goat [25-28]!

To the west lies an island called Ireland, fertile but not well cultivated by its people, and many say that if a wise people ruled this island, it would surpass Italy in its fertility. This island, offering a heavenly life on all sides, alas! rears

35 Nominibus sumptis passi discrimina furis,   fol. 2v
      Nitentis caeli lumina ferre sibi.
   His sibi concesso, pressa quoque mente sub artu
      Carnis, et ignari luminis Altithroni.
   Quantum per habitum, sectantur corpore scortum,
40   Est mihi perlatum, more cubant pecudum;
   Non braccas portant, ventri quia semper adherent.
      Illis namque Venus Martis amore decus.
   Phu! lectos violant, anni velut unius infans,
      Francia, quod cernis, Roma, aliquando tibi.
45 Sunt et adhuc de his Scottis mihi multa relata,
      Scribere quod nefas est quodque referre pudet.
   Sed quoniam Scottus Moriuht hac lege tenetur
      Precipue strictus, haec sibi sint volumus.
   Hic Moriuht stultus, de mortis origine dictus,
50   Tali gente satus, stat sibi grammaticus.
   Grammaticus, rethor, geometra, pictor, aliptes,
      Omnia sit vobis, est caper ipse mihi.
   Nam sibi nota magis propriae vesica capelle,
      Quam dialectica vis, quae geometrica sit.
55 Quid fecit Moriuht sapiens, qui talis habetur?
      Pro capra magnum pertulit exilium.
   Eia! nunc, nostrae, Scottum resonate, camenae,
      Naufragium passum conjugis ob puteum.
   Scottorum fines invadunt, pro dolor! hostes,
60   Femina mox capitur, ducitur et Moriuht.
   Nec mora, cum Moriuht, olidum mutatus in hyrcum,
      Naves ingreditur, Glicerium sequitur.
   Talibus his inhians, capitur mox stulta voluntas,
      Disponente Deo, cui patet omnis homo.
65 A Danis capitur, vinclis et forte ligatur,
      Ut latro permeritus, vel homo lunaticus.
   Truncus ut e manibus navis per plana rotatur,
      Ictus verberibus fortiter et manibus;
   Stant Dani circum, mirantur mobile monstrum,   fol. 3r
70   Mingentes calvi in medio capitis.
   Mentula decoquitur, per cornu fertur, ut hyrcus;

38 luminis Altithroni] luminis et Altithroni MS
43 Phu! lectos violant] Plectos violant MS
47 Moriuht] moriut MS, *corr.* moriuht
48 sint] sunt MS
51 geometra] geomeutra (?) MS

and supports the rude Irish, who, having acquired their names [as the "dark ones," "skotioi"], have suffered the hazards of the thief, trying to carry the light of heaven from them. By succumbing to these dangers, their minds have become enslaved to the power of the flesh, and they are ignorant of the light of the Almighty [29-38].

As for their dress, they seek out animal skins to cover their bodies, and I have been informed that they sleep like animals. They do not wear trousers, for trousers always cling to the belly, and Venus' adulterous love for Mars was honorable in their view. Phooey! They foul their beds, like year-old children, as you yourself, France, and you too, Rome, have seen. I have heard many other things about these Irish, things that are abominable to write about, shameful to relate [39-46].

And since the Irishman Moriuht is especially bound to such behavior, we wish him well. This stupid Moriuht, begotten of the Irish and named after death [i.e., *mors*], maintains that he is a scholar. Grammarian, rhetorician, geometer, painter, wrestler—let him be everything for you—he's still a goat to me. For the bladder of his she-goat is better known to him than dialectical power or geometry [47-54].

What did this wise Moriuht do, who is considered so great? On account of his she-goat he underwent exile. Ah! Now, my muses, sing of this Irishman, who suffered shipwreck because of his wife's pit [55-58].

Enemies [i.e., Vikings] invade Ireland—what a pity!—and Moriuht's wife is soon captured and led away. Then Moriuht, transformed into a stinking goat, boards a ship without delay and follows Glicerium. Eagerly engaged in this pursuit, he is soon enslaved by his own foolish lust, according to the plan of God, Who sees through everyone [59-64].

Captured by the Danes, he is bound tightly with fetters, just as a seasoned thief or madman would be, and while he rolls along the ship's deck as though he hadn't any arms, he is struck by fists and receives many blows. The Danes, standing around him, marvel at this monster rolling around, and they piss on the middle of his bald pate. His member becomes wasted, and he is led by his horn like a goat [65-71].

Reddita, quid ploras? nunc Rotomago capra.
Mille modis cantetur iners, et stultus, et amens,
    Tantus amor caprae; magne poeta, vale.
75 Subditur obprobriis et tunc pro conjuge Danis
    Conjugis officium cogitur esse suum.
Nudatur Moriuht, setis vestitus ut ursus,
    Et coram nautis ludis et, urse, feris.
Non tamen invitus fit rabula podice cunctis,
80   Percussus genio ingemuit, heu! misero.
Haec ita perpessus merito discrimina, Scottus
    In Corbric parvo distrahitur pretio.
Hic locus, a Scottis longe submotus amaris,
    Non modicam gentem sustinet atque fovet,
85 Nomine consimili, Scottorum semper amici,
    Dissimiles facie dissimilesque fide.
Hi Corbricenses infacti sunt meliores,
    Non melior Scotto est cane deterior.
Ad portum gentis hujus deducitur hyrcus,
90   Appositis hedere sed foliis capite;
Hoc signo Moriuht ut equus venalis habetur;
    Tres nummi tantum fit Moriuht pretium.
Tam parvo pretio venditus, setiger hyrcus
    Ducitur ad monachas a sibi jam dominas.
95 Cernentes monachae Moriuht, mirabile monstrum,
    Derident magnum depile calvitium;
Inquirunt cuncte Moriuht qua juveret arte.
    "Sum," canit, "Homerus, sum Maro Virgilius."
Diligit omne novum semper visus mulierum;
100   Idcirco Moriuht mox manet egregius.
Laudatur hyrcus pulchros sibi fingere versus,
    Minervae tepidus, sed Veneri calidus.
O monache, posite sub religionis honore,   fol. 3v
    Vulcanum stuppis stultus enim tribuit;
105 Inter vos habitat stupatus maximus hyrcus,
    Findendas gladio ipsius ex rigido.
Vos salvare potest, mentis castissimus heros,

74 magne] magnae MS
79 ravula] ravola MS
90 Appositis] Apositis MS
92 nummi] nummis MS
105 hyrcus] horcas MS
106 Findendas] Findendae MS

What lament do you make when your she-goat has been sent back to Rouen? Let this indolent and stupid and mad love be sung to a thousand melodies, so great is this love for your she-goat—great poet, I salute thee [72-74].

He is subjected to various abuses and is forced to assume conjugal duties like a Danish wife. Moriuht is stripped naked and then covered with a hairy skin [so he looks] like a bear, and then before the sailors, bear, you cavort and butt. Not, however, unwillingly does this braggart offer his rear to everyone, but when he has been struck through, he groans "alas!" in his wretched heart [75-80].

After enduring these perils deservedly, the Irishman is sold for a small price in Corbridge. The town is distant from the unpleasant Irish and contains a large number of people who have the same name as the Irish and who are always friendly with them, but they are unlike the Irish in their features and in their faith. These crude inhabitants of Corbridge are better [than the Irish]—to be worse than an Irishman is to be worse than a dog [81-88].

The goat Moriuht is led to the port of these people, and ivy leaves are placed upon his head. These indicate that Moriuht, like a horse, is for sale. Three cents, such is the price of Moriuht, and for this small fee he is sold to a group of nuns who, now his masters, lead the bristly goat away. The nuns, gazing at Moriuht, the amazing monster, make fun of his huge hairless head. Then they all ask Moriuht how he can help them. "I am Homer," he sings, "I am Maro Virgilius" [89-98].

Women's eyes always like new things. For this reason Moriuht soon achieves a reputation. The nuns praise this goat for writing pretty verses, tepid in Minerva but hot in Venus. O foolish nuns, sworn to holy chastity, only a fool places tow next to fire! A hairy goat resides among you, and you are about to be cleaved by his rigid sword. That Hero most chaste in mind, the Spirit sent from heaven by the Almighty, can save you [99-108].

Spiritus e caelo missus ab Altithrono.
Jam Moriuht cunctis coepit privatus haberi,
110   Crispando risum detegit hic veretrum;
Quid dicam? Moriuht cunctas ardere juvencas
Ex coito, ramo tangere necne suo,
Agnosci coepit cunctis ramoque pateri,
Plus jam non carus quam canis est rabidus.
115 Mos fuit, antiquo sapientum jure repertus,
Ilia quem novit, quae geminos peperit;
Hic mos corruptis monachabus pena perhennis
Dum corpus vivum, heu! pateretur humum;
Hunc morem dirum fera restaurare volebat
120   Corbric, Romano pretitulans titulo.
Heu! fratres gemini, genetrice lupa generati,
Vos Moriuht Corbric vult generare sibi,
Ilia sub quodam veluti violata sacratum,
Contra fas peperit, mors fuit unde sibi.
125 Hic Corbric cunctas voluit corrumpere vestas,
Romuleas centum traderet ut soboles;
His Corbric natis Romam super acta tyranam
Vastaret, totam gentibus Italiam.
Noluit Omnipotens urbem frustrare beatam
130   Nomine perpetuo semper et egregio.
Pro nefas! hic Moriuht, monacham deprensus ad unam,
A populo capitur, ut canis eicitur.
Nam sicut miserae tractabat crura puellae,
Pretendens ramum luxuria rigidum,
135 Sic peragendo nefas trahitur, quasi pellis ad undas,
Dignus morte fero sub crucis exitio.
Curritur ad Moriuht, magnum et mirabile monstrum,   fol 4r
Depile calvitium verberibus feriunt;
Ceditur hic tantum quantum lupus interceptus
140   A populo miseram dente ferendo capram.
Dissimulando loco tandem facto fugiendi,
Nolentes hyrcum perdere tam miserum,
Ingreditur parvam cum nullo remige cymbam,
Fortune velum cum prece dans proprium.
145 Incantator enim, postquam discessit ad illis,
Sacrificat ventis, immolat atque diis;

110 hic] he MS, *corr.* hec
112 ramo] ramoo MS
114 est] es MS
115 sapientum] sapientium MS

Now Moriuht begins to have intimate meetings with all of the nuns, and grinning broadly, he uncovers his private parts. What more can I say? Moriuht inflames all the young heifers with sexual desire and touches them with his rod. He begins to gain a reputation and his rod wins him fame, but he is no more loved than a rabid dog [109-14].

There was a law found in the ancient edicts of wise men that Ilia, who bore the twins, knew. This law condemned corrupt nuns to everlasting punishment when—horrors!—they would be buried alive. Savage Corbridge, which got its name from a Roman word, wanted to restore that cruel custom. Alas! You twin brothers who were born of a she-wolf, Moriuht wants to engender you for himself at Corbridge, just as Ilia, having violated sacred law by lying with a certain man, had borne a child unlawfully and as a result met death. Moriuht wanted to corrupt all the vestals of Corbridge in order to deliver a hundred Romuluses as offspring; with these sons of Corbridge he would once again lay waste tyrant Rome and depopulate all of Italy [115-28].

But the Almighty did not want Moriuht to bring to naught that blessed city's perpetual and ever-famous name. For shame! This Moriuht, caught in the company of a single nun, is seized by the people and cast out like a dog. For just as he was handling the wretched girl's thighs—his rod extended rigid with lust—in the act of committing his crime, he is hauled off, like a hide to water [i.e., to the washing tub], deserving a cruel death, even the punishment of crucifixion. The people run toward Moriuht, the great, wondrous monster, and strike his bald pate with lashes. He is beaten like a wolf, checked by the people just as he is bearing a wretched she-goat in his teeth [129-40].

Finally, keeping secret the place and act of his escape—for the people do not care to destroy such a miserable goat—Moriuht boards a small boat without an oar, entrusting his sail to Fortune with a prayer. For this wizard, having left Corbridge, sacrifices to the winds and makes offerings to the gods. But when

Sed cum forte deos inter maria alta profanos
  Advocat ex pici visceribus teneri,
A Danis rursus capitur strictimque ligatur
150 Perpessus merito deteriora mala.
Accidit hoc illi, sicut qui forte leoni
  Obviat, extractus dentibus ante lupi.
Si quis adhuc audire cupit discrimina Scotti,
  Perquirat genium corporis et vicium;
155 Inveniet magnas exstantes forte mariscas,
  Curandas magno nullius antidoto.
O! multum luitura tuam Saxonia gentem,
  Finibus in cujus distrahitur Moriuht;
Corruptos pueros juvenesque aliquando dolebis,
160 Diversis maculis istius et viciis.
Sed quia diversos retinet Saxonia portus,
  Inmemor hic portus nominis et fluvii,
Quo caper hirsutus, viciorum fleumate plenus,
  Ut merces vilis venditus est populis.
165 Ducitur ad portum gestans in vertice ramum,
  Venalem Moriuht nosceret ut populus;
Munere sat parvo vidua mercatus ab una,
  Pro Moriuht falsum dans ibi denarium.
Gaude jam, Moriuht! gaude, tu, magne poeta,
170 Mercatus falso qui bene denario.
Subjectus viduae patria qui gessit in illa,   fol. 4v
  Non tribuit venis ocia, nec Veneri.
Nam multos pueros, monachas, viduasque subegit
  Atque maritatas, esne, poeta, nefas?
175 Matres nobilium dum percipiunt puerorum
  Corruptas soboles jam fore sic proprias,
Libertate data, mox gente fugatus ab illa,
  Ut pecus a stabulo corporis ex vicio.
Nescio si dominam dignatus linquere castam,
180 Sed Moriuht ipsi non manet alma fides;
Ut dicunt, dominae lecto servivit amatae;
  Idcirco meruit liber ab hac fieri.

148 pici] puae MS
157 Saxonia] Saxoniam MS, *corr.* Saxonia
169 magne] magna MS
174 esne] est ne MS
180 ipsi] ipse MS

he is on the high seas and calls loudly upon the pagan gods from the entrails of a young woodpecker, he is again captured by the Danes and put in fetters, and deservedly he endures worse calamities. Thus it happens to Moriuht as it happens to a person who, after he escapes the wolf's teeth, by chance meets a lion [141-52].

If anyone would now like to hear about the distinctions of this Irishman, he should consider the nature and defects of his body. He will discover large piles greatly protruding, incurable by the strongest medicines [153-56].

O Saxony! Greatly will your people suffer, for Moriuht is sold within your borders. Long will you lament your corrupted youths and boys, thanks to Moriuht's many stains and vices [157-60].

Since Saxony has many ports, I forget the name and the river of the port where the shaggy goat, full of the phlegm [i.e., corruption] of vices, has been offered like cheap ware to the people. Led to the port, he holds up a branch so the people would know he is for sale. For a small price he is purchased by a widow, who gives a counterfeit coin for Moriuht. Rejoice now, Moriuht! Rejoice, O mighty poet! You have been rightly sold for a false coin [161-70]!

Made a slave to a widow living in that country, Moriuht did not give up his pleasure in pricks and in Venus. But he who has plowed many boys, nuns, widows, and wives—is he not wicked, O poet [171-74]?

When mothers of noble boys perceive that their daughters will soon be defiled, they grant Moriuht his liberty, and he is soon driven out by that people like a diseased animal from a stable. I don't know if he deigned to leave his mistress chaste, and you certainly cannot take his word for it. They say that he served the bed of his beloved lady, and for that act he deserved his freedom from her [175-82].

O! specimen magnum, tali virtute redemptum,
   Non sic a domino gratia Virgilio.
185 Tu gratus dominae pendentis munere coxae,
   Hic carus Rome carminis ex specie;
   Hic agros meruit pro stemmate carminis alti,
   Tu liber vulvae pro coitu rigide.
   Vindicta cesus, Germanis belua factus,
190   Currit ad invisum Beelzebub auxilium.
   Accipiens vita functae tenera exta puellae,
   Prospicit in fibris gausape Glicerii;
   Et dum sacra suo proferret verba labello,
   Distortis oculis et manibus tremulis,
195 Fertur ab adverso: "Vivit tua cara puella,
   Et magis intento i Rotomago cito;
   Illic amissos plorans tua cara furores,
   Expectat caprum pulchra capella suum.
   Ambulat ad portum, Moriuht ut cernat amatum,
200   Conlustrans cunctas undique naviculas;
   Te non invento, vult se conjungere Dano,
   Dicens quod dominus mortuus est Moriuht."
   His ita perceptis, Moriuht, saliens velut hyrcus,
   Ter caelo palmas sustulit ingeminans:
205 "O regina Venus, Gnidi Paphieque dicata,   fol. 5r
   Salva, quaeso, meam nunc Rotomago capram;
   Si facies salvam, feriam tibi rite columbam,
   Dum calvo capiti adfuerint oculi."
   His ita perceptis divisque ex cede placatis,
210   Tres tortas caldas ex humeris religat,
   Ut sibi per populum sic fas foret ire quietum
   Securumque suam cernere Glicerium.
   Arripiens iter ostensum sibi voce deorum,
   Nil parcit pedibus, ceu fugiendo lupus,
215 Et stimulatus Io sevique Cupidinis oestro,
   Inmemor est Rheni fluminis atque jugi.
   "O Moriuht, Moriuht! tantum cur, stulte, moraris,
   Adde tuis alas jam pedibus volucres."
   Haec secum dicebat enim currendo per omnes
220   Campos, per montes, per tribulos, silices.
   Nunc audire decet qualis quantusque poeta

191 functae] functa MS
200 naviculas] navi MS; "culas" v. 202 *terminat*
215 Cupidinis] cupidini MS

Ah! Great poet! Redeemed by such virtue! Not thus did Virgil receive favor from his lord. You were pleasing to your lady because you employed your hanging joint; Virgil was dear to Rome because of his song's beauty. He was given a farm in reward for his high poesy; you gained your freedom for stiffly poking a pussy [183-88]!

Made a beast by the Germans, struck by the liberating staff, Moriuht rushes to the hateful aid of Beelzebub. Taking up the tender entrails of a dead girl, he perceives Glicerium's cunt in the bowels, and while he was uttering holy words on his lips, with his eyes upturned and his hands trembling, the fiend says to him: "Your dear girl is alive. Moreover, I direct you to go quickly to Rouen, for there your dear wife, your pretty she-goat, laments her lost love and awaits her buck. She walks about the port, searching for her beloved Moriuht, inspecting every boat there. But she has not found you and, thinking that her lord Moriuht has died, she wishes to marry a Dane" [189-202].

Hearing these words, Moriuht, jumping like a goat, thrice held his palms up to heaven, repeating, "O divine Venus, worshiped in Gnidus and in Paphos, I beg of you to save my she-goat now in Rouen. If you keep her safe, I shall sacrifice a dove to you fitfully, so long as there are eyes in my bald head" [203-8].

After learning of these things and pleasing the gods with slaughter, Moriuht binds three hot loaves onto his shoulders so that he could pass through the people undisturbed and safely find his Glicerium. Taking the paths that the gods pointed out to him, he does not spare his feet at all, and like a fleeing wolf, stimulated by the gadfly of Io and of fierce Cupid, he does not concern himself with the Rhine or with the mountains [209-16].

"Moriuht, Moriuht! Why are you dragging your heels, you fool? Put birds' wings on your feet—quickly!" He said this to himself as he ran through fields and thistles, over mountains and rocks [217-20].

Now I would like to relate how this wise poet Moriuht distinguished himself

Claruit in habitu hic sapiens Moriuht.
Ante suum penem gestabat rabula pellem,
Ante nates caprae tegmina retro nigra,
225 Calceus et dexter consutus pelle asinina,
Et levus pariter nudus ad usque nates.
Et magis ut dicam, genitalia cuncta patebant
Podicis et nigri inguinis atque pili;
Insuper et podex tam semper hiabat aperte,
230   Cum flexo terram despiceret capite,
Cattus ut ingrediens annum requiescere totum
Posset cum catta huc hiemando sua;
Inguinis in silva nidum ciconia magna,
Uppupa vel proprium posset habere locum.
235 Hic incompositus, populis derisio factus,
Larva velut pueris sic erat horribilis;
Sic caput ad regni restans post sceptra mariti
Nobilis, egregii, divitis atque pii,
Scilicet ad dominam Moriuht veniens comitissam   fol. 5v
240   Corruit ante pedes, flebilis hoc referens:
"Tu pater et mater nobis et vita superstes,
Nunc consilium, rogo, Moriuht magnum fer.
Pro dolor! a Danis Moriuht predata capella
Partibus in vestris vendita cara fuit;
245 Quam reddas misero, rogo, multa pericula passo
Per mare perque solum, cernis ut ipsa, tuum;
Nocte, die vigilans non dormio plenus amore,
Unde mori Moriuht cogitat iste tuus."
Hic orator enim stultus, qui magnus habetur,
250   Non causas habitus rethoricae sequitur;
Rethoricam si sciret enim, non ista referret,
Astutis coram stroma serendo suum.
Sed quoniam non est Moriuht reprehendere nostrum,
Quid homo cum belua prosequar ipse mea?
255 His dictis, sapiens subrisit domna parumper
Et mitra pulchram supposuit faciem.
Tandem aperit vultum Scottumque ita fatur amice:
"Es Scottus patriae ut patet in facie;
Pone modum lacrimis, reddetur gloria dulcis

223 rabula] ravola MS
249 Hic orator enim stultus, qui magnus habetur] Hic orator enim stultus, is qui
    magnus habetur MS

in his manner of dress. This braggart wore a skin in front of his privates and the black hide of a goat over his buttocks. His right shoe was a sewn-up ass's skin, and his left leg was naked up to his rump. Indeed, I may say that his genitals were entirely exposed, as well as the black piles of his anus and groin, and his rear was always so wide open that when he bent his head down to look at something on the ground, a cat who entered there could hibernate a year with his female cat, a large stork could build a nest in the forest of his groin, or a hoopoe could construct a comfortable home. He was disheveled and mocked by the people, for he was as frightful as a bogeyman to boys [221-36].

In this condition Moriuht came to the countess who ruled the kingdom after the death of her noble, eminent, wealthy, and pious husband. When Moriuht was admitted to her presence, he fell at her feet and, weeping, said as follows [237-40]:

"You are our mother and father—indeed, you are life itself. I beg of you, give most needed advice to your servant Moriuht. What misery! Moriuht's little she-goat, carried off by the Danes, was sold—poor dear—in your country. I beg you to return her to me! I am a wretch who has endured bitter trials on the seas and, as you may easily see, in your country. I stay awake night and day, for I am so full of love that I cannot sleep. For that reason your servant Moriuht ponders his own death" [241-48].

Now this stupid orator, who is so greatly esteemed, does not follow the accepted rules of rhetoric, for if he really knew rhetoric, he wouldn't have spoken like that, patching together a disjointed tale before a learned audience. But since there's no point trying to reprehend our Moriuht, why should I, a man, continue to prosecute this beast of mine [that I am describing] [249-54]?

After he spoke, the wise lady smiled for a moment and hid her beautiful face under her veil. Then she uncovered her face and spoke to the Irishman in a friendly manner [255-57]:

"Your features clearly show that you are a genuine Irishman. You may now leave off weeping, for if your sweet love is anywhere in our country, she shall

260   In tota nostra si fuerit patria;
    I cito per regnum quaere et tua gaudia nostrum,
      Inventis ad me cuncta referre stude;
    Vendita servicio si forte tenetur ab illo,
      Ipsa tibi reddam, sed pretio referam."
265 His dictis domina, ridentibus undique cunctis,
      Cessit ab excelso mox Moriuht solio.
    Hoc monstrum circum juvenes puerique canebant:
      "Calvule, quere cappam, calvule, quere capram."
    Ille, redonatis iterum divisque placatis,
270   Audiit ex adito: "Est tua cara Rudoil."
    Hic portus domine non multum distat ab urbe;
      Sepius a Danis merce refertur opis.
    Huc adiens portum, Moriuht de conjuge certus   fol. 6r
      Perlustrat totum lumine navigium;
275 Illic non visa, lustrans habitacula cuncta,
      Pauperis in quadam conspicit ede suam.
    Haec, instans domine ferrato pectine telae,
      Ducebat vitam serva velut miseram,
    Nuda humero, infelix, et pulchris nuda mammillis,
280   Indicio quarum cognita Glicerium.
    Quod Moriuht cernens: "Utinam modo mortuus essem!
      Cur fera mors tardas?" ingeminat lacrimans.
    "O mea Glicerium! misero ploranda per aevum,
      Tot mala perpessam cerno tuam faciem."
285 Incipit effari mediaque in voce resistit,
      Ut Dido flammis interitura suis.
    Clibanus est, Moriuht, ardens tua femina presens;
      Hujus enim natibus te trahit Ascalaphus.
    Filius ipse Stigis, nigro detrusus Averno,
290   Gaudet luxuria, diligit atque nefas.
    Iste tuum semper bachando libidine pectus
      Ducit ad horrendum te, Moriuht, baratrum.
    O Moriuht, Moriuht, quae te dementia cepit!
      Cur Christum perdis, quem dedit unda tibi?
295 Quondam grammaticus, precurva caballia factus,
      Cur centumgemineus luxuria Briareus

261 gaudia] gaudi MS
268 Calvule] Calve MS
270 Rudoil] Ruduil MS, *corr. marg.* Rudoil
288 Ascalaphus] Aschalaphus MS
293 cepit] coepit MS
295 caballia] gabeliia MS

be returned to you. Go quickly and look for your love throughout our realm, and be sure to let me know everything you find out. If she has perchance been sold into slavery and is still a slave, I myself will return her to you, and I will also pay her ransom" [258-64].

After the lady said this, everyone broke out in laughter, and Moriuht quickly left the lofty throne as youths and boys, circling this monster, sang, "Look for your hat, little baldy, look for your goat, little baldy" [265-68].

When Moriuht was again sacrificing to the gods, he heard a voice at the shrine: "Your dear wife is in Le Vaudreuil." This port is not very far from the countess's court, and it is often frequented by Danes for the sake of gain [269-72].

When Moriuht is informed of his wife's whereabouts, he goes to the port and surveys every boat with his eyes. Not finding her at the port, he examines all the houses until he descries his wife in a poor man's dwelling [273-76].

She diligently worked at her mistress's loom with a metal shuttle and, as a slave, led a miserable existence. By the naked shoulders of this unhappy girl, by her pretty naked breasts, Glicerium was recognized [277-80].

When Moriuht sees her, he groans while he weeps, "I wish that I were dead! Why do you delay, cruel death? Oh, my Glicerium, forever to be wailed by wretched me, I see from your appearance all the sorrows you have endured" [281-84].

She begins to speak but in mid-stride stops, like Dido about to burn in the flames. She is an oven, Moriuht, your burning wife who is now present. Ascalaphus, himself a son of Styx, who was consigned to dark Avernus, draws you to her rump. He rejoiced in wantonness, delighted in evil. By debauching your breast with lust, he leads you, Moriuht, to the horrid pit. O Moriuht, Moriuht, what madness has seized you? Why do you lose Christ, whom the waters gave to you? Once you were a scholar, but now you've been made a swaybacked packhorse. Why have you become, unwilling, a hundred-armed

Invitus positus, jumentum stercore factus?
   Sexus femineus te facit esse pecus.
Cum caper os caprae tribuit dans oscula amoris,
300   Luctus erat talis, qualis adest pueris,
Cum patris aut matris plorantes ante sepulchrum
   Brachia dant collo, veque canunt mutuo.
Inter plorandum, Moriuht, ad pauperes orbam
   Fer hoc mancipium, cujus erit precium.
305 "En," contra Baucis, "mea, semper putida serva,
   Quaerit per populum fratrem amare suum;
Tot quoque gnationes illi popisma ferentes,   fol. 6v
   Quot terrae flores, quot corilis nuces.
Sicut vacca suum quaerit per devia taurum,
310   Sic hoc mancipium, gausape, vel veretrum."
Subridens Moriuht: "Mea quod si semper abusa,
   Hoc, Baucis, taceas, non minus inveniam."
"En," contra mulier, "si vis tu noscere mercem,
   Munere denarii est mihi dimidii."
315 His caper auditis, tendens ad menia castri,
   Munus Glicerii mox rogat atque capit.
Tam parvo caprae donatus munere carae;
   Ex humeris capram fert Rotomago suam.
Nec patitur pedetemptim incedere amicam,
320   Sed lectica suis efficitur humeris.
Sub coxis positus caprae carruca duabus
   Cantabat Martis dulcia furta sibi.
Cantando tandem Moriuht pervenit ad urbem,
   Deportans scapulis gaudia magna suis.
325 Conjuge donatur, sed vultu turbidus adhuc,
   Tristis pro caprae belua prole suae.
Domna velut sapiens Moriuht quid Scottus haberet
   Inquirit, sobolem dixit abesse suam.
Prole requisita, nummi quadrante redempta,
330   Panis precocti parteque dimidii,
Adductaque caprae Moriuht propriaeque capellae,
   Suscipitur magna non sine laetitia.

298 facit] facis MS
299 Cum caper os caprae tribuit] Cum caper os caprae os tribuit MS
303 pauperes] pauperis MS
306 fratrum] frater MS
315 ad menia] ad amenia MS
321 carruca] curruca MS
327 quid] quod Ms

Briareus for the sake of wantonness, made a mule in dung? A woman transforms you into a beast [285-98].

When the goat embraced his she-goat and gave her loving kisses, their sorrow was like that of two boys who, weeping at their father's and mother's graves, place their arms around each other's necks and moan with mutual woe [299-302].

While you're weeping, Moriuht, bring this orphan slave to Glicerium's poor owners as a ransom [303-4].

"Come now!" says Baucis [Glicerium's owner]. "This slave has always been a rotten one. She seeks to love her own brother among the people. As many buyers cluck their tongues at her as there are flowers on earth, nuts on hazel shrubs. Just as a cow seeks her bull through unfrequented tracks, just so this slave, this slut, this cunt [is looking for her brother]" [305-10].

Moriuht replies, "If you don't like this one, Baucis, stay calm—I'll find one just as good as her [Glicerium]" [311-12].

"Okay," says the woman. "If you want to possess this merchandise, she is worth a half *denarius* in cash to me" [313-14].

When Moriuht hears this, he makes for the walls of the castle, where he requests and receives the ransom money for Glicerium. Given the small sum for his dear she-goat, Moriuht carries his wife on his shoulders to Rouen. He does not suffer her to walk on her feet, but fashions a sedan out of his shoulders. He placed himself under her thighs as it he were a chariot and sang about the sweet thefts of Mars. Still singing, Moriuht finally arrives in Rouen, carrying his great joy on his back [315-24].

Moriuht now has his wife, but still his face is troubled. The beast is sad because of his she-goat's kid. The wise countess asks Moriuht what bothers the Irishman, and he said his offspring is missing. When Moriuht finds his progeny, he buys her with a quarter cent and half a loaf of half-baked bread. The kid is led to Moriuht and his she-goat, who receive her with great joy [325-32].

Suscepta capra Scottus capraeque capella
    Ausus se magnum dicere grammaticum;
335 Coepit doctiloquis semet preferre poetis,
    Homero magno, Virgilio, Statio;
Per totam cortem versus ructabat oberrans
    Dignos confectis stercore paginulis.
Sed dum sublimis versus ructator oberrat,
340   Empedocli similis in puteum cecidit.
"Foribus en clausis moratur pontifex Hugo."   fol. 74
    Quid sibi vult versus, claudicat, heu! Moriuht.
Gaude, mons Penton, costam tibi junximus unam,
    Gaudes ecce duo quod tibi tempora fero.
345 Mons Jovis, heu! plora, quia costa abduceris una,
    Syllaba *fex*, plora, longa brevis posita.
Pes fugat ecce pedem, rabidus frater quasi fratrem
    Unius matris visceribus geniti.
Dactilis amphymacro tribraco, spondee, fugaris;
350   I, spondee, viam; dactile, carpe fugam.
Non vobis locus est, neque gratia carminis ulla,
    Vos fugat a solio nunc Moriuht proprio;
Spondeum, iambus pellit te, dactile, curtus,
    Norma pedumque pudet carminis et species.
355 Da, Maro Virgili, flammis, da nobile carmen,
    Gratia nulla tibi ceu Moriuht cecinit.
Non Aurunca tibi palmas, neque Francia tendet,
    Si vacuus nobis fratribus es geminis.
Ecce duo plorate pedes, plorate sodales,
360   Perdentes normam carminibus legitimam.
Inter grammaticos pollentes laude fuistis
    Actenus et nostris versibus assidui;
Emeritos jam vos Moriuht vult esse per orbem,
    Foribus ex tribraco *pontifex* amphymacro.
365 Omnia miscentur, mundi confunditur ordo,
    Mons Jovis ardenti cingitur ceu busto;
Non retinent montes pecudes, atque ostrea montes,
    Si Maro deletur nobilis et Statius.
Si non esse potest mundo, neque stare decenter,

335 doctiloquis] doctiloquos MS
340 Empedocli] Empedocle MS
350 carpe fugam] carpe viam fugam MS, *corr.* carpe fugam
357 Aurunca] Aurumca MS
366 busto] buno MS
369 Si non esse] Si inquid non esse MS

After retrieving his she-goat and the she-goat's kid, the Irishman dared to call himself a distinguished scholar. He began to prefer himself to those erudite poets great Homer, Virgil, and Statius. As he rambled about the court, he belched forth verses worthy to be printed in shit [333-38].

But when this belcher of sublime verses was roaming about, like Empedocles he fell into a pit. [He composed this line:] "Lo! When the gates have been closed, Bishop Hugo delays" [339-41].

What kind of line is that, Moriuht? Alas! it limps! Rejoice, Mount Penton, for another rib has been joined to you. You may rejoice because look! I count two more measures for you. But the Hill of Jove horrors! you may as well weep, for you have been removed of one rib: the long syllable *fex* wail! has been placed as a short. Thus one foot drives away the other, just like a raving brother who drives away his brother, both born in the womb of the same mother. A dactyl [is driven out] by an amphimacrus [in the fifth foot], [another dactyl is driven out] by a trochee [in the third foot]. Spondee, you too are put to flight. Go your way spondee, and you too, dactyls, take flight. There is no longer a place for either of you, there is no longer any grace in poetry, for Moriuht has driven you from your proper seats. A short iamb expels both the spondee and the dactyl, and the rules of metrics and poetic beauty are violated [342-54].

Virgil, throw your noble poem to the flames. Surely there is no honor for you if Moriuht sings your song. Aurunca [i.e., Italy] does not extend palms to you, nor does France, if you lack the aid of the two brothers [i.e., the dactyl and the spondee]. See the two companions, the two feet, lament when the proper rules of poetry are abandoned. Among mighty scholars the dactyl and spondee received praise, and they were used even in my verse. Now Moriuht wants to remove them from the world, as he employs a tribrach for *foribus* and an amphimacrus for *pontifex* [355-64].

Everything has become confused. The world's order is utterly confounded. It's as if Jove's mountain is surrounded by a burning pyre. The mountains cannot retain their beasts, and oysters inhabit the mountains if noble Virgil is abolished along with Statius. Order cannot remain in this world, nor can the

370 Dum fuerint caelo lumina clara duo,
    Grammaticam Scottus Moriuht forsan sibi finxit,
      Dicens quod finis sit capiti similis,
    Spondeusque trocheus pariter sunt clausula versus,
      Spondeus curto longior est socio;
375 Clausula spondeo protenditur ultima longo,   fol. 7v
      Syllaba trocheo sit brevis a socio.
    His jungit tribracum Moriuht te, dactile, pellens
      Foribus apposito carminis in solio.
    Fertur ab hoc forsan quod sicut clausula versus,
380 Spondeum longe teque, trochee, tenet.
    Sic potis est tribrachum capiti prefigere versus,
      Quod non heroum carmina precipiunt.
    Grammaticam talem non nobis Beda reliquit,
      Componens librum carminibus habilem.
385 O Moriuht! nescit rursus vox missa reverti;
      Ructasti versum quam male compositum!
    Sub lodice tua melius recubare fuisset
      Te cum Glicerio, qua tibi caldus odor,
    Sic incompositum quam ferres rabula versum,
390 Quo risum Francis, dedecus et pueris.
    "Ludere qui nescit campestribus abstinet armis":
      Hoc cecinit Flaccus, nobilis, egregius;
    "Indoctusque pilae discive trochique quiescit";
      Immemor es Flacci, talia qui cecinit.
395 Credo tuum numquam Flacco tetigisse labellum,
      Vidisti tantam forte superficiem.
    Insanum, cuncti, Moriuht audite, poetae,
      Vos quorum mentes recta poesis habet;
    Cernite nunc verborum dogmate plenum.
400 Quis vidit caprum, dicite, grammaticum?
    Temporibus nostris redeunt spectacula multa;
      Ecce poeta asinus versifice loquitur,
    Cum natura sibi concedit rudere semper;
      Posthabitus phaleris versificare cupit.

383 reliquit] reliquid MS, *corr.* reliquit
385 vox] mox MS, *corr.* vox
389 rabula] ravola MS
395 labellum] labellum MS, *corr.* libellum
396 tantam] tantum MS

world remain stable—so long as there are two bright lights in the sky—if this Irishman Moriuht is allowed to establish the rules of prosody, claiming that the end of a line is identical to the beginning and that the spondee and the trochee are identical at the end of a line, the spondee being longer than its short friend. But the final foot should be lengthened by the long spondee. The second syllable of a trochee is shorter than its companion [365-76].

In addition to using these meters, Moriuht wants to employ the tribrach, abandoning the dactyl, as he shows when he places *foribus* at the beginning of the line. Hence we may conclude that a verse ends in two ways: either with a long spondee or with a trochee. Moreover, the tribrach may be affixed much earlier, at the beginning of a verse, a practice that epic prosody does not prescribe. Bede, writing a useful book about poetry, has left us no such rules [377-84].

But Moriuht, words once uttered cannot be drawn back: You belched forth a verse that was miserably composed! It would have been better if you had crawled under a blanket with Glicerium, with your hot stench, than clamorously produce faulty verses that provide laughter for Frenchmen and shame for boys. "He who cannot play a game shuns the weapons of the Campus"—this the noble, excellent Horace wrote—"and, if unskilled in ball or quoit or hoop, remains aloof." You forget Horace, who sang of such matters. I believe your lips never recited Horace. You probably saw only the surface [385-96].

Listen to the mad Moriuht, all ye poets, ye whose minds are ruled by true poesy! Seek out the man who is full of great dogma. Somebody tell me—has he seen the scholarly goat? Many a marvel has returned to our age: we may now see a poetic ass speak in verse as nature resigns herself to his constant braying. Lacking laurels, he nonetheless wishes to compose poetry. Who has ever seen

405 Talia quis vidit? Forsan mutatio secli
    Legis et Altithroni cogitat esse sibi.
    Quod non eveniat, Jesu, misere cito nostri,
    Gessisti nostram nempe diu faciem.
    Idcirco miserere tuis, et parce redemptis: fol. 8r
410   Versificare homini, rudere das asinis.
    Qui Moriuht non odit amet tua carmina, Scotte,
    Dilector Bavii est Moriuht similis;
    Nam quadrata domus spatiis distenditur equis,
    Rubricam fictor diligit unde suam.
415 Sic omnis sapiens verbis cautusque poeta
    Mentis in absconso carminatam trutinat,
    Librans spondeum pariter te, dactile, secum,
    Conjungens partes cum ratione sua,
    Donec incoeptum carmen deducat ad unguem,
420   Judicio dignum laudibus et meritum.
    Quod noscens Statius multos vigilata per annos
    Carmina descripsit, dans ea post populis,
    Et Maro Virgilius, Latiorum nobilis auctor,
    Ursa velut fetus, sic vomitabat opus.
425 Quod dictu mirum est, sicut vomit ore cruorem,
    Post lingit tantum donec habet catulum,
    Sic vir predictus, componens nobile carmen,
    Quod modo doctiloquis est honor atque decus,
    Mane incomposite versus ructabat abunde.
430   Quos detruncabat post relegendo die.
    Unde suum cum forte librum proferret Herotes,
    Querens infectos forte sibi numeros,
    Infecto cuidam, quo non prestantior alter,
    Apposuit subito vir bonus ille Maro;
435 Hujus enim menti semper bene vincta poesis,
    Recte scribendi fons et origo sibi.
    Idcirco nunc ejus opus per secula vivit,
    Servatur, legitur, laudibus et colitur.
    Esne memor horum, Moriuht, modo rabula Scotte?
440   Ut patet, in versu es, Moriuht, fatuus.
    Cur te jactasti tantum, caper, esse poetam?

406 Altithroni] Altithrono MS, *corr.* Altithroni
406 cogitat] cogit MS
407 cito] scito MS
422 descripsit] descripsis MS, *corr.* descripsit
439 rabula] ravola MS

the like? Perhaps it is the end of the world and he thinks the Almighty's laws are his own. May such an event never occur—Jesus, pity us! You yourself bore human form for a time, so pity your faithful, spare those who are saved. You allow men to versify, asses to bray [397-410].

Let him who does not despise Moriuht love your songs, O Irishman. One who likes [the poetry of] Bavius is like one who likes [the poetry of] Moriuht. But just as a square house has four equal walls, and just as a painter loves his red paint, every provident poet, wisely using words, weighs his compositions in the recesses of his mind, considering the dactyl as well as the spondee, joining each part according to his sound judgment, until he composes the undertaken poem perfectly and has made it worthy of judicious praise. Knowing this method, Statius drafted poems but kept them for many years before publishing them, and Virgil, that noble writer of the Romans, would discharge his work like a she-bear her cub. It is amazing, but just as a she-bear vomits a bloody mess from her mouth and later licks it until she has a whelp, Virgil, composing noble poetry that is now greatly respected and valued among the learned, would belch forth abundant disordered verses in the morning that he would later lop off at the end of day. So when Herotes happened to present his book to Virgil, complaining that some of the meter was imperfect, that good man Maro would approve of a certain defective line because it was no worse than any other. He had good control over his subject matter, and he himself was a fount, an originator of correct writing. For that reason his work flourishes throughout the world. It is preserved, read, covered with praise [411-38].

Are you not aware of these facts, Moriuht, you clamorous Irishman? Since it is clear from your poetry that you are a fool, why, goat, do you boast so much

En pudet egregios hos imitare viros!
Quid facient? hiatu pereunt tua carmina! Horati,   fol. 8v
    Virgili, plora, te caper ecce fugat.
445 Cedamus patria, pereunt jam grammata nostra,
    Scottia grammaticam protulit ecce suam.
O caper! ante tuae manduces gausape caprae
    Et vulvam pariter funditus atque nates,
Virgilii pereant quam docta poemata nostri.
450   *Fo* duo *mo* habeant tempora, *fex* habeat:
"Foribus en clausis moratur pontifex Hugo";
    Fo modo *mo*, gaude, syllaba *fex*que geme.
Ni fallor, Moriuht, vesicae intentus amatae,
    Ructasti versum non bene compositum.
455 Nudus cum nuda recubans cur, stulte, capella
    Ut pecus ad pecudem retro tenes faciem?
Esne mnemor quod te nudum nudamque capellam
    In feno vidi mane jacere fimi?
Non jurare potes, neque te purgare decenter;
460   Vidi ceventes, Hercule, vos mutuo.
Nam si vis jurare mihi non esse quod audis,
    Produc reliquias conjugis ipse nates;
Si super hanc orcam mihi tu juraveris ordam,
    Oscula dans illi, crimine liber abi.
465 Vis, Moriuht, hujus vicii sic perdere famam?
    Jejuna contra fortia forte sacra,
Et mane caput fluvio ter subrue nocte,
    Ut totus purus basia des natibus.
Contigerit si forte tuum non esse labellum
470   Forte repurgatum, nec satis esse sacrum,
Tollas inde lupo quod caprae pancia mittit
    Stercore genzivas atque habeas humidas.
Jam satis est Moriuht Scottum risisse petulcum
    Illius nomen jamque iterare pudet.
475 Posthabito capro procino melle cibando,
    Ad melius carmen nos properare decet;
Non debemus enim calamum corrumpere nostrum   fol. 94
    Pro Moriuht capro atque caprae puteo.
Facturam Moriuht numeris quis scribere posset?

443 hiatu] latu MS
443 Horati] honorati MS
444 Virgili, plora, te] Virgili, plorate MS
450 Fo] o MS, *corr. marg.* Fo
456 pecudem] pecudim MS, *corr.* pecudem

that you are a poet?   Come!   You should be ashamed to imitate such distinguished men! What will your poems do? They perish because of a hiatus! Horace, Virgil, weep! See the goat put you to flight. We may as well leave our country, since the rules of prosody have perished and Ireland has produced her own grammar [439-46].

You goat! I would rather see you devour your she-goat's beard, her cunt as well as her rump, than see the brilliant poems of my Virgil perish. *Fo* and *mo* are made long, as should be *fex*. "Lo! When the gates have been closed, Bishop Hugo delays." *Fo* and *mo* are lucky [because they are short syllables placed in positions where long ones are required], but the syllable *fex* groans [because it is used as a short instead of a long syllable]. Unless I am mistaken, Moriuht, always intent upon your love's bladder, you have belched forth poorly composed poetry [447-54].

When you lie naked with your naked she-goat, why, stupid, do you copulate from behind like a beast on a beast? Do you remember when I saw you both naked, lying in the hay and dung one morning? You cannot deny it, nor can you excuse yourself. By Jove, I saw you both screwing [455-60]!

But if you want to swear that what I say is untrue, show me what is left of your wife's rump. If you swear to the truth on that stinking barrel—and you must kiss it—you may go acquitted. Would you like to lose your notoriety for this vice, Moriuht? Fast reverently at a holy tomb and in the morning and at night dunk your head in a river three times so that all pure you may kiss your wife's buttocks. If it should occur that your lips are still not holy enough, take from the wolf the same thing that your she-goat's belly sends forth and hold the gums wet with dung [461-72].

Now I have sufficiently ridiculed this wanton Irishman Moriuht, and it would be shameful for me to repeat his name. This goat, who can only be fed with porcine honey, should be rejected, and I should attempt a higher subject. For I should not sully my pen on account of this goat Moriuht and his she-goat's pit.   Who can describe this creature Moriuht in verse?   He is indescribable, just like

480   Est indicibilis sicut arena maris.
    Hic factis finem Moriuht imponere possem,
      Sed me cogit adhuc fama volans Moriuht.
    Cuculus in silvis hiemali tempore cantat:
      "Cuc cuc cuc, Moriuht, te voco, cuc, Moriuht!
485 Nam, Moriuht, vigila, recubans ne forte capella
      Juxta te lenem dicat adesse bovem,
    Qui lingendo nates capre succedat amice,
      Poplitis et retro stans." Crebra popismata ait:
    "Sis cautus, Moriuht, jaceas ne forte retrorsum,
490   Ut bos non veniens linguat amice nates."
    Imponam finem dictis, ne talia fando
      Corrumpam calamum mentis et ingenium.
    Jam pereat Moriuht, vas perditionis, et illud
      Quod fert ad tabulam presulis egregiam;
495 Accidit unde modo quod factus hyrundo bibendo,
      Heu! resupinatus cum vomitu geritur.
    Tu, presul, valeas, valeat per tempora cuncta
      Domna, decus regni, lumina clara suis.

483 Cuculus] Cucculus MS
487 succedat] subcadat MS
493 Jam pereat Moriuht, vas] Jam pereat Moriuht, et vas MS

Petri Pictoris, *De matronis*

    Matronarum pudicarum   bona continentia
    Veneretur et laudetur   digna reverentia:
    He decorant et honorant   maritalem copulam,
    Fugientes et verentes   male fame maculam.
5   Sed sunt quedam que rem fedam   committunt in latebris,
    Nomen clarum, falso clarum,   fama facit celebris:
    Harum vana et prophana   falsaque religio
    Est cavenda et spernenda   nec digna coniugio.

    Nuper ait quidam michi: "Sponsam nutrio fidam.
    Vix, nisi quando videt ridentem me sibi, ridet,
    Non male lascivit, quasi Penelopes michi vivit.
    Aut legit aut orat simul aut operando laborat.

Prologus 3 maritalem] maritale MS

the sands of the sea [473-80].

Now I should place an end to this story of Moriuht, yet Moriuht's reputation, which flits about, drives me on. The cuckoo in the winter forest sings, "Coo, coo, coo, Moriuht, I'm calling you, Moriuht. For Moriuht, watch out, lest by chance your she-goat, lying down, should say that a gentle bull is nearby and is next to you. Standing behind her knees, it may lick her rump and mount her in a friendly fashion." Making clucking sounds, it says, "Be careful, Moriuht, not to lie on your back, so the ox, wandering by, does not lick your friend's rump" [481-90].

Let me end my words, lest by saying too much I corrupt my craft and my wit. Let Moriuht die, this vessel of damnation, along with everything he brings to my patron's distinguished table. For what happens now once happened to the swallow while drinking: alas! he is carried out flat on his back with his vomit [491-96].

Farewell, my prelate, farewell, my lady, glory of the kingdom. Bright lights of the people, fare thee well for all time [497-98].

Peter the Painter, *On Married Women*

> The virtuous chastity of modest wives
> Should be praised and honored reverently;
> They grace and ennoble the marriage bond,
> Fleeing and fearing the stain of evil fame.
> 5   But some wives engage in foul deeds in secret;
> Great fame makes their names well known well known for falsity.
> Their meaningless, perverse, phony show of religion
> Should be shunned and rejected; they're not worthy of marriage.
>
> Recently someone said to me: "I cherish a faithful
> Wife who hardly laughs unless she sees me laughing.
> She is not wicked or wanton, but like Penelope, she lives for me alone.
> She reads, prays, and works very hard.

5   Otia non curat hec nec super omnia iurat.
       Quod si perdiderit me, non alium sibi querit,
       Quin iugulo cultra defiget quam nubat ultra.
       Hinc, recolens Annam viduam castamque Susannam
       Et matronarum sacros mores aliarum,
10   Has preponendas aliis docet, has imitandas,
       Et male ludentes reprehendit acerba clientes.
       Vtque scias tandem laus quanta sequatur eamdem:
       Non habet uxorem vir quisquam me meliorem."
          Sic michi laudabat, sic sponsam iustificabat,
15   Hanc etiam solitus aliis laudare maritus.
       Vix ego, vix vere risum potui cohibere
       Post hunc sermonem, dum falsam religionem
       Eius miratur miser utque deam veneratur.
       Nam quod amatorum sit amatrix innumerorum
20   Iamdudum novi, quod sit meretrix bene novi.
       O serpens prudens, mala sponsa, virum male ludens,
       Fraude vel arte pari tibi quid valet assimilari?
          Cedit, concedit tibi sponsus, obaudit, obedit.
       Matronis mille prefert te credulus ille
25   Fame laude bone, doctrina, religione.
       At tu deceptrix mala mechorumque receptrix
       Furtim mecharis, cum casta viro videaris.
       Nocte sub obscura peragis sine coniuge plura,
       Dum per posticum trahis intro latentem amicum,
30   Aut subagenda viris egros aut templa requiris.
       Sepe viro dicis: "De nostris unus amicis
       Languet; ad hunc ibo solandum iamque redibo."
       Dicis vera quidem, sed suis sit languidus idem
       Ille tuus nescit dominus qui cetera nescit.
35   Quem petis egrotus puer est aliquis tibi notus,
       Cuius lesuras languentis languida curas,
       Quando per amplexus alternos est tibi nexus,
       Quem camera clausa demulces quelibet ausa,
       Dans huic antidotum vobis medicis bene notum.
40   Sic consolaris languentem, sic medicaris,
       Sic morbum iuvenis dulci lenimine lenis.
       Inde regressa cito sic inquis casta marito:

8 recolens] lecolens MS
9 mores] mares MS
35 notus] natus MS
39 vobis] nobis MS

5   She does not seek leisure time, nor does she swear by anything.
So if she lost me, she would not look for another husband,
But would cut her throat with a knife rather than wear a veil for long.
Reflecting on the widow Anna and the chaste Susanna
And the saintly ways of other wives,
10 She maintains that these women should be preferred to others, that they
      should be imitated,
And she severely censures those women who sport with lovers wickedly.
So you should know how much people praise her.
No man has a better wife than I do."
   Thus did he praise his wife to me, thus did he justify her;
15 This husband also would praise her to others.
Really, I could scarcely contain my laughter
After this speech, as the fool admires his wife's false show of religion
And worships her like a saint.
For I have long known that she is the mistress of
20 Innumerable lovers; I have known very well that she is a slut.
O wily serpent, evil wife, wickedly deceiving this man,
What can be compared to you in fraud and cunning?
   The husband yields, submits, obeys, complies.
Credulous, he prefers you to a thousand wives
25 Because of your fame for good repute, principles, religion.
But you, evil deceiver and receiver of adulterers,
Stealthily commit adultery, while you seem chaste to your husband.
In obscure night you execute vile deeds without him
When through a back door you visit your sweetheart hiding within.
30 Sometimes, when you're going to get plowed, you inquire after the sick or
      go to the churches.
You often say to your husband: "One of our friends
Is sick. I'm going to comfort him and return right away."
Indeed you speak the truth, but your lord does not know
The sick person, just as he does not know other things.
35 The sick boy whom you visit is known only to you.
You, sick one, care for the invalid's affliction
When he entwines himself around you in mutual embraces.
You stroke him when the bedroom door is shut, you dare everything,
And you give him that remedy well known to you doctors.
40 Thus you console the sick one, thus you doctor him,
Thus you alleviate the youth's illness with sweet medication.
Then, quickly returning home, you say to your husband,

"En ope divina nostraque simul medicina
Quem gravis afflixit dolor eger in orbe revixit.
45   Febre gravi plenam miseri tetigi modo venam,
Sed me tangente fugit febris inde repente,
Carmen enim unum per me fugat omne nocivum."
      Gaudet et applaudit quia talia vir suus audit;
Laudat, credit idem quia credidit omnia pridem,
50   Huicque refert grates propter tantas bonitates.
      Ergo qui queris prescire dolos mulieris,
Ne fallat forte simili te perfida sorte,
Audi quam docte fingit mendatia nocte
Coniunx astuta Veneris documenta secuta.
55   Audi serpentem virus sub melle vomentem,
Et male fallentem sponsum male nil metuentem.
"Nunc est surgendum," dicit, "lacrimisque luendum
Quicquid nocturnus suasit furor atque diurnus.
Surgendum David de nocte propheta probavit,
60   Vt mens tunc pura Domino libet pia thura.
Hoc Domino gratum tempus, reor, estque beatum,
Templa Dei munda iam cum prece sunt adeunda,
Quare devote factura precamina pro te,
Vir meus, illa peto: curam de rebus habeto!
65   Tu res carnales, ego tractem spirituales."
Ista quidem fando suspiria dat lacrimando,
Mox fictas tergit lacrimas securaque pergit
Ad loca que novit, votumque quod impia vovit
Solvit amatori cuius et iunxit amori,
70   Et subigi gaudet et quicquid non decet audet,
Quod nec homo nec himen laudet, patrat impia crimen.
Sic flexis orat genibus, sic crimina plorat,
Sic matutina iacet hora facta supina,
Sordibus implicitum sic expiat illa maritum.
75   At male sollicitus de rebus in ede maritus
Estimat orantem, putat in templo vigilantem,
Condolet uxorem vigilandi ferre laborem
Falsoque tristatur miser, ignorans quid agatur.
      Hec ubi transacta furtim sunt nocte peracta,

75 in ede] inde MS

"So! With God's help, and my medicine,
The sick boy who was afflicted with a serious disease has returned to the living.
45 I only felt the wretch's pulse, checked his high fever,
And when I touched him, his fever quickly subsided.
Because of me, a single spell put everything injurious to flight."
    Her husband rejoices and approves when he hears these
Words. He believes her and praises her, just as he did
50 Before, and he thanks her for her great goodness.
    So you who would like to know about women's wiles before [you get married],
Just in case an unfaithful woman should someday befall you too,
Listen how she cleverly invents lies at night,
How this wife knows the clever tricks of Venus.
55 Listen to the serpent, vomiting forth poison disguised
As honey, wickedly deceiving her husband, wickedly fearing nothing:
"Now is the time to rise," she says, "and to expiate with tears
Whatever the passions of day and night have driven us to do.
David the prophet favored rising at night
60 So that with a pure and holy mind we could make an offering of incense to the Lord.
I believe this time is most pleasing to the Lord and is blessed by Him.
One should now go to God's holy churches to pray.
So, my husband, while I am ready to pray devotedly for you,
I ask you to take good care of our possessions.
65 You take care of worldly things; let me handle the spiritual ones."
While she speaks, she sighs and weeps,
But she soon wipes off the feigned tears and, confident, proceeds
To her well-known haunts, and the prayers that the unfaithful woman promised her husband
She fulfills for her lover, as she joins him
70 And rejoices to be plowed and dares everything that is indecent.
The faithless woman commits crimes that neither mankind nor the marriage institution approves.
Thus she prays on bent knees, thus she laments sins,
Thus she lies supine till the break of dawn,
Thus she atones for the sins of her husband, who is entangled in baseness.
75 Her husband is at home and is untroubled by this state of affairs;
He thinks she is praying and holding vigil at church.
He grieves that his wife maintains this heavy vigil;
The fool is saddened by her falsity and does not know what is really going on.
The woman, after performing her business secretly at

80 Prima puellarum loca circuit ecclesiarum,
Psalmos cantando, sua fletibus ora rigando,
Ceu nocturnarum non conscia nequitiarum.
His operam dantem studiis, his invigilantem
Quilibet errator dum cernit sive viator,
85 Talia facta viro defert narramine miro
Dicens: "O felix, homo vere coniuge felix,
Coniuge formosa, prudenti, religiosa!
Quam bene successit tibi dum talis tibi cessit
Femina, que sane non cessat vespere, mane
90 Visere sanctorum loca sive domos miserorum.
Religione pia modo Martha modoque Maria,
Sic et sic orat, sic inrequieta laborat
Pervigili cura celi tibi regna datura.
Ergo leteris quia vir suus esse mereris,
95 Prospera fortuna tibi coniuge cessit in una."
        Audit, miratur sponsus miser, exhilaratur
Coniuge de iusta quam laudat fama venusta.
Sed noctu gesta res non est huic manifesta,
Quam mox odiret, si que sunt abdita sciret.
100   Orandi fessa post mane domumque regressa
Prudens matrona, sponsi decus atque corona,
Quid misero dicit, quem fraudis carmine vicit?
"Vir meus, exulta," dicit, "quia te prece multa
A laqueo mortis dissolvi femina fortis!
105 Non opus orandi tibi, non opus est vigilandi,
Nam si scire velis quam sim tibi sponsa fidelis:
Nocte laboravi pro te, nostros iteravi
Himnos cum psalmis, tensis ad sidera palmis,
Vt sic salveris precibus fide mulieris,
110 Ergo salvandus et per me iustificandus
Dormis securus, per me celos habiturus."
O fraus serpentis miserum male decipientis!
Pulcra quidem verba facit, at latet anguis in herba:
Edit verba foris melliti plena saporis,

81 cantando] cantandos MS
93 Pervigili] Per vigili MS
100 Orandi] Oravi MS
102 dicit] dicet MS
109 salueris] saluaris MS
111 Dormis] Darmi MS

80 Night, is the first of the maidens to circle [the stations of] the churches [at dawn].
She sings psalms and wets her face with tears,
As if unaware of her nocturnal debauchery.
She takes pains to perform her duty carefully, paying close attention to detail,
And any passerby who sees her
85 Reports her activities to her husband in a wonderful little story,
Saying, "O happy man, truly happy husband,
To have such a beautiful, wise, religious wife!
How well things have gone for you, since such a woman
Has fallen to your lot, who does not cease evenings,
90 Mornings, to visit the altars of the saints and the houses of the sick.
She is devoutly religious, sometimes like Martha, at other times like Mary,
Praying like one or the other. Thus she cultivates
The tireless concern of ever-watchful heaven, the kingdom that will someday be yours.
Therefore you should rejoice because you have deserved to be her husband;
95 A prosperous fortune befell you in your unique wife."
    The stupid husband listens, marvels, rejoices
In his upright wife, whom repute praises as lovely.
But he is not shown the deeds she performs at night;
He would soon hate her if he knew what she concealed.
100   Later that morning, when she tires of praying and returns home,
What does this crafty matron, the honor and crown of her husband,
Say to the wretch, whom she conquers with a tune of deceit?
"Rejoice, my dear," she says, "for with much praying
I, your vigorous wife, have released you from the snares of death!
105 It is not necessary for you to pray and keep vigil,
For if you want to know how true I am toward you,
At night I labored on your behalf, I repeated hymns
And psalms, with my palms stretched toward heaven.
So you have been saved through your trusty wife's prayers.
110 Therefore, saved and pardoned through me,
You sleep soundly. Through me you will attain heaven."
Oh, fraud of the serpent wickedly deceiving the wretch!
Truly she utters pretty words, but a snake lies in the grass.
She speaks words ladened with honey on the surface,

115 Intus habet plenum cor fraude latensque venenum.
Os aliud fatur, mala mens aliud meditatur,
Iusticiam iactat coram, clam crimina tractat.
Celum promittit sponso, delicta remittit,
Quam sua culpa gravat magis actio sordida pravat.
120 Sponsum securum reddit misere periturum,
Qui nisi speraret vitam per eam, vigilaret,
Arctius oraret, fleret, delicta piaret.
Nunc miser ignorat rem, sponsam laudat, honorat,
Dum putat hypocritam sinceram ducere vitam,
125 Cui quia se credit, animam cum corpore ledit,
Demone captivat, se celi lumine privat.
     Sed concedatur nunc ut prior hic moriatur,
Quid vidua tristis faciet sub casibus istis?
Thesauros, vestes, gemmas dabit ipsa superstes,
130 Vt qui dampnatur baratro sponsus redimatur?
Non dabit! Imma dabit iuveni quem mox adamabit,
Cui coniunx grata sit amicitia sociata.
Huius amatoris coniunx oblita prioris,
Quicquid inornatum tulit ante nec arte paratum,
135 Nec bene composito studio, vivente marito,
Docta reformabit modo seque novam reparabit,
Se fingens Helenam facie cultuque serenam,
Vt stupratorem succendat sic ad amorem.
Et cum deberet miseris dare quicquid haberet
140 Pro sponsi mendis precio, precibus redimendis,
Clausa die tota thalamo satur et bene pota,
Pro foribus stantes inopes victumque rogantes
Negliget, expositum penis neglecta maritum
Cui dum vivebat celos dare sepe solebat.
145 Et quas sollicitus terraque marique maritus
Res desudavit et inaniter accumulavit,
Distrahet, expendet leviter, dabit aut male vendet,
Se pariter vendens et ad omnia crimina tendens.
     Ergo matrone pro falsa religione
150 Non est credendum, sed ab eius amore cavendum.

121 nisi] non MS
138 stupratorem] stupratarem MS
146 desudavit] desudarat MS

115 But within she harbors a heart full of fraud, hiding venom.
    Her mouth says one thing; her wicked mind plans something else.
    Openly she speaks of upright behavior; secretly she engages in sin.
    She promises her husband heaven; she remits his transgressions.
    But her sordid deeds deprave her, even more than her sins bother her.
120 She makes her husband complacent, though he will suffer the worse for it.
    If he did not expect eternal life through her, he would have held vigils,
    He would have prayed devoutly, wept, and propitiated his transgressions.
    Now the fool ignores the truth and praises and honors his wife
    While he thinks this hypocrite leads a holy life.
125 Because he entrusts himself to her, she destroys him body and soul.
    He is taken captive by the devil; he deprives himself of the light of heaven.
      Let us assume that this husband dies before his wife.
    What widow would not be saddened in such circumstances?
    Will this woman, this survivor, distribute treasures, garments, jewels,
130 So that her husband, who is condemned to hell, may be redeemed?
    No, she will not! Rather, she will give gifts to the youth whom she will
      soon love,
    Whom she pleases with warm affection.
    The wife forgets her first lover.
    However unadorned she bore herself before, not wearing makeup,
135 Lacking interest in her clothes while her husband was alive,
    Now she will cleverly transform herself and make herself a new woman,
    Pretending her face is Helen's, fair and refined,
    In order to enflame a defiler to lust.
    And though she ought to have given everything she had to the poor
140 So she could acquire their prayers for her husband's sins,
    She shuts herself up in her room, well fed and well drunk,
    And she neglects the needy standing outside, asking for victuals.
    She neglected her husband, exposed to torments,
    To whom she offered heaven when he was alive.
145 And those things that her solicitous husband
    Sweated for and idly accumulated upon land and sea
    She will scatter, valuing them lightly; she will give them away or sell them
      for nothing,
    Just as she sells herself and heads toward every kind of sin.
    Therefore wives, because of their false show of religion,
150 Should not be trusted, but one should beware of their love.

Bibliography

PRIMARY SOURCES

Manuscripts

Biblioteca Apostolica Vaticana:
  Vat. Palatinus 1710 [f. 16r, *Modus Liebinc*]
  Reg. lat. 61 [f. 23r-23v, *De Iohanne abbate*]
  Reg. lat. 278 [f. 39r, *Ridmus de Iohanne parvulo*]
  Reg. lat. 344 [f. 40v, Hildebert, *De Milone mercatore*]
  Reg. lat. 1357 [f. 121r-124v, Radulfus Tortarius, *Ad Sincopum*]
  Reg. lat. 1762 [f. 226, *De Iohanne abbate*]
Bibliothèque Municipale de Beauvais:
  Beauvais MS. 11 [Fulcoius of Beauvais, *Epistles*]
Bibliothèque Nationale (Paris):
  BN lat. 242 [f. 114v-r, *De Lantfrido et Cobbone*, rhythmic version]
  BN lat. 2872 [f. 26v, *De Iohanne abbate*]
  BN lat. 3705 [f. 146r, Hildebert, *De quodam servo*; f. 146r-v, Hildebert, *De Milone mercatore*; f. 146v, *Parvus erat limes*]
  BN lat. 3761 [f. 67r, Hildebert, *Ad Milonem*; f. 68v, Hildebert, *Quid sit vita pudica*; f. 73r-75v, Peter the Painter, *De muliere mala*]
  BN lat. 8121A [f. 2r-8v, Warnerius of Rouen, *Satire against Moriuht*]
  BN lat. 8427 [f. 5, Hildebert, *De virgine seni nupta*]
  BN lat. 8433 [f. 114v, *Sepe lupus quidam*; f. 118r, *Parvus erat limes*; f. 118r, *Dum vir dormit*]
  BN lat. 8865 [f. 157v, Peter the Painter, *De muliere mala*; f. 158r-159v, Peter, *De illa que filium impudenter adamavit*]
  BN lat. 13768 [f. 1r, Peter the Painter, *De mala muliere*; f. 3r-4r, Peter, *De matronis*]

BN lat. 14193 [f. 8v, Gautier, *Aeole, rex fortis*]

BN lat. 14194 [f. 160v, Hildebert, *De Milone mercatore, Ad Milonem*; f. 164r, Hildebert, *De quodam servo*]

BN lat. 16699 [f. 176r-176v, Peter the Painter, *Prologus de mala muliere*; f. 176v-177v, Peter, *De illa que impudenter filium suum adamavit*; f. 173v, *Exacta cena*]

Collection Etienne Baluze no. 120 [f. 321r-v, Hildebert, *De quodam servo*; f. 325v, Hildebert, *Milo domi non est*; f. 326v, Hildebert, *Ad Milonem*; f. 326v, *Foedere nupta viri nolebat sene potiri*; f. 327r, Hildebert, *De virgine seni nupta*; f. 328v, *De quodam rustico*; f. 332r, *Fertur, erat binis meretricibus unus amator*]

Bibliothèque Royale (Brussels):

MS. 10078-95 [f. 38v-42v, *Unibos*]

Bodleian Library (Oxford):

Oxon. Laud. 86 [f. 94r, *Cum de latrina lapsum salomona ruina*; f. 111v, Hildebert, *De Milone mercatore, Ad Milonem*; f. 114r-v, Hildebert, *De quodam servo*; f. 114v, Hildebert, *Quid sit vita pudica*]

Rawley G.109 [f. 40, Hildebert, *De virgine seni nupta*; f. 71, *Potus Milo sapis*; f. 89, Hildebert, *Ad Milonem*; f. 97, *Virginis insano Iulianus captus amore*; f. 98, *Grecinum virgo puerum grecinus amabat*]

British Library (London):

Cotton Vit. A XII [f. 131r, *De Judeo in latrinam lapso, De marito ab uxore turpiter interempto*]

Harl. 2621 [f. 33v, Hildebert, *Quid sit vita pudica*]

MS. Add. 24199 [f. 44r, Hildebert, *Quid sit vita pudica*; f. 44v, Hildebert, *De quodam servo*; f. 75v, *Res mea*; f. 77v, *Magnus Alexander*]

Royal MS. 8 D XIII [f. 83v, *De Iohanne abbate*]

Cambridge University Library:

MS. Gg.5.35 [f. 432r-441v, *Cambridge Songs*]

Kölner Dombibliothek (Cologne):

MS. 196 [Egbert of Liège, *Fecunda ratis*]

Collections

Barbazon, Etienne, and D. Méon, eds. *Fabliaux et contes des poètes françois des XI, XII, XIII, XIVe et XVe siècles*. 4 vols. Paris: Warée, 1808.

Benson, Larry, and Theodore Andersson, eds. and trans. *The Literary Context of Chaucer's Fabliaux*. Indianapolis: Bobbs-Merril, 1971.

Boutémy, André, ed. "Le recueil poétique du Manuscrit Additional 24199 du British Museum." *Latomus* 2 (1938): 30-52.

The Cambridge Songs: A Goliard's Song Book of the XIth Century. Edited by Karl Bruel. Cambridge: Cambridge University Press, 1915.

Die Cambridger Lieder. Edited by Karl Strecker. Berlin: Weidmann, 1966.

Cohen, Gustave, et al., eds. *La "comédie" latine en France au XIIe siècle.* 2 vols. Paris: "Belles-lettres," 1931.

Eichmann, Raymond, and John DuVal, eds. and trans. *The French Fabliau B.N. MS. 837.* 2 vols. New York: Garland, 1984.

Elliott, Alison Goddard, trans. *Seven Medieval Latin Comedies.* New York: Garland, 1984.

Faral, Edmond, ed. *Les arts poétiques du XIIe et du XIIIe siècle.* Paris: Champion, 1923.

Grimm, Jakob, and Wilhelm Grimm. *The Complete Grimm's Fairy Tales.* Edited by Padraic Colum and Joseph Campbell. New York: Pantheon, 1972.

Harrison, Robert, ed. and trans. *Gallic Salt.* Berkeley: University of California, 1974.

Hauréau, Barthélemy. *Notices et extraits de quelques manuscrits latins de la Bibliothèque Nationale.* 6 vols. Paris: Klincksieck, 1890-93.

Hervieux, Léopold, ed. *Les fabulistes latins depuis le siècle d'Auguste jusqu'à la fin du moyen âge.* 5 vols. Paris: Firmin-Didot, 1893-99.

Langosch, Karl, ed. and trans. *Waltharius, Ruodlieb, Marchenepen.* Basel: Schwabe, 1956.

Luria, Maxwell, and Richard Hoffman, eds. *Middle English Lyrics.* Norton: New York, 1974.

Migne, Jacques-Paul, et al., eds. *Patrologiae cursus completus, seria latina . . .* 221 vols. Paris, 1841-79.

Montaiglon, Anatole de, and Gaston Raynaud, eds. *Recueil général et complet des fabliaux des XIIIe et XIVe siècles.* 6 vols. Paris: Librairie des bibliophiles, 1878.

Monumenta Germaniae Historica [MGH] inde ab anno Christi quingestesimo usque ad annum millesimum et quingentesimum, Libelli de lite imperatorum et pontificum saeculis XI et XII conscripti. 3 vols. Hanover: Hahnian, 1891-97.

Monumenta Germaniae Historica . . . , Poetarum Latinorum medii aevi. 6 vols. (vols. 1-5 = *Poetae Latini aevi Carolini*). Berlin: Weidmann, 1881-1964.

Monumenta Germaniae Historica . . . , Scriptorum. Edited by G. H. Pertz, et al. 32 vols. Hanover: Hahnian, 1826-1934.

Noomen, Willem, and Noco van den Boogaard, eds. *Nouveau recueil complet des fabliaux.* 2 vols. to date. Assen, Netherlands: Van Gorcum, 1983- .

Röhrich, Lutz, ed. *Erzählungen des späten Mittelalters und ihr Weiterleben in Literatur und Volksdichtung bis zur Gegenwart.* 2 vols. Bern: Francke, 1962.

Werner, Jakob, ed. *Beiträge zur Kunde der lateinischen Literatur des Mittelalters aus Handschriften gesammelte.* 2d ed. Aarau: Sauerlander, 1905.

Wright, Thomas, ed. *The Anglo-Latin Satirical Poets and Epigrammatists of the Twelfth Century.* 2 vols. London: Longman, 1872.

———, ed. *A Selection of Latin Stories.* London: Richards (Percy Society), 1842.

Individual Writers and Works

Adalbert of Laon. *Les poèmes satiriques d'Adalbéron*. Edited by G. A. Hückel. Bibliothèque de la Faculté des Lettres de Paris 13. Paris: Université de Paris, 1901.

Aeneas Silvius Piccolomini. *Chrysis, comédie latine inédite*. Edited by André Boutémy. Bruxelles: n.p., 1939.

Alphanus of Salerno. "Verse des Erzbischofs Alfanus von Salerno für Monte Cassino." Edited by B. Albers. *Neues Archiv* 38 (1913): 667-69.

Arnulf of Orléans. "Zur Geschichte der mittellateinische Dichtung: Arnulfi 'Delicie Cleri.'" Edited by J. Huemer. *Romanische Forschungen* 2 (1886): 211-46.

Baudry of Bourgueil. *Les oeuvres poétiques de Baudri de Bourgueil (1046-1130)*. Edited by Phyllis Abrahams. Paris: Champion, 1926.

Boccaccio, Giovanni. *The Decameron*. Translated by G. H. McWilliam. New York: Penguin, 1981.

———. *Filocolo*. Edited by Carlo Salinari and Natalino Sapegno. Turin: Einaudi, 1976.

Bracciolini, Poggio. *Facezie*. Edited and translated by Marcello Ciccuto. Milan: Rizzoli, 1983.

Cena Cypriani. Edited by Karl Strecker. *MGH, Poetae Latini aevi Carolini* 4: 857-900.

Chronicon Novaliciense. *Monumenta novaliciensia vetustiora*. Edited by Carlo Cipolla. Fonti per la Storia d'Italia 31-32. Rome: Instituto storico italiano, 1898-1901.

De nuncio sagaci. Edited by E. H. Alton. *Hermathena* 46 (1931): 61-79.

De uxore Cerdonis. Edited by H. Niewohner. *Zeitschrift für deutsches Altertum*, N.F. 65 (1928): 65-92.

Ecbasis cuiusdam captivi per tropologiam. Edited by Karl Strecker. *Scriptores rerum germanicarum in usum scholarum ex Monumentis Germaniae historicis separatim editi*. Hanover: Hahnian, 1935.

Egbert of Liège. *Fecunda ratis*. Edited by Ernst Voigt. Halle: Niemeyer, 1889.

Evangelium secundum Marcas Argenti. Edited by Paul Lehmann. *Parodistische Texte* 7-8.

Facetus. "The 'Facetus': or, The Art of Courtly Living." Edited and translated by Alison Elliott. *Allegorica* 2 (1977): 27-57.

Froumond of Tegernsee. *Die Tegernsee Briefsammlung (Froumond)*. Edited by Karl Strecker. *MGH, Epistolae selectae* 3. Berlin: Weidmann, 1925.

Fulbert of Chartres. "Hymni et Carmina Ecclesiastica." In Migne et al., *Patrologiae cursus completus* 141: col. 339-52.

Fulcoius of Beauvais. "Fulcoii Belvacensis Epistolae." Edited by M. Colker. *Traditio* 10 (1954): 191-273.

Gallus et Vulpes. Edited by Léon Hermann. *Scriptorium* 1 (1946-47): 260-66.

Gautier. "Un mystérieux ami de Marbode: Le 'redoutable poète' Gautier." Edited by Maurice Delbouille. *Moyen Age* 6 (1951): 205-40.

Geoffrey of Vinsauf. *Poetria Nova.* Translated by Margaret Nims. Toronto: Pontifical Institute of Medieval Studies, 1967.

Geoffrey of Winchester. *Godefridi Prioris Epigrammata.* In Wright, *Anglo-Latin Satirical Poets* 2: 149-50.

Gesta Apollonii. Historia Apollonii regis Tyri. Edited by Alexander Riese. 2d ed. Leipzig: Teubner, 1893.

Gesta Romanorum. Edited by Hermann Oesterley. Berlin: Weidmann, 1872.

Guibert de Nogent. *Histoire de sa vie (1053-1124).* Edited and translated by Georges Bourgin. Paris: Picard, 1907.

Herimannus Contractus. "De octo vitiis principalibus." Edited by Ernst Dümmler. *Zeitschrift für deutsches Altertum* 13 (1853): 385-434.

Hildebert of Lavardin. *Carmina Minora.* Edited by A. Brian Scott. Leipzig: Teubner, 1969.

———. "Carmina Miscellanea." In Migne et al., *Patrologiae cursus completus,* 171: col. 1381-1458.

Historia septem sapientum. Edited by Alfons Hilka. Sammlung mittellateinischer Texte 4. Heidelberg: Carl Winter, 1912.

Hrotsvitha. *Hrotsvithae opera.* Edited by Paul von Winterfield. Berlin: Weidmann, 1892.

———. *The Plays of Roswitha.* Translated by Christopher St. John. New York: Blom, 1966.

Jacques de Vitry. *The Exempla of Jacques de Vitry.* Edited by Thomas F. Crane. London: Nutt (Folklore Society), 1890.

La Fontaine, Jean de. *Fables.* Paris: Garnier-Flammarion, 1966.

Lehmann, Paul. *Parodistische Texte.* Munich: Drei Masken, 1923.

Leo of Vercelli. "Zu den Gedichte Leo's von Vercelli." Edited by Hermann Bloch. *Neues Archiv* 27 (1902): 752-54.

Marbod of Rennes. "Carmina Varia." In Migne et al., *Patrologiae cursus completus* 171: col. 1647-86.

———. "Liber Decem Capitulorum." In Migne et al., *Patrologiae cursus completus* 171: col. 1693-1716.

———. "Liebesbriefgedichte Marbods." Edited by Walther Bulst. In *Liber Floridus,* edited by Bernhard Bischoff, 287-301. St. Otillien: Eos Verlag der Erzabtei, 1950.

Marcabru. *Poésies complètes du troubadour Marcabru.* Edited by J.-M.-L. Dejeanne. Bibliothèque Méridionale 12. Toulouse: Privat, 1909.

Marie de France. *Die Fabeln der Marie de France.* Edited by Karl Warnke. Bibliotheca Normannica 6. Halle: Niemeyer, 1898.

——. *Fables.* Edited and translated by Harriet Spiegel. Toronto: University of Toronto, 1987.

Moniage Guillaume. Edited by Wilhelm Cloetta. 2 vols. Paris: Firmin-Didot, 1906-11.

Pamphilus. Edited by F. G. Becker. *Beihefte zum mittellateinischen Jahrbuch* 9 (1972): 1-340.

Petrus Alfonsi. *Disciplina Clericalis.* Edited by Alfons Hilka and Werner Soderhjelm. Heidelberg: Carl Winter, 1911.

——. *The Disciplina Clericalis of Petrus Alfonsi.* Translated by Eberhard Hermes. Berkeley: University of California, 1970.

——. *Disciplina Clericalis (English Translation) from the Fifteenth Century Worcester Cathedral Manuscript F.172.* Edited by William Hulme. Western Reserve University Bulletin 22, Cleveland, 1919.

Peter the Painter. *Petri Pictoris Carmina.* Edited by L. von Acker. Corpus Christianorum 25. Turnhout: Brepols, 1972.

——. "Quelques oeuvres inédites de Pierre le Peintre." Edited by André Boutémy. *Latomus* 7 (1948): 51-69.

Phaedrus. *Phaedri Augusti Liberti Fabularum Aesopiarum.* Edited and translated by B. E. Perry. Cambridge, Mass.: Loeb, 1984.

Querolus. Le Querolus, comédie latine anonyme. Edited by Louis Havet. Paris: Vieweg, 1880.

Radulfus Tortarius. *Carmina.* Edited by Marbury Ogle and Dorothy Schullian. Papers and Monographs of the American Academy in Rome 8. Rome: Tipografica editrice, 1933.

Richars li biaus. Edited by Wendelin Foerster. Vienna: Hölder, 1874.

"'Richeut,' Old French Poem of the Twelfth Century, with Introduction, Notes and Glossary." Edited by I. C. Lecompte. *Romanic Review* 4 (1913): 261-305.

Roman d'Alexandre. The Medieval French Roman d'Alexandre. Edited by Edward Armstrong, et al. 2 vols. Princeton: Princeton University Press; Paris: Presses Universitaires de France, 1937.

Roman d'Eneas. Eneas: A Twelfth-Century French Romance. Translated by John Yunck. New York: Columbia University Press, 1974.

Roman de Renart. Edited by Mario Roques. 6 vols. Paris: Champion, 1972-83.

Roman de Thèbes. Edited by Guy Raynaud de Lage. 2 vols. Paris: Champion, 1966-67.

Ruodlieb: The Earliest Courtly Novel (after 1050). Edited and translated by E. H. Zeydel. Chapel Hill: University of North Carolina Press, 1959.

Sextus Amarcius. *Sexti Amarcii Galli Piosistrati Sermonum libri IV.* Edited by Maximilianus Manitius. Leipzig: Teubner, 1888.

Sponsus: Dramma delle virgini prudenti e delle virgini stolte. Edited and translated by D'Arco Silvio Avalle. Documenti di Filologia 9. Milan: Ricciardi, 1965.

Theodulf of Orléans. "Theodulfi Carmina." Edited by Ernst Dümmler. *MGH, Poetae Latini aevi Carolini* 1: 525-26 and 551-52.

"Tractatus Garsiae." Edited by Ernst Sackur. *MGH, Libelli de lite imperatorum et pontificum* 2: 423-35.

"'Unibos': The Earliest Full-length Fabliau (Text and Translation)." Edited and translated by Marc Wolterbeek. *Comitatus* 16 (1985): 46-76.

Versus Eporediensis. "Gedichte aus Ivrea." Edited by Ernst Dümmler. *Zeitschrift für deutsches Altertum* 14 (1869): 245-53.

Walter Map. *De nugis curialium.* Edited by Montague R. James. Oxford: Clarendon, 1914.

Warnerius of Rouen. "Satire de Garnier de Rouen contre le poète Moriuht (Xe-XIe siècle)." Edited by Henri Omont. *Annuaire-Bulletin de la Société de l'Histoire de France* 31 (1894): 193-210.

——. "Le satiriste Garnier de Rouen et son milieu (début du XIe siècle)." Edited by Lucien Musset. *Revue de Moyen Age Latin* 10 (1954): 237-66.

William IX of Aquitaine. *Les chansons de Guillaume IX, Duc d'Aquitaine (1071-1127).* Edited and translated by Alfred Jeanroy. Paris: Champion, 1972.

William of Blois. "Alda." Edited and translated by Alison Elliott. *Allegorica* 1 (1976): 58-93.

Ysengrimus. Edited by Ernst Voigt. Halle: Waisenhaus, 1884.

Ysengrimus: Text with Translation, Commentary and Introduction. Edited and translated by Jill Mann. Leiden: Brill, 1987.

SECONDARY SOURCES

Allen, Philip. *Medieval Latin Lyrics.* Chicago: University of Chicago, 1931.

Bar, Francis. *Les épîtres latines de Raoul le Tourtier (1065?-1114?), Etude de sources.* Paris: Droz, 1937.

Bédier, Joseph. *Les fabliaux: Etudes de littérature populaire et d'histoire littéraire du moyen âge.* Paris: Champion, 1911.

Bergson, Henri. *Le rire: Essai sur la signification du comique.* 303d ed. Paris: Alcan, 1972.

Beyer, Jürgen. *Schwank und Moral: Untersuchungen zum altfranzösischen Fabliau und verwandten Formen.* Studia Romanica 16. Heidlberg: Carl Winter, 1979.

——. "The Morality of the Amoral." Translated by Linda Pickle. In *The Humor of the Fabliaux: A Collection of Critical Essays*, edited by Thomas Cooke and Benjamin Honeycutt, 15-42. Columbia: University of Missouri Press, 1974.

Bloch, R. Howard. *The Scandal of the Fabliaux.* Chicago: University of Chicago, 1986.

Bolte, Johannes, and George Polívka. *Anmerkungen zu den Kinder- und Hausmärchen der Brüder Grimm.* 5 vols. Leipzig: Dieterich'sche Verlagsbuchhandlung, 1915.

Boutémy, André. "Autour de Godefroid de Reims." *Latomus* 6 (1947): 231-55.

———. "Foulcoie de Beauvais et l'intérêt pour l'archéologie antique au XIe et au XIIe siècle." *Latomus* 1 (1937): 173-86.

Certain, Eugène de. "Raoul Tortaire." *Bibliothèque de l'Ecole de Chartes* 4 (1853): 425-63.

Chambers, Edmund K. *The Mediaeval Stage.* 2 vols. Oxford: Clarendon, 1903.

Cooke, Thomas, and Benjamin Honeycutt, eds. *The Humor of the Fabliaux: A Collection of Critical Essays.* Columbia: University of Missouri Press, 1974.

Curtius, Ernst Robert. *European Literature and the Latin Middle Ages.* Translated by Willard Trask. Bollingen Series 36. Princeton: Princeton University Press, 1973.

Dronke, Peter. *Medieval Latin and the Rise of the European Love Lyric.* 2 vols. Oxford: Clarendon, 1965.

———. *Poetic Individuality in the Middle Ages.* Oxford: Clarendon, 1970.

———. "The Beginnings of the Sequence." *Beiträge zur Geschichte der deutschen Sprache und Literatur* 87 (1965): 43-73.

———. "A Note on 'Pamphilus.'" *Journal of the Warbourg and Courtauld Institute* 42 (1979): 225-30.

———. "The Rise of the Medieval Fabliau: Latin and Vernacular Evidence." *Romanische Forschungen* 85 (1973): 275-97.

Ehrismann, Gustav. *Geschichte der deutschen Literatur bis zum Ausgang des Mittelalters.* Munich: Beck, 1954-55.

Faral, Edmond. "Le fabliau latin au moyen âge." *Romania* 50 (1924): 321-85.

Feibelmann, James. *Aesthetics: A Study of the Fine Arts in Theory and Practice.* New York: Duell, Sloan and Pearce, 1949.

Franceschini, Ezio. "Il teatro post-carolingio." In *I Problemi Comuni dell'Europa Post-Carolingia,* 295-312. Spoleto: Centro Italiano di Studi sull'Alto Medioevo, 1955.

Freud, Sigmund. *Jokes and Their Relation to the Unconscious.* Translated by James Strachey. New York: Norton, 1960.

Friedman, Lionel. "Gradus Amoris." *Romance Philology* 19 (1965): 167-77.

Grant, Mary. *The Ancient Rhetorical Theories of the Laughable.* University of Wisconsin Studies in Language and Literature 21. Madison: University of Wisconsin Press, 1924.

Hart, W. M. "The Fabliau and Popular Literature." *PMLA* 23 (1908): 329-74.

Hauréau, Barthélemy. *Notice sur les mélanges poétiques d'Hildebert de Lavardin.* Le Mans: n.p., 1882. Also published in *Notices et extraits des manuscrits de la Bibliothèque Nationale et autres bibliothèques* 28.2 (Paris: Imprimerie Nationale, 1878), 289-448.

———. "Notice sur un manuscrit de la Reine Christine à la Bibliothèque du Vatican." *Notices et extraits des manuscrits de la Bibliothèque Nationale et autres bibliothèques* 29.2 (Paris: Imprimerie Nationale, 1880), 231-362.

Helsinger, Howard. "Pearls in the Swill: Comic Allegory in the French Fabliaux." In Cooke and Honeycutt, *The Humor of the Fabliaux*, 93-105.

Hunt, Tony. "Chrestien and the 'Comediae.'" *Medieval Studies* 40 (1978): 120-56.

Kögel, Rudolf. *Geschichte der deutschen Literatur bis zum Ausgänge des Mittelalters*. Strassburg: Trübner, 1897.

Lacy, Norris. "Types of Esthetic Distance in the Fabliaux." In Cooke and Honeycutt, *The Humor of the Fabliaux*, 107-17.

Lauter, Paul, ed. *Theories of Comedy*. New York: Doubleday Anchor, 1964.

Leblond, Bernard. *L'accession des Normands de Neustrie à la culture occidentale (Xème-XIème s.)*. Paris: Nizet, 1966.

Lehmann, Paul. *Die Parodie im Mittelalter*. Munich: Drie Masken, 1922.

Leyen, Friedrich von der. "Märchen und Spielmannsdichtung." *Germanisch-Romanische Monatsschrift* 10 (1922): 129-38.

Magoun, F. P., and H. M. Smyser, eds. *Walter of Aquitaine: Materials for the Study of His Legend*. New London: Connecticut College, 1950.

Maigne d'Arnis, W. H. *Lexicon manuale ad scriptores mediae et infimae latinitatis ex glossariis Caroli Dufresne, D. Ducangii, D.P. Carpentarii, Adelungii, et aliorum, in compendium accuratissime redactum*. Paris: J. P. Migne, 1858.

Ménard, Philip. *Le rire et le sourire au moyen âge*. Geneva: Droz, 1969.

Menner, Robert. "The Man in the Moon and Hedging." *Journal of English and Germanic Philology* 48 (1949): 1-14.

Meyer, Wilhelm. "Fragmenta Burana." In *Festschrift zur Feier des Hundertfünfzigjährigen Bestehens der königlichen Gesellschaft der Wissenschaften zu Göttingen, Abhandlungen der Philologisch-Historischen Klasse*, 1-21. Berlin: Weidmann 1901.

Moos, Peter von. *Hildebert von Lavardin, 1056-1133: Humanitas an der Schwelle des hofischen Zeitalters*. Pariser Historische Studien 3. Stuttgart: Hiersemann, 1965.

Müllenhoff, Karl, and Wilhelm Scherer. *Denkmaler deutscher Poesie und Prosa aus dem VIII-XII Jahrhundert*. 3d ed. Berlin: Weidmann, 1892.

Muscatine, Charles. *The Old French Fabliaux*. New Haven: Yale University, 1986.

Nichols, Stephen. "'Canso-Conso': Structures of Parodic Humor in Three Songs of Guilhem IX." *L'Esprit Créateur* 16 (1976): 16-29.

Nicoll, Allardyce. *Masks, Mimes, and Miracles*. New York: Harcourt, Brace, 1931.

Nykrog, Per. *Les fabliaux: Etude d'histoire littéraire et de stylistique médiévale*. Copenhagen: Munksgaard, 1957.

Ogilvy, J. D. A. "'Mimi,' 'Scurrae,' 'Histriones': Entertainers of the Early Middle Ages." *Speculum* 38 (1963): 603-19.

Paris, Gaston. "Les fabulistes latins." *Journal des Savants* (January 1885): 37-51.

———. "Lantfrid et Cobbon." *Le Moyen Age* 2 (1889): 285-89.

Pearcy, R. J. "Realism and Religious Parody in the Fabliaux: Watriquet de Couvin's 'Les Trois Dames de Paris.'" *Revue Belge de Philologie et d'Histoire* 50 (1972): 744-54.

Raby, Frederic J. E. *A History of Christian Latin Poetry*. Oxford: Clarendon, 1927.

———. *A History of Secular Latin Poetry in the Middle Ages [SLP]*. 2 vols. Oxford: Clarendon, 1934.

Schenck, Mary Jane Stearns. *The Fabliaux: Tales of Wit and Deception*. Purdue University Monographs in Romance Languages 24. Philadelphia: John Benjamins, 1987.

Schupp, V. "Der Dichter des 'Modus Liebinc.'" *Mittellateinisches Jahrbuch* 5 (1968): 29-41.

Skeat, Walter. *A Concise Etymological Dictionary of the English Language*. New York: Capricorn, 1963.

Suchomski, Joachim. *"Delectatio" und "Utilitas": Ein Beitrag zum Verständnis mittelalterliche komischer Literatur*. Bibliotheca Germanica 18. Bern: Francke, 1975.

Sudre, Léopold. *Les sources du Roman de Renart*. Paris: Bouillon, 1892.

Thiener, Paul. "Fabliaux Settings." In Cooke and Honeycutt, *The Humor of the Fabliaux*, 119-36.

Thompson, Stith. *Motif-Index of Folk-Literature (T-Z)*. Indiana University Studies 22. Bloomington, Ind.: Indiana University Press, 1934.

Trimpi, Wesley. *Muses of One Mind*. Princeton, N.J.: Princeton University Press, 1983.

Wallner, A. "Reinhart Fuchs: Lesungen und Deutungen." *Beiträge zur Geschichte der deutschen Sprache und Literatur* 47 (1923): 173-220.

Yunck, John. *The Lineage of Lady Meed: The Development of Mediaeval Venality Satire*. Notre Dame, Ind.: University of Notre Dame, 1963.

Young, Karl. *The Drama of the Medieval Church*. 2 vols. Oxford: Clarendon, 1933.

Index

(Italicized page numbers refer to the primary discussion.)

About the Author

MARC WOLTERBEEK is Assistant Professor and Head of the Department of English at the College of Notre Dame, Belmont, California. His previously published articles include " 'Unibos': The Earliest Full-length Fabliau (Text and Translation)." He is presently completing "The Priest and the Poet: The Lives and Works of Robert of Arbrissel and William IX, Duke of Aquitaine."